A Narrative Approach to Social Media Mourning

This book investigates how social media are reconfiguring dying, death, and mourning. Taking a narrative approach, it shows how dying, death, and mourning are shared online as *small stories of the moment*, which are organized around transgressive moments and events with motivational, participatory, or connective scope. Through the different case studies discussed, this book presents an empirical framework for analyzing small stories of dying, death, and mourning as practices of sharing that become associated with specific modes of affective positioning, i.e. modulations of different degrees of distance or proximity to the death event and the dead, the networked audience(s), and the affective self. The book calls for the study of affect as integral to narrative activity and opens up broader questions about how stories and emotion are mobilized in digital cultures for accruing audiences, social value, and visibility. It will be of interest to researchers in narrative analysis, the anthropology and sociology of emotion, digital communication, media and cultural studies, and (digital) death and dying.

Korina Giaxoglou is Lecturer in Applied Linguistics and English Language at the Open University, UK, where she leads the Health Discourse Research Group. Her research on mourning, narrative, affect, and sharing has appeared in edited volumes, special issues, and peer-reviewed journals including *Pragmatics, Applied Linguistics Review, Discourse, Context and Media* and *Social Media +Society*.

Routledge Research in Narrative, Interaction, and Discourse

A Narrative Approach to Social Media Mourning
Small Stories and Affective Positioning
Korina Giaxoglou

For more information about this series, please visit: www.routledge.com/Routledge-Research-in-Narrative-Interaction-and-Discourse/book-series/RRNID

A Narrative Approach to Social Media Mourning
Small Stories and Affective Positioning

Korina Giaxoglou

Routledge
Taylor & Francis Group

NEW YORK AND LONDON

First published 2021
by Routledge
605 Third Avenue, New York, NY 10017

and by Routledge
2 Park Square, Milton Park, Abingdon, Oxon, OX14 4RN

First issued in paperback 2022

Routledge is an imprint of the Taylor & Francis Group, an informa business

Publisher's Note
The publisher has gone to great lengths to ensure the quality of this
reprint but points out that some imperfections in the original copies may
be apparent.

Library of Congress Cataloging-in-Publication Data
A catalog record for this title has been requested

ISBN: 978-1-138-28602-3 (hbk)
ISBN: 978-0-367-52066-3 (pbk)
ISBN: 978-1-315-26867-5 (ebk)

DOI: 10.4324/9781315268675

Typeset in Sabon
by Apex CoVantage, LLC

To my grandmother, Kiki: everywhere I go, she's going with me.

Contents

Figures

Tables

Image

Acknowledgements

As the losses, encounters, readings, and emotions that motivated this book are now dusted by language and serialized as chapters in this book, what remains is the continued importance of mourning as a force that emanates from encounters with others' words and worlds, past and present. It is this relentless relevance of mourning for social life in an age of social media that I have sought to bring out in this book.

The editors of the series, Anna De Fina, Alexandra Georgakopoulou, and Ruth Page, and their cutting-edge research on Narrative, Interaction, and Discourse have been a vital source of inspiration for this book. Without their insightful comments and much-needed encouragement throughout, the completion of this book would not have been possible. All mistakes and omissions remain mine.

Many thanks to the commissioning editor Elyssée Preposy and all the Routledge editors for their work and patience with the production process.

Earlier versions of some sections in the book have been previously published in the following journals: "'Everywhere I go, you're going with me': Time and space deixis as affective positioning resources in shared moments of digital mourning", *Discourse, Context and Media* 9 (2015), pp. 55–63; "JeSuisCharlie? Hashtags as narrative resources in contexts of ecstatic sharing", *Discourse, Context, and Media* 22 (2018), pp. 13–20; (with Tereza Spilioti) The Shared Story of #JeSuisAylan on Twitter: story participation and stancetaking in visual small stories, *Pragmatics. Quarterly Publication of the International Pragmatics Association*, IPrA 30: 2 (2020), pp. 277–302.

I would like to thank colleagues in the School of Applied Linguistics and English Language at the Open University and especially Ann Hewings, Philip Seargeant, Frank Monaghan, Caroline Tagg, and Laura Paterson for transforming work into a creative experience.

Special thanks to Marcel Burger, Laura Delaloye, and Gilles Merminod, convenors of the Digital Communication workshop at the University of Lausanne, for our discussions on parts of my work as it was developing. I would also like to thank the Death Online Research Network for welcoming me to their vibrant interdisciplinary group.

I am grateful to my partner, Dimitris, who's been a pillar of support and a true source of radical happiness.

I am ever grateful to my parents for their unwavering encouragement and patience and to my formidable nieces Ioanna, Lila, and Anthi, for all our joyful moments. Heartfelt thanks to my friends for sharing life roots and routes in our precious chats.

To my uncle Evgenios, whose painful loss led me into the worlds of online mourning in the first place.

The last word is a tribute to Charlotte Eades, the vlogger whom I never had the opportunity to meet in person, but whose videos have been an inspiration for part of this book.

Barking, April 2020.

1 Introduction

Why Mourning?

Mourning is the reckoning with death, the dead, and the self with(in) and with(out) the other. This reckoning is poignantly illustrated in Jacques Derrida's (2001) essay-tributes to fourteen of his eponymous friends and colleagues, among whom Roland Barthes, Paul De Man, Michel Foucault, and Louis Althusser. In his *work of mourning*, Derrida enacts his memorial gestures to those who passed away before him, as if walking on a tightrope between the refusal to speak and the need to speak of his dead friends; between inscribing death as something absolutely unique and yet as something shared and public, subject to the iterations of conventional rhetorical moves. Derrida's reflections exemplify the double-edged nature of mourning as a personal *response* to loss and a *responsibility* to the dead and their memorialization.

In mourning the singular and the iterable, the personal and the social are weaved together, providing a unique window to the practices and politics of how subjects, affective relationalities, and socio-political bodies are formed. It is this intricate connectedness of the personal, the social, and the political that has turned mourning into an object of academic study across different disciplines, as much as into a topic of public interest.

As seventeenth-century French author François de la Rochefoucauld, notes "death, like the sun, cannot be looked at steadily or directly" (cited in Manning, 2009, p. 379). The question is, then, what kinds of 'filters' are made available in different societies for 'looking' at death, dying, and bereavement at various degrees of distance. One such common filter, for example, is talking about death: Even though the raw experience of dying and grieving may be more difficult to put into words and share with others, talking about death as an event, e.g. a funeral, a memorial ceremony, or a media event, often makes for an engaging topic of conversation or story material that allows death to be embedded, at least in part, to the everyday – even if, often, at some distance from the painful realities it can evoke.

The recognition that some aspects of death are routinely talked about in specific contexts – in line with local conversational norms – suggests that death is not as much of a taboo or 'banished' as it has often been assumed (see Gorer, 1955; Ariès, 1981, pp. 579–583). As Jupp and Walter (1999) note, the *death-as-taboo* thesis has become something of a journalistic cliché, a conventional formula used to frame public discussions on death in terms an assumed need to discuss it more openly – consider, for example, the motto 'Let's talk about death' featured in many Death Café events.[1] This idea has been also pervading the public discourse about grief –consider, for example, the online support network 'Let's talk about loss: talking through the taboo[2]' (for a more detailed discussion of the death-as-taboo thesis, see Chapter 2).

If, however, death and mourning were banished, forbidden, or hidden, it would be invisible. And yet, death is all around. As Tony Walter points out (2014), the need to talk about death or mourning does not really emerge from its 'repression' in contemporary society. It is, rather, motivated by the need to make sense of the ongoing and substantial changes in dying, mourning rituals, and beliefs about the afterlife, as well as by an incessant need to reflect on the implications of death for personal and social life. Other scholars have also pointed out the importance of approaching death not so much as 'taboo' but in relation to the particular structures that configure the ways we encounter and experience it (see for example Noys, 2005, p. 3).

In this book, death, dying, and mourning are approached as *tellable*, *narratable*, and thus, *visible* in social life under particular conditions of tellership and participation, which are worthy of empirical investigation. My aim is to shed light onto the narrative, affective, and identity modes, which are constituted by – as much as they constitute – the diverse and changing frames for tellership and participation in mourning. The chapters that follow focus specifically on mourning in social media contexts inspired by the narrative approach to interaction and social media communication known as the *small stories* research paradigm (Georgakopoulou, 2015; see Chapter 3 for a discussion of this approach). Taken together, the chapters of this book address the question of *how contemporary technologies of communication and connectedness online are mobilized for dealing with the end of life, for remediating existing rituals, story forms, and affective norms for mourning and memorialization, and for assessing technologies' potential and limits.*

Mourning and Social Media

The questions addressed in this book resonate with ongoing scholarly and public debates on the opportunities and the risks of internet technologies or the "unintended negative consequences of benevolent design" as the creator of the web, Tim Berners-Lee (2019, n.p.), puts it. These debates are not new, given that the technologies we live with are not entirely new, either. In her introduction to the edited collection on *Networked Self and Birth, Life and Death*, Papacharissi (2019) notes that we have always lived – and died – with *technology* or *techne*, i.e. the art of getting through everyday life by doing things in optimal, imaginative, and gratifying ways; and all too often, our worries about technology have reflected and continue to reflect our misunderstanding of our complex relationship to it (p. 1).

As is the case with every technology, digital technologies of communication and sharing through computers, mobile devices, and social media applications have been reconfiguring existing modes for the production of events, stories, and subjectivities (in parts of the world with access to these technologies). These modes are inflected by – as much as they inflect – the ways in which 'new' media refashion or *remediate* prior media forms (Bolter and Grusin, 1999, p. 273) in the broader contours of dominant and emerging social structures.

The impact of structures on social life has been described under various labels branding societies, for example, as *network societies* (Castells, 2004) or cultures of *participation* (Jenkins, 2006) and *connectivity* (van Dijck, 2013). These descriptions, appealing as they may seem to be, are grounded in a culturist approach to the internet and make part of the positive techno-social imaginaries of the so-called *Information Age* (Castells, 2000). As Fuchs (2014, pp. 60–61) notes, culturalist approaches tend to reify and overstate the creativity and agency of users on the web, while underplaying the commodification and exploitation of such creativity. And yet, the commodification of users' online activity is increasingly intensified in the so-called *Age of Sharing*, where the positive connotations of sharing serve to reinforce at the same time as to camouflage the commercial aspect of social media platforms (John, 2017, p. 64). The rhetorical mobilization of personal and relational vocabulary for commercial ends is further attested in the recent rebranding of the Information Age in current business and technology writing as the *Age of Experience* (BA Times, 2019; Tech Crunch, 2016). The buzzword is used to foreground the potential of sharing the moment for creating 'experiences', which foster strong emotional interconnections as well as help to increase the social and monetary value of shared content. Such emotion-tinted 'experiences' are constitutive of 'visceral data', i.e. affective states, such as 'flow', 'engagement', and 'boredom', generated in the use of technological devices and circulated via them (Powell, 2018, pp. 13–14).

The emphasis on generating and disseminating emotion attests to the broader importance that emotion has been accumulating in everyday and professional domains (Illouz, 2007) as well as in the media, where they form the basis of aesthetic experience, entertainment, but also collective identities, values, and modes of action (Eder et al., 2019). Anne-Cécile

Robert (2018) discusses this turn to emotion and addresses the discontents of what she calls "the emotion doctrine" (echoing Naomi Klein's 'shock doctrine', 2008), whereby catastrophes are put to the service of capitalist reproduction, dominating the news and fostering tears over reasoned reflection and meaningful social and political action.

While Robert's approach takes a critical pessimist angle on the emotionalization of society in and through media events, this book takes a more nuanced, empirical angle on such phenomena drawing on evidence from social media, which have been acknowledged as an important affective platform for communication about illness, death, and mourning (Stage and Hougaard, 2018). The practices that will be discussed are viewed as intricately connected to processes of mediatization and social-mediatization, which are briefly discussed in the remainder of this introduction in relation to death, dying, and mourning.

Mediatization

Mediatization is a sensitizing concept, which is useful insofar as it helps draw attention to the media's increasing permeation of "all aspects of private, social, political, cultural and economic life, from micro (individual) to the meso (organizational) and the macro (societal) level of analysis" (Strömbäck and Esser, 2014, p. 10). Mediatization processes impact the way we approach death, given that they entail specific frames for encountering and experiencing death. As Jacobsen (2016) notes, in contemporary culture, death (often gory and dramatic) is exposed and made instantaneously available globally through the screens of television, computer, or mobile phone, calling forth momentary affective reactions on the part of the viewers. This "spectacular death", which "inaugurates an obsessive interest in appearances that simultaneously draws death near and keeps it at arm's length" (p. 10), textures the new *mediated and mediatized visibility* of death and mourning.

This visibility is always selective, and it is revealing of dominant forms of *thanatopolitics*, whereby some types of death attract high levels of visibility and turn into media spectacles (see Kellner, 2002), reinforcing the grievability of certain lives over that of others (Butler, 2004). Poignant examples of media spectacles of death in recent times have been the September 11, 2001 attacks against targets in the United States and more recently, the attacks across different targets in Europe from 2015 to 2017, which have taken a terrible toll on human life and called forth widespread public mourning. In the extensive media coverage of these disasters, mourning has been recurrently mobilized as a resource for national unity and as a political communication strategy of confidence building and grief management (Sontag, 2001). As Edwards and Martins (2004) note, sharing sympathy or pity and negotiating public solidarity has been typically articulated along the drawing up of sharp distinctions between 'us' and 'them', as part of broader practices of negotiating and discursively constructing "the boundaries of identity" (p. 153) and creating collective identities, i.e. "conceptual structures comprising beliefs and knowledge, norms and values, attitudes and expectations as well as emotions, [. . .] reinforced and negotiated in discourse" (Koller, 2012). In other words, in conditions of a heightened sense of fear, death and mourning become key resources for displaying emotional alignment (or disalignment) with specific groups of people, values, and moral stances.

The mobilization of death and mourning in contemporary media has been (re)producing a sense of *intimacy at a distance* fostered by modern mass media, especially radio and TV (Horton and Wohl, 1956, p. 215 cited in Montgomery, 1999, p. 5).[3] As Jacobsen (2016) notes, "spectacular death" is something that we witness at a safe distance with equal amounts of fascination and abhorrence, we wallow in it and want to know about it without getting too close to it" (p. 10).

The media coverage of large-scale death events, such as attacks and disasters, especially since 2001, and their extension to immediate reactions on social media have further pushed this blending of intimate styles with the public construal of mourning as a collective affective experience.

Social Mediatization

Social media audiences witness death events through *shared stories* (Page, 2018), which are opened up to public scrutiny as well as to ecstatic modes of affective participation (see Chouliaraki, 2006; Papacharissi and de Fatima Oliveira, 2012; Giaxoglou, 2018). Shared stories emerge in – and through – media events reconfigured into *hybrid media events*, where elements of ceremonial and vernacular mass communication forms converge in complex networks of mass media, internet-based, and mobile communication technologies; hybrid media events foster (and accelerate) social intensifications between and among different actors in line with the affordances and constraints of social media platforms (Sumiala et al., 2018, pp. 14–16). The hybridization of media events with social media communication formats points to the extension of mediatization processes into processes of *social-mediatization* (Georgakopoulou and Giaxoglou, 2018), where social media logics permeate the making and sharing of stories, subjectivities, and collectivities online.

The hybrid media event of the school shooting at Virginia Tech's Blacksburg campus in 2007 is taken to be emblematic of this turn to the social-mediatization of death and mourning (Reuters, 2007; Computer World, 2011). While the shooting that resulted in the death of thirty-two people (CNN Library, 2009) was still unfolding, updates were being posted on Facebook by people who were still hiding across the campus, allowing people to witness the events live. The Missouri Review (2013) cites Amanda Dawn Toth's updated status while she was taking refuge in a computer lab in Shanks Hall:

> *22 people are reported dead and 25 more are reported injured. They say that the shooter is dead, but we are unsure if there are more shooters . . . so yeah I am freakin out right now . . . well so is everyone else . . . but I'm gonna try to keep this up-to-date with what's going on down here . . . this is being reported as the worst school shooting in US history . . . wow . . . I honestly can't believe I'm here while this is taking place . . . absolutely unbelievable.*

In addition to live news-broadcasting, Facebook also became a bulletin board for students to post they were safe on a group called "I'm OK on VT", while other groups were set up to discuss the shooting or share tributes after the news of the victims' death was announced. Many college students replaced their profile pictures with the logo of Virginia Tech as a sign of solidarity.

Even more groups and pages sprang up in the days following the shooting, where people across the U.S. and the world shared their personal reactions to the news. In these updates, users often made explicit reference to the immediacy or recency of the news of the shooting that reached them, using that media connection as a frame for projecting their identification or sympathy with the victims and their bereaved families, even if they had never been acquainted with them (see Examples 1–2).

Example 1

what a horrible thing to have happened. i can't imagine what is going through the minds of everyone involved. **just seeing the news reports and interviews**, *i can't help but feel sick to my stomach. i know that i'll keep those people in my thoughts and prayers.*

> [Source: Facebook Group *R.I.P. Virginia Tech*;
> emphasis added]

Example 2

when i heard about the virginia tech shooting *my heart dropped. one of my friends goes there and i have never been so terrified. God bless the families who lost their children today. This just teaches everyone how life can be taken so quickly and we must live for those moments that make life unbelievably amazing.*

> [Source: Facebook Group *R.I.P. Virginia Tech*;
> emphasis added]

The focus of these posts on the here and now of the sharer contrasted with the here and now of the victims helped create a shared spatio-temporal frame between the two, placing witnesses in a sense of close proximity to the events and those involved in them. Such frames are part of what Papacharissi and de Fatima Oliveira call *affective news streams*, which are produced as networked users participate in the news stream, combining news, opinion, and emotion with an 'always-on' affective feed (2012, p. 280). Sharing reactions to media events in affective news streams online echoes in some respect the ecstatic modes of live news reporting on global spectacles of tragedies and suffering, which (re)produce a sense of instant proximity and position viewers as intimate witnesses to others' suffering (Chouliaraki, 2006). This mode of online sharing of reactions to attacks and tragedies attests to modes of *ecstatic sharing* (Giaxoglou, 2018). Ecstatic sharing is not so much about distributing factual information; it's about prompting affective participation in happenings and events in the instantaneous proximity of the here and now and enhancing, as well as mobilizing, the visibility of these happenings and events for identity purposes. This mode is discussed in more detail in the case studies presented in Chapters 6 and 7.

The ecstatic sharing of reactions to spectacular death online has been argued to create social media *spectacles of affect* (Klastrup, 2015). This direct mode of witnessing invites social media users' participation, irrespective of where they are located, and creates a sense of collectivized mourning that helps amplify the visibility of some types of death. The more removed people are from the time and place of the events, the more likely it is that their displays of mourning are cases of *parasocial* grief, i.e. grief which has to do with the lives and deaths of people the mourners don't know personally (DeGroot and Leith, 2018; Klastrup, 2018). And yet, these expressions should not be straightforwardly dismissed as 'insincere' and 'fake', as they arguably allow "grieving to be experienced both privately and collectively, and even at community level" (Julier-Costes, 2018).

Online reactions to mass death are not restricted to solidary participation in affective news streams online, showing sympathy with the victims and their families. Offensive counter-reactions are also common, as illustrated, for example, in the case of posts claiming that the story shared by conspiracy groups on Facebook that the Sandy Hook Elementary school shooting was a hoax (*The Guardian*, 2018). Other types of trolling involve the posting of disruptive, distracting, and offensive posts targeting user communities of memorial sites as well as the hijacking of stories and pictures of the dead and their viral circulation as memes. A common trope of this type of trolling is the social media circulation of photographs of alt-right 'comedian' Sam Hyde as the perpetrator in the wake of the Las Vegas attacks or other mass shootings and terror attacks.

Activities of this type are known among users of social media subcultures (e.g. users frequenting the social media network *4Chan*) as 'RIP trolling' or 'LOL trolling' and are discussed by Whitney Phillips (2011, 2015). Trolling behaviour is often condemned in the media as evidence of lack of sensitivity to the pain of others or as a direct outcome of the anonymity of the internet. Some of the trolls that Phillips interviewed, however, said that their trolling activity was attacking 'grief strangers', who are not really connected to the death they are reacting to and are not really in mourning; trolls are seen to take it upon themselves to act as the 'grief police', making judgments about what counts as 'sincere' or 'fake' mourning. Trolls also claimed they target memorial pages 'for the lulz' – i.e. the antagonistic laughter derived from the infliction of emotional distress – and often in reaction to media's sensationalizing coverage of death events turning tragedy into merchandise (Phillips and Milner, 2018). As much as these trolling behaviours are outrageous, insensitive, and offensive to the bereaved, they also constitute important sites for underscoring the degree to which immediate affective reactions to death news are normalized among large parts of the public and for surfacing the tensions and ambivalences that such reactions raise. Trolling activities, although important, are beyond the scope of this book, whose aims and structure are summarized in what follows.

Structure of the Book

This book sets out to investigate the extent to which social media are reconfiguring mourning in contemporary networked societies. It challenges the popular thesis that 'death is taboo' and draws attention to how, when, and why death and mourning become tellable and shareable in online environments. The book has been, more specifically, motivated by the following questions:

1. *How do people use social media to share dying, death, and mourning in different contexts?*
2. *What kinds of online storying and participation does the sharing of mourning make possible?*
3. *What does the study of mourning in social media reveal about the broader continuities and shifts in the way we engage narratively and affectively with death, dying, and grief?*

Based on the empirical study of four different cases of mourning in social media, I show how dying, death, and mourning are shared online as *small stories* affording sharers positions of a *teller*, a *co-teller*, or a *witness* to death. The different chapters offer empirical analyses of how different types of small stories of mourning are used as *affective positioning* resources that allow the sharer to modulate their degree of proximity or distance to (i) the death event and the dead, (ii) (known and unknown) audiences, and (iii) their own sense of their emotional self.

Sharing small stories of mourning online arguably attests to emerging modes of *death-writing of the moment*, in which mourning is variously mobilized as a motivational force, a connective and participation affordance, or a resource for displaying cosmopolitan emotion, amplifying the semiotic, affective, relational, and social scope of death and mourning.

The book consists of eight chapters, including the present one, whose content is summarized in what follows. Chapters 2 and 3 provide the theoretical and methodological background to the study's narrative approach to mourning. Chapters 4 and 5 focus on the social-mediatization of the personal experience of dying, death, and mourning and contribute insights into the ways in which grief is constructed as a shared and shareable story for and with networked audiences. Chapters 6 and 7 focus on forms of social-mediatized witnessing of spectacular death and shed light into how mourning is collectivized and mobilized for different purposes. Chapter 8 summarizes the key aspects and implications of the narrative-affective framework developed for the study of mourning in social media and discusses the potential and limits of sharing dying, death, and grief online.

In Chapter 1, Mourning in Social Media, I introduce the topic of the book and delimit its scope. I present the importance of mourning as a unique site for the study of continuities and shifts in narrative, affective, and identity forms in an age of media and social media sharing. I also sketch out the content of each of the chapters that follow and highlight the threads that connect them.

Chapter 2, Histories of Mourning, revisits general understandings of the terms *mourning* and *grief* commonly organized around contrasts between public and private domains of emotional expression and experience. It calls for a move beyond the popular thesis that 'death is taboo' to a concern with conditions of tellability, which in an age of sharing, further extend to conditions of shareability. Drawing on linguistic anthropology's insights on mourning as situated performances of emotion whose narrative trajectories can carry important social, political, and (meta) cultural meanings, the chapter outlines the key principles of a narrative approach to the study of death and mourning. This approach can encompass a wide range of mourning practices across ritual and non-ritual, 'traditional' and contemporary, offline and online contexts. In addition, this chapter distils key insights and research directions from the study of death online.

Chapter 3, A Narrative Approach to Social Media Mourning, presents the key ingredients of a small stories approach to the study of digital mourning. After briefly overviewing the different narrative turns and their associated views of narrative, it proposes a framework for the empirical study of digital mourning as *small stories*, paying attention to different levels of sharing, namely *selecting*, *storying*, and *positioning*. The concept of *affective positioning* is introduced and defined as the use of linguistic and discourse cues for modulating degrees of distance from or proximity to events and characters, audiences, and the self. The chapter also presents the data and methods, which have guided the selection and analysis of the different case studies, including the main ethical principles and challenges raised by the selected data.

Chapter 4, Small Stories of Illness and Dying on YouTube, considers emerging modes of death-writing of the moment in video-blogging (aka vlogging) on the video-platform YouTube, where young adults diagnosed with a terminal illness can assume the position of *teller*, documenting and broadcasting their unique personal experience with and despite illness. The analysis of a selected vlog brings to the fore the emergence of this new mode of telling and sharing the illness experience as *small stories*, which draws on the conventions of fashion and beauty vlogging on YouTube. Story making in this context is characterized by an emergent and cumulative plotline over video segments and a focus on the past, the very recent past, or the here and now, depending on how the vlogger affectively positions herself to her illness, her viewers, and her emotional self.

Vlogging on (terminal) illness serves as a way of reclaiming some control over life with illness as well as over one's posthumous legacy; inadvertently, it also emerges as a site for mourning, making available specific types of affective positioning for viewers as supporting and supported by the vlogger, but also as mourners inspired and motivated by her life and resilience. This mode of curated storying of the illness experience attests to the mobilization of illness as an authenticating resource for creating networked empathic connection, visibility, and value (personal, social, economic). In such vlogs, mourning is mobilized as a resource for motivating and inspiring intimate publics, part of the growing commoditization of the 'wound' and vulnerability of the illness experience.

Chapter 5, Small Stories of Everyday Mourning on Facebook, turns to the examination of modes of death-writing of the moment on Facebook memorials and brings to the fore practices of memorialization, which afford sharers participation in mourning as co-tellers of a loved one's grievable life. The focus is on a Facebook group created in memory of a young adult by his friends who become co-tellers of his life. Participation in this collective mourning unfolds along two main participation modes, *ritual* and *knowing participation*, which have been recognized as key formats of digital interaction (Georgakopoulou, 2016). Ritual participation is enacted through mirroring acts of generic remembrance, which serve to signal membership to a group of mourners, while *knowing participation* is achieved through one-off acts of personalized remembrance, termed here *memorial outbursts*. Memorial outbursts are found to be shared as different types of small stories: (i) *breaking news stories of mourning*, i.e. acts of remembrance in the here and now or the recent past, (ii) *projections*, i.e. stories about the sharer's plans in the (near) future, inviting the dead's support or participation and (iii) *habitual* stories of grief, i.e. small acts of remembrance in the everyday. The analysis also draws attention to a sharer's use of temporal and spatial deixis as indexical of her changing identity and affective positioning at different levels. The chapter provides an empirical account of practices of forming *continuing bonds* with the dead, mobilizing mourning as a resource for vernacularizing, personalizing, and at the same time collectivizing the experience of grieving for the loss of a love one and challenging ideas of bereavement as a 'big' event of rupture and crisis.

Chapter 6, Small Stories of Ecstatic Mourning on Twitter, examines the emergence and circulation of small stories and the associated types of affective positioning in the context of reactions to the attack at the offices of the satirical magazine *Charlie Hebdo* in Paris, January 7, 2015. The chapter draws on *The Guardian*'s live news blog on the events as well as on Twitter reactions and examines a mode of affective news engagement called, here, *ecstatic sharing*, which echoes modes of ecstatic news in the live broadcasting of disasters (Chouliaraki, 2006). As I show, this mode engenders participation positions along dividing lines of identification and create affective positions that signal different degrees of proximity to the event and the victims. This case study illustrates how small stories of mourning can be mobilized for symbolic purposes and scaled up at a national and global scale.

Chapter 7, Visual Stories of Mourning on Twitter, examines the use of visual small stories for mobilizing and scaling up mourning on Twitter in the case of Alan Kurdi's death, the three-year old boy who drowned on September 2, 2015, when the inflatable boat he was on capsized. The analysis looks at different phases of the circulation of images portraying his death, which became iconic, and the different types of reactions provoked by their circulation on Twitter. It shows how visual small stories of ecstatic mourning in this case contributed to the sharing of cosmopolitan emotions and identities. As I argue, these identities were enacted through types of affective positioning, which signaled distance from, rather than proximity to, the death event and the dead boy, illustrating the mobilization of mourning as a resource for engaging in cosmopolitan modes of digital mourning.

In Chapter 8, Small Stories of Mourning and Affective Positioning, I overview the main components of the narrative approach to the study of mourning in social media and outline the framework proposed in this book for the study of affective positioning. I provide a summary of the key insights from the analysis of the different case studies discussed in the previous chapters. I also reflect on the promises and limits of mourning in social media and discuss the broader implications of this book for the study of death online, affect, and narrative.

This book calls for the critical study of how stories, affect, and identities are mobilized in digital cultures as commodities that can drive audience engagement and increase affective, social, and economic value and visibility. This intense mobilization raises important questions about the ownership of the stories and emotions shared as well as about the legacies that these emerging modes of sharing leave behind.

Notes

1. Death Café is a UK-based international movement in which people drink tea, eat cake, and discuss death with the aim to increase awareness of death to help people make the most of their (finite) lives. More details about the Death Café movement can be found in its official website: https://deathcafe.com.
2. Let's Talk About Loss. Talking Through the Taboo is founded and directed by Beth French and supports bereaved people across the UK.
3. The sense of intimacy at a distance cultivated in mass media has reconfigured not only the discourse style of the media coverage of death and mourning but also the style of tributes paid by public figures in response to expectations for displays of emotion invested with sincerity. As Martin Montgomery (1999) has shown, for example, public tributes paid to the death of Diana by Tony Blair (then British Prime Minister), the Queen, and Earl Spencer were publicly scrutinized by media commentators for the degree of sincerity they displayed, attesting to a broader trend of private values erupting into the public domain – a trend that was driven as much by the awfulness of the event as by the requirements of live broadcasting media (ibid, p. 29).

References

Ariès, P. (1981) *The Hour of Our Death*. New York: Alfred A. Knopf.

BA Times (Bennett, S.) (2019) The experience age has arrived. *BA Times* [online]. Available at: www.batimes.com/articles/the-experience-age-has-arrived.html. Accessed: 22 Nov. 2019.

Berners-Lee, T. (2019) 30 years on: What's next #ForTheWeb? *Web Foundation* [online]. Available at: https://webfoundation.org/2019/03/web-birthday-30/. Accessed: 22 Nov. 2019.

Bolter, J.D. and R. Grusin (1999) *Remediation: Understanding New Media*. Cambridge, MA: MIT Press.

Butler, J. (2004) *Precarious Life: The Powers of Mourning and Violence*. London: Verso.

Castells, M. (2000) *The Rise of the Network Society*. Cambridge, MA: Blackwell Publishing.

Castells, M. (Ed.) (2004) *The Network Society: A Cross-Cultural Perspective*. Cheltenham, UK: Edward Elgar Publishing.

Chouliaraki, L. (2006) *The Spectatorship of Suffering*. London, Thousand Oaks, and New Delhi: Sage Publications.

CNN Library (2009) Virginia Tech shootings fast facts. *CNN*. Available at: https://edition.cnn.com/2013/10/31/us/virginia-tech-shootings-fast-facts/index.html. Accessed: 11 Aug. 2019.

Computer World (Gohring, N.) (2011) Virginia Tech shooting shows benefits of social networking sites. *Computer World* [News], Apr. 18. Available at: www.computerworld.com/article/2544701/networking/virginia-tech-shooting-shows-benefits-pitfalls-of-social-networking-sites.html. Accessed: 10 Jan. 2018.

DeGroot, J.M. and A.P. Leith (2018) R.I.P. Kutner: Parasocial grief following the death of a television character. *OMEGA* 77 (3): 199–216.

Derrida, J. (2001) *The Work of Mourning* (Edited by P.A. Brauet and M. Naas). Chicago and London: Chicago University Press.

Eder, J., J. Hanich, and J. Stadler (2019) Media and emotion: An introduction. *NECSUS* (Special Section: #Emotions), Spring. Available at: https://necsus-ejms.org/portfolio/spring-2019_emotions/. Accessed: 22 Oct. 2019.

Edwards, J. and J.R. Martin (2004) Introduction: Approaches to tragedy. *Discourse & Society* (Special Issue: Interpreting Tragedy: The Language of 11 September 2001) 15 (2–3): 147–155.

Fuchs, C. (2014) *Social Media: A Critical Introduction*. Thousand Oaks, CA: Sage Publications.

Georgakopoulou, A. (2015) Small stories research: Methods-analysis-outreach. In De Fina, A. and A. Georgakopoulou (Eds.), *Handbook of Narrative Analysis*. Malden, MA: Wiley-Blackwell, pp. 255–272.

Georgakopoulou, A. (2016) From narrating the self to posting self(ies): A small stories approach to selfies. *Open Linguistics* 2 (1): 300–317.

Georgakopoulou, A. and K. Giaxoglou (2018) Emplotment in the social mediatization of the economy: The poly-storying of economist Yanis Varoufakis. *Language@Internet* 16, Article 6.

Giaxoglou, K. (2018) #JeSuisCharlie? Hashtags as narrative resources in contexts of ecstatic sharing. *Discourse, Context, and Media* (Special Issue on Discourse of Social Tagging, edited by C. Lee) 22: 13–20.

Gorer, G. (1955) The pornography of death. In Gorer, G. (Ed.), *Death, Grief, and Mourning*. New York: Doubleday, pp. 192–199.

The Guardian (2018) An open letter to Mark Zuckerberg: Our child died at Sandy Hook: Why let Facebook lies hurt us even more? Leonard Pozner and Veronique De La rosa, parents of Noah Pozner. *The Guardian [Opinion]*, July 25. Available at: www.theguardian.com/commentisfree/2018/jul/25/mark-zuckerberg-facebook-sandy-hook-parents-open-letter. Accessed: 20 Jan. 2019.

Illouz, E. (2007) *Cold Intimacies: The Making of Emotional Capitalism*. Cambridge, UK: Polity Press.

Jacobsen, M.H. (2016) "Spectacular death": Proposing a new fifth phase to Philippe Ariès's admirable history of death. *Humanities* 4 (2): 1–20.

Jenkins, H. (2006) *Confronting the Challenges of Participatory Culture: Media Education for the 21st Century* (with R. Purushotma, M. Weigel, K. Clinton, and A.J. Robison). The John D. and Catherine T. MacArthur Foundation Reports on Digital Media and Learning. Cambridge, MA: The MIT Press.

John, N. (2017) *The Age of Sharing*. Malden, MA: Polity Press.

Julier-Costes, M. (2018) L' expérience du deuil d'un(e) ami(e) chez les jeunes à l'ère du numérique. In Cottin, P., A. Lanchon, and A. Le Pennec (Eds.), *Accompagner les adolescents: Nouvelles pratiques, nouveaux défis pour les professionels*. Toulouse: Erès, pp. 73–83.

Jupp, P. and T. Walter (1999) The healthy society: 1918–98. In Jupp, P. and C. Gittings (Eds.), *Death in England: An Illustrated History*. Manchester: Manchester University Press, pp. 256–283.

Kellner, D. (2002) *Media Spectacle*. Abingdon: Routledge.

Klastrup, K. (2015) "I didn't know her, but . . .": Parasocial mourning of mediated deaths on Facebook RIP pages. *New Review of Hypermedia and Multimedia* 21 (1–2): 146–164.

Klastrup, L. (2018) Death and communal mass-mourning: Vin Diesel and the remembrance of Paul Walker. *Social Media + Society* (Special Issue: Mediatization of Emotion on Social Media: Forms and Norms in Digital Mourning Practices edited by K. Giaxoglou and K. Döveling) 4 (1): 1–11.

Klein, N. (2008) *The Shock Doctrine: The Rise of Disaster Capitalism*. London: Allen Lane, Penguin Books.

Koller, V. (2012) How to analyse collective identity in discourse: Textual and contextual parameters. *Critical Approaches to Discourse Analysis across Disciplines* 5 (2): 19–38.

Manning, M. (2009) "Death, like sun cannot be looked at steadily": (François de la Rochefoucauld-1678). *Studies: An Irish Quarterly Review* 98 (392): 379–391.

The Missouri Review (Landfair, A.) (2013) Facebook of the dead. *The Missouri Review*, Oct. 8. Available at: www.missourireview.com/article/facebook-of-the-dead/. Accessed: 20 Jan. 2019.

Montgomery, M. (1999) Speaking sincerely: Public reactions to the death of Diana. *Language and Literature* 8 (1): 5–33.

Noys, B. (2005) *The Culture of Death*. Oxford: Berg Publishers.

Page, R. (2018) *Narratives Online: Shared Stories in Social Media*. Cambridge: Cambridge University Press.

Papacharissi, Z. (2019) Introduction. In Papacharissi, Z. (Ed.), *A Networked Self and Birth, Life, Death*. New York and London: Routledge.

Papacharissi, Z. and M. de Fatima Oliveira (2012) Affective news and networked publics: The rhythms of news storytelling on #Egypt. *Journal of Communication* 62 (2): 266–282.

Phillips, W. (2011) Loling at tragedy: Facebook trolls, memorial pages and resistance to grief online. *First Monday*. Available at: http://firstmonday.org/ojs/index.php/fm/article/view/3168/3115.

Phillips, W. (2015) *This Is Why We Can't Have Nice Things: Mapping the Relationship between Online Trolling and Mainstream Culture*. Cambridge, MA: MIT Press.

Phillips, W. and R.M. Milner (2018) *The Ambivalent Internet: Mischief, Oddity, and Antagonism Online*. Cambridge and Malden, MA: Polity Press.

Powell, H. (2018) Introduction to part I. In Sampson, T.D., S. Maddison, and D. Ellis (Eds.), *Affect and Social Media: Emotion, Mediation, Anxiety and Contagion*. London and New York: Rowman & Littlefield.

Reuters (Pelosfky, J.) (2007) Facebook becomes bulletin board for Virginia Tech. *Reuters*, Apr. 18. Available at: www.reuters.com/article/us-usa-crime-shootings-facebook/facebook-becomes-bulletin-board-for-virginia-tech-idUSN1742895920070418. Accessed: 10 Jan. 2018.

Robert, A.C. (2018) *La stratégie de l'émotion*. Paris: Editions Lux.

Sontag, S. (2001) Tuesday, and after: New Yorker writers respond to 9/11, September 24. *The New Yorker*. Available at: www.newyorker.com/magazine/2001/09/24/tuesday-and-after-talk-of-the-town. Accessed: 29 July 2019.

Stage, C. and T.T. Hougaard (2018) *The Language of Illness and Death on Social Media: An Affective Approach*. Bingley, UK: Emerald Publishing.

Strömbäck, J. and F. Esser (2014) Mediatization of politics: Towards a theoretical framework. In Esser, F. and J. Strömback (Eds.), *Mediatization of Politics: Understanding the Transformation of Western Democracies*. Basingstoke: Palgrave Macmillan.

Sumiala, J., K. Valaskivi, M. Tikka, and J. Huhtamäki (2018) *Hybrid Media Events: The Charlie Hebdo Attacks and the Global Circulation of Terrorist Violence*. Bingley, UK: Emerald.

Tech Crunch (Wadhera, M.) (2016) The information age is over: Welcome to the experience age. *Tech Crunch* [online]. Available at: https://techcrunch.com/2016/05/09/the-information-age-is-over-welcome-to-the-experience-age/. Accessed: 3 Nov. 2019.

van Dijck, J. (2013) *The Culture of Connectivity: A Critical History of Social Media.* Oxford: Oxford University Press.

Walter, T. (2014) The revival of death: Two decades on [blog post, October 17]. *End of Life Studies Blog*, University of Glasgow. Available at: http://endoflifestudies.academicblogs.co.uk/the-revival-of-death-two-decades-on-by-tony-walter/. Accessed: 29 July 2019.

2 Histories of Mourning

Introduction

This chapter provides the entry point to this book by looking into key linguistic and sociocultural dimensions of mourning in 'traditional', 'modern', and 'network' societies[1] in an attempt to locate death in contemporary social life. I start by discussing general understandings of the terms *mourning* and *grief* in contemporary language use, arguing that they inflect and are inflected by meaning distinctions between *private* and *public*, among other binaries. These largely Western-based dualistic understandings of emotion are nuanced in this chapter through a historicizing angle on (meta)cultures of mourning (Wilce, 2009a). This angle is grounded in insights from linguistic anthropology and the broader perspective that they offer into *mourning as social and cultural practice*. The chapter also revisits the widespread thesis that 'death is taboo' in favor of a narrative approach to death and mourning, concerned with the conditions of their tellability and storyability and, in an age of sharing, the conditions of shareability. The main principles underlying this approach are sketched out, framing the analysis of the selected case studies, which will be discussed in the following chapters.

Coming to Terms With Death

Death is a window to life, both an individual's biographical life, as well as cultural and social life; it calls forth different approaches to its uncanny certainty and the use of largely shared tropes (e.g. *death as a transition*), clichés (e.g. *death is the great leveler*), and euphemisms (e.g. *he passed away, she's in a better place*). Facing death is, after all, fraught with ambivalence, even when one has lived long enough or even too long (as in the case of the absurdly long-lived king raging against his impending death in Ionesco's play *Exit the King*).

Equally – and perhaps even more so – experiencing the death of the other is fraught with ambivalence. Witnessing someone else's death turns the prospect of death into an irrevocable reality. Experiences of loss, as variable as they may be in intensity and complication, depending on the type of loss, stir up fundamental questions about who we are, who we were (with the other), and who – and how – we will be without them. They affirm, thus, the inter-subjective constitution of our self with(in) the other. As Judith Butler (2004, p. 22) notes:

> On one level, I think I have lost 'you' only to discover that 'I' have gone missing as well. At another level, perhaps what I have lost 'in' you, that for which I have ready vocabulary, is a relationality that is composed neither exclusively of myself nor you, but is to be con-ceived as *the tie* by which those terms are differentiated and related.

Death as an existential fact and as a reality that is experienced situates its subject in a liminal time and space, where the body, the self, but also the social body becomes vulnerable. In this time-space, language proves an inadequate means of expression. Societies have addressed this inher-ent ambivalence and liminality of death in various ways through rituals, belief systems, community practices, interactional norms, and emotional regimes. In some societies, death is defined as a medical fact where the dead are seen as no longer functional biological organisms. In others, death is seen as a transition to a new state structured by ritual, and the dead are envisaged as an acting presence among the living. Coming to terms with death can take the form of denying, accepting, or defying death (or all of these alternately), and it involves more or less regimented ways of expressing, displaying, and controlling emotions, such as sorrow, rage, and grief.

The extent of some of these differences, which are attested across and within national boundaries (Rosenblatt, 2015), becomes apparent when considering how well some of the terms relating to death and loss translate – or not – in other languages. For example, as Lutz (1982) observes, for the Ifaluk islanders on a Pacific Ocean atoll, the word *fago* denotes a blend of compassion, love, and sadness, which is difficult to translate in English. Difficulties in translating loss-related terms also arise within any one lan-guage. In English, for example, there is no absolute consensus about what the terms *mourning* and *grief* denote exactly and what are their main meaning differences. English author Julian Barnes (2014), in his literary autobiographical foray into his personal experience of loss, describes *grief* as vertical and vertiginous and *mourning* as horizontal: "Grief makes your stomach turn, snatches the breath from you, cuts off the blood supply to the brain; mourning blows you in a new direction" (p. 88). But not all English speakers would necessarily feel that these definitions resonate with their own understanding of the terms and their personal experience of the emotional turmoil they involve. Even though corresponding words for *grief, mourning, crying, anger,* or *sadness* can be found in other lan-guages, it is unlikely that the cultural meanings and practices invoked by each of these words travel well across – or even within – language and cultural boundaries. These first-level terminological matters reveal that death and its associated emotions and practices are socially and culturally embedded. They also provide a useful starting point for probing further into death and mourning as socio-cultural practices.

Mourning or Grief?

In English, the terms *mourning and grief* (and their associated verb forms *mourn* and *grieve*) are often used interchangeably. Some dictionaries even provide the same definitions for the two terms. Cambridge English Dictionary, for example, defines both terms as follows: "to feel or express great sadness, especially because of someone's death". Other dictionaries, like the Collins Dictionary, treat the two terms as synonyms.[2] As much as dictionary definitions can be illuminating in terms of the common and general uses of terms, they don't always capture their diverse understandings in use.

One of the difficulties in 'fixing' the meaning of any of these two terms is their generally low frequency of use. According to the corpus-based Collins Dictionary, both verbs *mourn* and *grieve* are used only *occasionally*, i.e. one in 30,000 words (based on the corpus-based Collins Dictionary's scale of *extremely common, very common, common usage, occasional usage, rare usage*). Even though it is not incorrect to use the two terms interchangeably, the meaning of the two terms has slightly different nuances in English. In language users' *metacommentary* – "second-order descriptions of emblematic language features" (Rymes and Leone, 2014, p. 33) – for instance, *mourning* tends to be associated with formal and public domains as opposed to *grief*, which is used to refer predominantly to more personal and private domains.

Even though an analysis of the uses of these terms in English is beyond the scope of this study, metacommentaries elicited by 11 Twitter users in September 2018 who volunteered their responses to the author's question: "Do you use the verbs *mourn* and *grieve* interchangeably or not?" pointed to general differences between the two terms under a range of dimensions, including:

  i. *Register*, i.e. the degree of formality or informality each term is associated with (e.g. "*Mourning* seems more formal, e.g. a day of national mourning").
 ii. *Duration* covered by each term, i.e. a defined versus an undefined time period (e.g. "I think mourning is more communal and linked with time, whereas grief is personal, and for most, never leaves you").
iii. *Domain of use*, for example ritual vs. non-ritual; public vs. private. (e.g. "Does *mourning* not carry some sort of public display or ritual? Marking someone's death in a way that is culturally recognized? *Grieving* seems more about private feelings").

iv. *Affective intensity*, i.e. less or more intense. (e.g. "*Mourn* seems less intense than *grieve*").

v. *Agency*, i.e. being within or outside someone's control. (e.g. "*Mourning* is something you actively do – as others have said, connected with ritual etc. *Grieving* was something I had no choice about, like breathing").

vi. *Semantic prosody*, that is associated with negative vs. positive connotations (e.g. "It [mourn] has really traditional and uncomfortable connotations for me, I'm not sure where they have come from though!").

vii. *Ontology*, i.e. the nature of mourning and grief (e.g. "To *mourn* is to solemnly think about the loss of someone/thing, to *grieve* usually includes suffering, different behavior, a process").

Understandings of meaning differences between mourning and grief in the everyday, such as the ones cited above, arguably inflect and are inflected by positions of "modern subjectivity", i.e. reflective understandings of self with an emphasis on the individual as a site of emotional richness and conflict (Abu-Lughod, 2000), which locate loss-related emotions firmly within the realm of the individual and the degree of control over emotional states. The seeds of these understandings are to be found in broader uses of the terms in the specialist domain of psychology and their further circulation in public domains.

Approaches to Mourning and Grief

Sigmund Freud, who is often credited with the pioneering of the psychoanalytic study of mourning and showed a particular interest in its pathological development into states of *melancholia*, defines *mourning*[3] as "the reaction to the loss of a loved person, or to the loss of some abstraction which has taken the place of one, such as fatherland, liberty, an ideal, and so on", thus recognizing the metaphorical and symbolic dimensions of such states" (Freud, 1917, p. 153). It is in later clinical and academic psychology that *grief* becomes a focal concern as "the psychobiological response to bereavement" (Shear, 2012, p. 120). The term became widely associated with the process of recovering from loss (*grieving*), which, according to Kübler-Ross and Kessler (2005), unfolds in five interrelated stages: *denial* (one simply refuses to accept the fact), *anger* (when one can no longer deny the fact but resists accepting it), *bargaining* (when one tries to somehow postpone or diminish the inescapable fact), *depression* (libidinal disinvestment), and *acceptance*. This idea of grief as a state leading to recovery through a set of stages or phases has been often reduced to a sequential process and has attracted various criticisms since its initial formulation, while remaining popular in public and media discourse. Later theories put forward views of grief as a process by which one works through tasks, which allow the bereaved to re-orient to their new circumstances (Worden, 1983), or as a dual-process, where the bereaved oscillate between an orientation to the loss and an orientation to restoring a sense of order (Stroebe and Schut, 1999). More recently, views of grief as a state or a process of *letting go* of the dead or *moving on* are giving way to views of grief as a process oriented to maintaining meaningful bonds with them, also known as *continuing bonds* (Klass et al., 1996).

While Freud opened the way for the study of mourning and melancholia, modern psychologists have focused on the process of grief understood as an individual's experience of loss that is gradually or continuously worked through. These understandings of grief have been widely popularized.

News headlines, for example, tend to feature uses of *grief*, *grieving*, and *grieve* to refer to private experiences of loss. An advanced Google search for UK English pages for news published in 2018 including these search terms returned article headlines focused on grieving families, bereaved parents sharing their experiences of how they grieved or needed to take time off work to grieve, or lessons on coping with grief. A similar search for news pages featuring the search terms *mourn* and *mourning* returned headlines of articles focusing on public reactions to the loss of a public figure, public displays of grieving in the context of a funeral, and examples of metaphorical uses, e.g. the expression of sorrow for the end of the *Love Island* series. These results attest to the widespread use of mourning to refer to public (and cultural) displays of loss-related emotions.

Popular uses of the two terms suggest the organization of understandings of *mourning* and *grief* terms around binary oppositions. These are invoked as language ideologies of differentiation (Gal, 2008), whereby the feeling experience is discursively set apart from its public, normative display (see Giaxoglou, 2017). In this book, the two terms will be used interchangeably, recognizing that the personal experience of pain in the face of loss cannot be separated from the social and cultural norms and conditions for its expression. This integrated understanding of mourning and grief is couched in the work of linguistic anthropologists. Their insights into death-related practices around the world, from pre-capitalist societies to (late) modern societies furnish an approach to mourning and grief as social and cultural practice and as *meta*culture, i.e. as evaluations about such practices that guide the conditions of their circulation (Urban, 2001; Wilce, 2009a). I will selectively present some of these insights and offer, thus, a historicized angle to mourning as a solid theoretical foundation for venturing into the understanding of the place of mourning in contemporary, networked social life.

Cultural Performances of Mourning

Mourning for the dead is attested across cultures as diverse as South America, South Greece, and the Middle East among many others. Although the nature of practices as well as the forms of emotional expression that make them up may differ across these different contexts, the social functions of mourning are largely shared. The need for some form of reverence or bereavement for the dead appears to be universal (Parkes et al., 1997), as is the need for communities and individuals to restore social order and mean- ing in the face of irrevocable loss (Wilce, 2009b). Mourning is often seen as a duty or responsibility to the dead on the part of the living, which helps forge connections between past, present, and future through personal and collective memory making. It is also an integral part of articulating the expe- rience of bereavement based on existing expressive and affective repertoires.

One of the genres typically associated with mourning is *lament* (*mirolói* in Greek verbal art traditions or *dirge* in Irish). Laments refer to a genre of crying performed predominantly by women in a collective ritual context associated with mourning – even though their relevance and significance extends beyond funerals (Giaxoglou, 2008). Laments are best defined as "stylizations that performatively embody and express complex social issues connecting largely female gendered discourses on death, morality, and memory to the aesthetic and political thematization of loss and pain, resistance and social reproduction, and to the ritual performance of emo- tion" (Feld and Fox, 1994, p. 39). They perform therapeutic functions (for the living) and honouring functions (for the dead), but they also serve political functions. For instance, checking on shamans' power or stirring revenge killings and vengeance in different cultures, including parts of Greece, Corsica, and Sardinia (Wilce, 2009b, pp. 28–29).

Laments have been intricately woven into the fabric of social life, par- ticularly in pre-capitalist societies, intertwined with pain, women's labour, and counter-voicing. They have also been integral in sustaining and repro- ducing closely knit communities in the face of loss. Such close links of death songs to the survival of communities are also acknowledged by members of indigenous communities, where laments constitute a power- ful and socially effective cultural practice. For instance, among the Warao indigenous people in northeastern Venezuela, locals assert that if women did not wail, residents would be unable to return to their subsistence tasks (Briggs, 1992, p. 349). The social role of the lament is also illustrated in the case of Inner Mani (Greece). Mourning in Maniat laments is discussed briefly in what follows to illustrate key points about mourning as a social and cultural practice interlocked with narrative and affect performances.

Mourning, Narrative, and Affect

Ritual performances of mourning in Inner Mani are organized around laments, which are typically performed by a leading lamenter, who draws on conventional rhythms (e.g. the eight-syllabic metre), formulaic expressions, and a rather archaic language bracketing the performance as distinct from everyday language registers. The acoustic structure of the ritual is characterized by alternation between *sobbing and telling* by the leading lamenter and a group of lamenters, whose participation not only supports the leading lamenter, but also serves to validate and memorialize the performance (Seremetakis, 1991, p. 99). The combination of stylized weeping, heavy, ingressive breathing, breathlessness, and syllabic prolongation directly calls for the – often tearful – participation of those present and gives the resulting performances their meaning (Wilce, 2009a, p. 14).

In these rituals, words are uttered as "shared substance" to be touched and shared. In other words, laments are substantial and material: using the technique of antiphony, women entextualize the words in a memorable way and insert these words in a collective oral history and archive of life and death in the community (Seremetakis, 1991, pp. 100–105). The technique of antiphony is a key resource for validating discourse within the particular time and space of the mourning ritual and for ensuring the lament's entextualization and circulation beyond that setting. Entextualization is realized by extracting stretches of discourse from their setting(s) (*decontextualization*), fostering their circulation beyond a particular setting, into new settings (*contextualization)* again and again (*recontextualization*; Bauman and Briggs, 1990, p. 73; Foley, 1997, pp. 371–372). This mode of witnessing the Inner Maniat lament creates chains and histories of tellings and feelings, which circulate long after a particular death event. As Seremetakis suggests, "to 'witness', to 'suffer for, or 'to come out as representative for' are narrative devices in laments" (1991, p. 102).

Laments travel as shared substance, words, and feelings in and through stories of mourning, which are essentially stories of life and death. In the case of the Inner Maniat lament, in particular, the content of these stories typically revolves around the recounting of the specific details of the deceased person's life and events leading up to the death or killing, interspersed by evaluations of characters, including the praising of the dead's life and character and the assignment of blame for their death (which secures that their death will be avenged). The transportability of these stories sustains them – although in changed forms – to this day, when they can be invoked often as emblems of local identity and affiliation. Their performance unfolds on the continuum of speaking and singing in the typical monotone of lamentations and shows regularity in their musical tone and their poetic, ethnopoetic, and narrative patterning. The attested regularity at different levels signals the lament's high degree of crystallization shaped by and shaping culturally specific norms for encoding past events, affect, and forms of relationality. Locals refer to these laments as 'old laments' or just 'stories'. These (more or less) crystallized versions constitute representations of ritual wailing and index local mourning norms; they also serve as displays of locals' skill in remembering and performing them, furnishing opportunities for participation in local practices of memory keeping (Giaxoglou, 2019).

The narrativity of Maniat laments is attested in other types of lament, too. Wilce (2009a, p. 10), for example, notes that "laments weave stories – stories of the lamented dead and the lamented family and community. They respond to moral cracks in the moral structure of local universes, asking why *this* sickness, *this* death, *this* destruction or loss". As a genre, laments are not restricted to ritual performance, but they also constitute an everyday genre for articulating pain and narrativizing death and mourning. This process creates chains and histories of tellings and associated positions of participation and witnessing death. In other words, lament is simultaneously "a revelation, a disclosure, a witnessing and an objectification of pain and suffering" (Seremetakis, 1991, p. 105).

The important role that laments play in people's everyday life beyond rituals of mourning is attested across cultural contexts. For example, as Mary Hegland has shown (1997), among Shi'a Muslim women in contemporary Pakistan, performances of mourning rites, locally known as *majles*, become sites for the contestation of women's subordinate position and the claiming of new socially and culturally emancipated female identities. Similar uses of *majles* have been pointed out among Iraqi Shi'a Muslim women in Wales for whom these sacred religious practices become key sites for constructing diasporic identities (Al-Bundawi, 2018).

Furthermore, the ethnomusicologist Estelle Amy de la Bretèque (2013) has shown how melodized speech among the Yezidis, which is known locally as *kilame sur* (translated as words about someone or something) is not only performed in funerals or graveyard feasts but can also be inserted in daily conversations when the topic evokes sad memories (ibid, p. 198). De la Bretèque argues that this use of melodization among the Yezidis serves as a way to regulate distance so that narration of traumatic events becomes possible and as a way to enable emotional sharing with others (ibid, pp. 104–107, p. 198).

As Urban notes, lamenting is a sociocultural practice and a culture-specific semiotic sign (Urban, 1988), which furnishes a window to local socio-emotional structures and agency. Mourning lamentations are inextricably linked to social institutions (Seremetakis, 1991), discourse bodies (Briggs, 1992), and techniques or processes of cultural circulation (Wilce, 2009b), the sharing of pain and affect and the construction or (re)claiming of identities. Looking at key dimensions of diverse cultural performances of mourning points to the need to avoid cultural or modernist essentialism that relegates such practices to the realm of the pre-modern, rural, female, 'traditional' past (Bauman and Briggs, 2003).

Taking as a starting point a historicized understanding of mourning is useful for approaching public displays of loss-related emotion in contemporary contexts in their interconnected social, cultural, and emotional dimensions and the web of ideologies they index. Importantly, it helps us move beyond understandings of grief as a privately 'owned' experience (Wilce, 2009a, p. 99) or a form of emotional 'catharsis' and, instead, attend to its broader socio-affective and political dimensions. As Willerslev et al. (2013, p. 5) note "[d]eath is inherently social in the sense that it pre-exists us, we handle it socially and we experience death through the death of others". Based on these considerations, mourning is *a socially and culturally situated vernacular expression, interlocked with narrative activity, which is shaped by and shapes our values and understandings of life and death.*

Mourning in (Late) Modernity

Mourning is not just worthy of scholarly attention as a cultural phenomenon. James Wilce (2009, pp. 4–11) points out that mourning is an important site in which modernist discourses are being created and reaffirmed. Scholarly representations of lament, for example, tend to promote its understanding as a pre-modern genre, relegated to the past. Such representations emerge out of modernist constructions of the *urban* and the *rural*, the *public* and the *private*, the *global* and the *local* as fundamentally opposed to each other. Genres of mourning, like lament, emerge, thus, as a trope for creating the 'modern' as 'new' at a distance from the 'traditional' and 'old' – unless if in commodified forms. Mourning is also used as a trope for addressing a more general sense of loss and uncertainty characterizing modern, particularly urban, life. Such tropes are based on understandings of mourning as an emotional genre.

However, mourning was never purely a matter of passion, but it has always carried stark political undertones. Associations of lament to emotion are not as straightforward as they may appear to be at first sight, given that they are mediated by ideologies about their appropriacy and function. For example, ancient Greek mourners' laments were considered as emotionally excessive and were banned during fifth- and sixth-century Athens in an attempt to curb their force and suppress them (Holst-Warhaft, 1992). Maniat laments in modern Greece have also been associated with notions of 'rural', 'backward', and 'female' domains, leading to their relegation to traces of ancient traditions and samples of local and national folklore (Giaxoglou, 2008). In other words, evaluative assessments about mourning determine their circulation or marginalization as a form of appropriate cultural expression. Such metacultural dimensions tend, however, to be missing in the majority of studies of mourning.

Associations of mourning with emotion are also taken up in accounts of modern practices, and as we will see later in assessments of social media mourning. Laments or 'traditional' forms of mourning continue to be invoked today, for discursively constructing contrasts between premodern and (post) modern, digital cultures. These sharp contrasts tend to be driven by an over-emphasis on Western – mostly urban, white, middleclass contexts – and the reliance on those specific contexts for making generalizations about the whole of society.

Even in highly individualistic cultures, however, contradictions around mourning continue to exist. Belshaw and Purvey (2009) observe that "contradictory responses to mortality and mourning rituals survived throughout the twentieth century, during which time established spiritual authority was increasingly questioned, the family and the community took on new and different roles, the individual came to mean something different, and the physical space of villages, towns, and cities was encircled by suburban housing tracts" (p. 17).

Despite the common assertion that mourning and death are private, there are plenty of examples of public mourning, for example public mourning for war victims, politicians, and celebrities. Princess Diana's death in 1997 remains very much still an emblematic event, one that has led even to the addition of a new word, *dianafication*, to the popular lexicon. The word came into use to refer to the reaction of sociological and psychopathological interest and "the orgy of demonstrative pseudo-grief" that the death of Princess Diana provoked (Darlymple, 2007) or more broadly, to the widespread idea that contemporary public mourning is driven more by selfishness and secularism than sincerity of emotion. Death sociologist Tony Walter (2008), however, noted how acts of public mourning for the death of Princess Diana, such as the laying of flowers and the creation of shrines in everyday places, "materialized a close-knit, public society" (p. 507).

Another popular example of contemporary public displays of grief are roadside shrines and memorials – also known as RDMs – which, as Belshaw and Purvey (2009) suggest, make part of a longer and complex story about the meaning of both death and grieving in a particular time and place (p. 15) – in their case in the Canadian province of British Columbia.

Therefore, instead of looking at practices of mourning and grief in contrastive terms of 'private' versus 'public', arguing about which one is least 'aberrant', it is more useful to approach them as situated practices, which are inherently social and inflected by local as much as by broader ideologies of culture and emotion.

Is Death Taboo?

Contrastive frames for discussing mourning have also been extensively used in discussions about death. Often contrasted to 'the cult of death' in Victorian times, modern death has been described as highly privatized. References to the 'hidden death' or the 'denial of death' (Becker, 1973) abound in accounts of death and mourning in late modernity, which tend to take as their starting point the loosening of social bonds and the rise of radical individualism (Giddens, 1990) to make the point that death no longer disrupts communal worlds but rather individual ones. Walter et al. (2011), for example, note that while "premodern societies tended to produce a bereaved community, modern societies tend to produce bereaved individuals" (p. 289), leading to the privatization of death, its experience, and its sequestration from everyday life. This is manifest in the notable decrease in the public space afforded to death, a shrinkage of the scope of the sacred in terms of the experience of death in favor of the medicalization of death and a fundamental shift in the corporeal boundaries, symbolic and actual. In these claims, "private" death becomes equated with "institutionalized, hidden and thus de-ritualised" (de Vries and Roberts, 2004, p. 1) and associated with the idea that 'death is a taboo' in modern Western societies.

In his 1955 article "The Pornography of Death", Geoffrey Gorer was noting a shift in prudery in the twentieth century that has affected Western society's approach to death: "whereas copulation has become more and more 'mentionable', particularly in the Anglo-Saxon societies, death has become more and more 'unmentionable' *as a natural process*" (Gorer, 1955, p. 51). Furthermore, Philippe Ariès, in his landmark book *The Hour of Our Death* asserted the denial of death as "a significant trait of our culture" interlinked with the refusal to mourn publicly: "The tears of the bereaved have become comparable to the excretions of the diseased. Both are distasteful. Death has been banished" (Ariès, 1981, p. 580).

The idea that 'death is taboo' is also regularly making headlines in media articles and charity campaigns, as the selection below illustrates:

1. "BJ Miller: 'Death and dying continues to be seen as a big taboo'".
   (*The Guardian*, 2017, May 9)

2. "A charity is calling for a 'national conversation' about dying, saying the topic has become 'taboo' and a source of anxiety for many".
   (BBC, 2018, Feb. 26)

3. "Discussing death and funerals continues to be a taboo for many people, according to latest research from the Funeral Planning Authority (FPA)".
   (*The Telegraph*, 2018, Mar. 12)

4. "Joan Bakewell and her panel discuss death and dying, exploring the choices open to us and confronting the questions we fear the most".
   (BBC Radio 4, 2016–2017)

In addition to journalists who see the 'death taboo' as a problem in need of a solution, be it improved palliative care support or better funeral planning, this 'problem' is also emerging as a central topic in the discourse and campaigns of health-related charity organizations, such as Marie Curie's "Help us break the taboo around death" (2017), Age UK's "Let's Talk about Death" (2017) or Dying Matters mission "to help people talk more openly about dying, death and bereavement, and to make plans for the end of life". The need to tackle the 'death taboo' by talking more openly about death has even given rise to the movement of the Death Café, a not-for-profit organization that encourages meet-ups of (often urban) strangers, who get together to talk about death, tea, and cake with the goal of raising public awareness of death and dying. As noted in one of the many calls for such a Death Café get-together:

5. "Death is often taboo in our society, yet it's a part of life. It will happen to us all and will touch us all many times before that. I believe it's always healthier to speak about the things that trouble us and that's why I was inspired to run death cafes".

(Death Café, Aug. 11, 2018)

This public thematization of death as the ultimate taboo is not new, though. Some twenty years ago, death sociologist Tony Walter was citing the following examples from media and broadcasting sources, which strike a strong chord of resemblance to the examples cited earlier:

6. 'Death – and talk about it – is one great taboo of our age'.

(*Radio Times*, February 24, 1990)

7. 'Death, in a world of uncertain beliefs, has become something of a taboo subject'.

(Office of Fair Trading report, Funerals, January 1989)

8. 'In our society the subject of death is taboo; we don't talk about it' (Bereavement, leaflet produced jointly by Help the Aged, Cruse, and the National Association of Funeral Directors, 1989/90).

(Walter, 1991, p. 293)

These examples illustrate how the assertion that 'death is taboo' has turned into a type of discourse frame, which helps to draw attention to social matters, campaigns, or organizations relating to death and dying. At the same time, this thesis organizes approaches and interpretations of death, dying, and bereavement around specific social 'problems' and possible 'solutions' and around negative emotions, such as fear and denial, typically associated with death in parts of the Western world. As Jupp and Walter (1999) put it, the 'death as taboo' thesis has become "a popular journalistic cliché" (p. 256).

Criticisms to scholarly accounts of the 'death as taboo' thesis have been raised, noting their generality and their failure to offer contextualized and nuanced understandings of contemporary death (and mourning). As Jupp and Walter (1999, p. 278) point out, "death is nowhere to be seen, but it is everywhere", considering that death is often the topic of everyday talk. In addition, Walter (1991) has critiqued the death taboo thesis, arguing that this thesis is rarely followed by clarification as to how death as a subject matter is different to socially and culturally specific "conversational norms against speaking of death" (p. 296). He has proposed five modifications to the death taboo thesis so as to connect it more explicitly to changing attitudes to and practices of death. First, he acknowledges cultural shifts to a more expressive culture as contributing to the discovery of the death taboo and clarified that death in modern medicalized society tends to be 'hidden' rather than 'forbidden'. He also notes the gap between the death anxieties of institutions, including the media and the public, and cautions to avoid conflating the two. Lastly, he points out that in an increasingly secular and diverse society, there are multiple frames for handling death and that these often result in embarrassment around death rather than in its invisibility or outright banishment (Walter, 1991, p. 297). More recently, Walter (2014) has altogether denied the death taboo thesis, proclaiming that "death is not taboo in contemporary Britain". His break with this accepted truism draws attention to the importance of conversational norms about what and when to talk about death (see also Chapter 1).

The death-as-taboo thesis needs to be revisited, then, by attending to which aspects of death are thought to be taboo, but also whose death, and when, is considered to be grievable and tellable. In other words, a linguistic-discourse angle is called for that can draw attention to the interactional norms, the social discourses (or ideologies) surrounding death and mourning, and the specific conditions for death talk and stories of life and death in specific contexts.

The Reportability and Tellability of Death

A step towards moving beyond the 'death as taboo' thesis is the closer consideration of the conditions of the reportability and tellability of death.[4] Labov suggested that some types of stories are inherently *reportable*, such as the stories of near-death experience that he and Waletzky (1997 [1967]) elicited in the context of their sociolinguistic study of vernacular speech. This type of reportability refers to the subject matter, irrespective of the context in which a story is told. For Labov, the themes that prime the flow of speech involve three universal centres of interest which surface in socially and culturally variable forms, depending on local social norms. These centres of interest, which are conflated in some narratives, are the following:

- *Death and the danger of death*: violence, fighting, sickness, fear, dreams, premonitions and communication with the dead.
- *Sex and relations between the sexes*: dating, courtship, proposals, marriage, breaking off relationships, affairs, intermarriage.
- *Moral indignation*: assignment and rejection of blame, unfairness, injustice, gossip, violations of social norms.

(Labov, 2013, p. 4)

The reportability of these types of subject matter, as Labov is careful to acknowledge, is contextually variable. The situated character of a story's reportability is best captured by the term *tellability*, which has emerged from the study of conversational storytelling before it extended to all kinds of narrative, referring to features that make a story worth telling, in other words, its noteworthiness (Baroni, 2013).

Tellability is not inherent to a particular subject matter or story topic and point, but it's negotiated *in situ* between the interlocutors present – or in some cases absent, as for instance in the opening of a story by a preface like the following: 'Mary wouldn't want me to tell you this but . . .". This notion of tellability extends understandings of reportability as a situated, interactional accomplishment rather than an inherent feature of stories. Ochs and Capps (2001), for example, treat tellability as one of the gradient dimensions of narrative, while Norrick (2005, p. 324) proposes the need for a two-sided notion of tellability:

> Some events bear too little significance (for this teller, this setting, these listeners) to reach the lower bounding threshold of tellability, while others are so intimate (so frightening) that they lie outside the range of the tellable in the current context. Similarly, one narrative rendering of an event may fail to bring out its significance (humor, strangeness), and thus fail to reach the threshold of tellability, while another telling might render the event so frightening (intimate) that the story is no longer tellable.

Death as an event that irrevocably disrupts life – both the biological flow of life and the everyday life of those left behind – is a unique event that is inherently worth reporting. Whether this report will turn into a public performance of mourning, a subject of talk, or a story depends on a number of other factors, including whose death it is, who is reporting it, to whom, when, how, and why. In case of a personal loss or a traumatic experience, the transformation of a reportable death to a tellable death can become even more problematic due to gaps in memory or an unwillingness to verbalize this experience. These are cases that point to the limits of tellability and offer a window to liminal states of being and feeling, in addition to revealing social and cultural norms and ideologies of emotion.

In digital environments, where stories are co-constructed and shared, the conditions of tellability become enmeshed with conditions of *shareability*, which include a shared story's visibility and value potential, i.e. what kind of story can gain widespread reach and impact, how, and when. Shareability raises differential *telling rights* (Shuman, 2015), i.e. when is a story deemed to be shareable, by whom, and how. Shareability, then, refers both to the design of a story for sharing and its potential for dissemination through retellings and reworkings. Emerging norms of shareability online call for the reformulation of questions like 'Is death a taboo?' or 'Is death tellable?' as follows:

1. *What makes it possible for a death event or for the experience of mourning to be transformed into a story of mourning that is deemed appropriate for sharing with and for others in specific online contexts?*
2. *How do the sharing and narrative affordances of specific platforms impact the design of stories about death or mourning as stories that have the potential of gaining online visibility through retellings?*

The next section considers in more detail the broader context of sharing in which these conditions of shareability of death and mourning have been emerging, offering a summary of key insights from research in the interdisciplinary field of death online, which form the basis for this study.

Mourning and Death in the Age of Sharing

Digital media uses relating to mourning the dead have existed at least since the 1990s. Cyber-memorials, web memorials, virtual cemeteries, and shrines, for example, described as emerging post-death rituals (Roberts and Vidal, 2000), have been said to play an important role in the recovery process for grieving individuals (see, for example, Cable, 1996; Roberts, 2006).

The internet has offered increased opportunities for creating and maintaining bereavement groups, such as the online grief support group Grief-Net.org (Lynn and Rath, 2012) and the special online support groups focused on specific kinds of traumatic events, like school shootings in the U.S. (Gary and Remolino, 2000) or the bereavement of a child, which is often experienced as a disenfranchised loss (Refslund Christensen et al., 2017). Since the 2000s, social network sites (SNSs) rapidly emerged as sites for mourning, grieving, and memorializing the dead, extending the scope of mourning temporally, spatially and socially (Brubaker et al., 2013). Even though the majority of the body of work on digital death and mourning has focused on social media, some scholars have also drawn attention to uses of mobile media for loss-related practices and rituals, noting how their emotive power and intimate affordances ends up heightening and intensifying these remediated practices and rituals (Hjorth and Kim, 2012; Cumiskey and Hjorth, 2017).

The body of research in the interdisciplinary area of death online suggests that the use of internet and Web 2.0 technologies for mourning "brings death back into everyday life" (Walter et al., 2011, p. 295), affording the creation and maintenance of (online) communities of the bereaved in which mourning re-emerges as a group experience. Web-based online support groups for coping with traumatic events, social network sites, blogs, and, more recently, vlogs (aka video blogs), as well as mobile media and instant messaging have been recognized as sites for narrating, commemorating, expressing, and experiencing death and mourning (Sofka et al., 2012), and more recently also as sites for engagement in entrepreneurial activities, associated with charity action and potential social change (Stage, 2017).

As norms of grief appear to be 'relaxing' or shifting in some of these 'new' sites (Jakoby and Reiser, 2013), a wider group of mourners including those who are disenfranchised in 'traditional' rituals (Doka, 2009) is feeling entitled to participate in public mourning (Hensley, 2012), while, at the same time, the potential for conflict among the bereaved increases, as their grieving norms may clash (Bell et al., 2015). In addition, the publicness of many of these sites and practices leaves them open to scrutiny and even attacks that, in some, cases takes the form of organized trolling behavior on Facebook, for example (see Chapter 1). In other words, the mediation of private experiences as a public process can, in some cases, result in loss of control over the personal experiences broadcast to known and unknown audiences, attesting to the way that the texture and visibility of public life and the frameworks available for its interpretation and participation are being more generally reconfigured (see Thompson, 2005; Baym and boyd, 2012; Giaxoglou et al., 2017).

Sharing is not just mediated by specific technologies of communication, but it is *mediatized*, that is it is subject to media logics, i.e. specific forms and formats of communication (Mazzoleni and Schulz, 1999).[5] In addition, it is also shaped by (and shapes) the digital affordances of social networking sites. These include *persistence* (what we share stays online), *replicability* (what we share can be reshared and even become viral), *scalability* (local indexicalities can quickly attain global meanings), and *searchability* (our lives and selves can be tracked, and we can track the lives of others; boyd and Ellison, 2007, p. 45). These affordances result in a higher level of self-reflection, self-awareness, and self-monitoring on the part of users, for whom performing the self online has become part of routine ways of being and relating to others (Papacharissi, 2012).

General digital affordances, but also platform-specific ones, are part of the social media logics that drive sharing practices of mourning. For example, the rising trend of taking funeral selfies, i.e. pictures of a smiling person taken next to a corpse, attests to users drawing on the platform-specific visual affordances of sites like Instagram, part of a wider turn to the visual (Gibbs et al., 2015). As Meese et al. (2015) point out, these visual practices can be understood as a subtle form of *presencing*, an integral part of the "vernacular (and ongoing) tradition of online memorialisation" (p. 1828), which facilitate a personal, affective response in the context of attempts to capture "the flamboyant and internationally gazed-upon memorial event" (p. 1827). Platform-specific and social media logics have an important impact on the shape and content of representation and dissemination of moments of life and death, giving rise to networked, vernacular forms of witnessing, testimony, and memorialization, which produce and are produced by networked publics (Bourdeloie and Julier-Costes, 2016).

The Interdisciplinary Study of Death Online

The study of using digital technologies as thanatology resources – or *thanatotechnologies* (Sofka, 1997) – has been growing and developing as the web has been developing and changing. Even though the main body of this work has had its origins in healthcare, palliative care, and social work, responding to the need for a better understanding of the implications of these technologies for practitioners (see Sofka et al., 2012), in recent years it has grown into an interdisciplinary field that brings together scholars who recognize the digital embeddedness of death-related practices. Such international dialogue has been particularly fostered since 2013 in the context of the Death Online Research Network (DORN),[6] which invites the study of death online with a focus on "cultural change, identity performances, social bonding, legal matters, design innovations, business opportunities and more". In their introduction to the Special Issue on Online Cultures, Refslund Christensen and Gotved (2015) acknowledge the rapid maturation of the field as an interdisciplinary field concerned with the potential impact of the internet and social media on ways of grieving and mourning as well as on social concepts of death and bereavement (p. 2).

A broad way of classifying studies of death online is based on the type of practices they focus on, i.e. whether these relate to *ante-mortem* (before death), *peri-mortem* (at or around the time of death), or *post-mortem* (after death) activities. It seems that the largest part of studies deals with *post-mortem* practices of death-related communication, including announcements about death and various kinds of memorialization activities, which have seen a huge growth with the advent of social media. Studies of death online can also be differentiated depending on their analytic focus. In their overview of studies in the field, Reflsund Christensen and Gotved (2015) identify three different social levels (which can variously overlap), which include: (1) *the individual level*, which refers to coping with personal loss, (2) *the community level*, that is mourning and commemoration in the extended social network by relatives, friends, colleagues, acquaintances, and the broader community, and (3) *the cultural level*, which covers memorial practices for people not personally known to those engaged in these practices, for example tragic death, disaster death, or celebrity death, attesting to the expansion of the cultural repertoires of grief and memorialization (p. 5).

As a field, death online has drawn attention to the technological as much as to sociocultural aspects of remediated rituals of grief and commemoration (Reflsund Christensen and Gotved, 2015). A growing body of work in the field of death online has also been looking at the mediatization of affect online (see, for instance, Reflsund Christensen and Sandvik, 2014; Giaxoglou et al., 2017; Stage, 2017; Giaxoglou and Döveling, 2018), converging in recognizing the blurring of the boundaries between formal and informal, institutional, commercial and personal, public and private in practices of sharing death and mourning online. Other scholars have pointed out the inherent ambivalence and tensions in these vernacular or 'folkloric' practices (Phillips and Milner, 2017, p. 21), highlighting the important role of *vernacular creativities* in their constitution and their connection to earlier folkloric practices (and reactions to these) both offline and online. Some of the key findings that have emerged from studies in the field can be summarized as follows:

1. Death-related practices online are material practices, which are not clearly separated from offline practices; rather, the online and the offline are interconnected and variously navigated by users, depending on their practical, emotional, and social needs (Madianou and Miller, 2013).

2. Remediated practices of death online draw on the use of digital resources for communicating, interacting, and performing emotion and the self, featuring in particular vernacular language (Jones and Haffner, 2012). The language used in digital mourning features digital writing features, such as emoji and hashtags, and also draws on platform-specific vernaculars, for example images in photo-sharing websites (see funeral selfies in Gibbs et al., 2015; Meese et al., 2015).

3. Given the intense impression management work (Goffman, 1959) required in digital contexts, increased work is needed for negotiating and controlling (i.e. minimizing or maximizing) the visibility of grief across a spectrum, depending on the type of loss involved, context-design aspects of the specific interactional situation, and the broader sociocultural norms users draw on in the process of remediating their grief. Navigating this "spectrum of visibility" (Giaxoglou et al., 2017, p. 5) raises important dilemmas and tensions (see also Baym and boyd, 2012) related to existing and emerging hierarchies of mourning (Marwick and Ellison, 2012). As Julliard and Quemener (2018) have argued, these tensions point to the way practices of sharing death and grief online structure and are structured by affect logics in specific contexts, depending on the type of loss, but also the target audience of emotional performances (p. 19).

4. Grief emerges as a process of identity reconstruction, integration, and reintegration for the bereaved through the creation and maintenance of *continuing bonds* (Klass et al., 1996) rather than a process

of "letting go" of the dead and "moving on" (Kasket, 2012; Reflsund Christensen and Gotved, 2015, p. 4).

5. In digital contexts, small-scale (i.e. non-institutional) ritualizations and repetitions are central (Reflsund Christensen and Gotved, 2015, pp. 2–5).

The majority of studies on death online have foregrounded the benefits of the internet and social network sites, in particular as a resource for grieving "alone, together" (Turkle, 2011), which can prove especially beneficial for those who are disenfranchised in the 'real world' (Sofka et al., 2012). This recurrent finding is, in part, the result of these studies' overprivileging of individual or small-group experiences of coping with loss, which can be explained as much by convenience as by discipline-specific research approaches to social media practices. Less systematic attention has been paid so far to the narrative dimensions of mourning from a sociolinguistic perspective and the broader implications of these practices for social life, which has scope for making a broader, critical contribution to research in identities and emotion. This book aims to bridge this gap and offer an empirical account of social media mourning informed by developments in the sociolinguistic and discourse analysis of narrative, identities, and affect.

Key Tenets for the Study of Social Media Mourning

The approach used in this book has emerged from a combination of insights in anthropological research on cultural performances of mourning and recurrent findings in the study of death online selectively discussed in this chapter. In this final section, I will present the main tenets of this approach, summarized in three pivot points:

1. Mourning and grief are social and cultural performances of emotion, used as affective resources which have the power to move and mobilize others towards a range of purposes.
2. Performances of grief and mourning are not restricted to death-related rituals or ceremonies. They extend spatially, temporally, and socially beyond such occasions through narratives, which are subject to linguistic adjustments of the intensity of affect as appropriate to the context and audience. This social extension of mourning in everyday contexts creates opportunities for participation in individual and collective witnessing and memory making.
3. Mourning is a window to different cultural approaches to life and death, as much as it is a window to *metacultures*, that relate to forms of self-reflexivity framing semiosis (Urban, 2001, p. 4; see also Wilce, 2009b, p. 14). The study of mourning as metacultural discourse can shed light into local and global ideologies of self and emotion, which

are central in the making of modernities and networked (post)modern subjectivities.

An approach to mourning as narrative practice, both cultural and metacultural, provides a critical lens into the different forms mourning can be attested in. This helps us avoid confining our focus to 'traditional' lament as 'authentic' expressions of mourning or assume that 'tradition' and 'modernity' are distinct evolutionary stages in the history of humanity, given that tradition and modernities co-exist in various, overlapping ways (Bauman and Briggs, 2003).

The empirical approach used in this study has been informed by the body of work in digital death, discussed earlier, which has been bringing to the fore how practices of digital mourning vary just as platform affordances and users vary. The different dimensions of variation of these, used as a starting point for selecting the different case studies discussed in this book, are summarized below:

1. *the type of loss*, which largely determines the specific kind of role relationship in which grief is experienced and shared;
2. the (intended) *purposes of sharing*, i.e. who shares, what, when, what the envisaged *duration* of the sharing is (is the sharing envisaged as a more or less permanent material entity?)
3. the *degree* and *types of interactivity* in the sharing, which are linked to the specific affordances of the site of sharing. This dimension draws attention to who interacts with whom and how, for example groups of mourners interacting with each other or individual mourners interacting with the dead.

These three general dimensions account for the different narrative positions for participants as *tellers*, *co-tellers*, or (more or less distant) *witnesses* to a death and mourning spectacle. In the context of mourning in social media, *tellers* appropriate social media sites for sharing their personal story of loss or their unique experience of dying with networked audiences, known and unknown. An example of this form of mourning tellership designed for a large-sized audience is Sheryl Sandberg's long emotional post on Facebook[7] following the death of her husband. In addition to one-off cases like this that relate to post-mortem death-writing, teller positions can be also taken up in the context of ante-mortem and peri-mortem activities, as illustrated by the appropriation of social media by users for voicing their unique experience of illness and dying. This is illustrated in the case of young teenagers vlogging on cancer, attesting to users' attempt to take control of one's life with illness but also of their legacy. These are discussed in Chapter 4.

Co-tellers contribute tributes, memories, and updates and participate in the creation of the collective mosaic of someone's life, even if they had known them only briefly or in some cases, not at all. Co-tellers can be expected to post one-off messages, as for example in R.I.P. messages on Twitter, using hashtags to connect with others, or they can post recurrently on a memorial site, as in the case of memorial Facebook pages created by and for a group of bereaved. Co-tellers often address the dead directly, either publicly or privately, reconstructing and continuing the bonds between those who are gone and those are left behind. This type of practice will be discussed in Chapter 5.

Lastly, *witnesses* to death events contribute their personal affective reactions to disasters and tragedies by noting, for instance, where they were when they heard the news, how they felt at the time, and who they feel is to blame. This is most notable in the case of the multitude of Facebook groups created after the Sandy Hook shootings in 2012 or the Twitter storm that followed the school shootings in Florida in 2018. These kinds of messages are posted immediately after the related press coverage of the events, showing that media hype is a key driver of these reactions (Klastrup, 2015). Witnesses to media death events engage mainly in hashtag mourning, given the potential this particular mode offers for connecting users to bigger audiences, as illustrated in the case of global reactions in the wake of attacks or natural disasters. Examples of these practices will be discussed in Chapters 6 and 7.

These narrative positions make possible specific kinds of *affective positioning* at a relative proximity or distance to the death event, the audiences (known and unknown), and the affective self. Affective positioning is suggested in this book as a powerful heuristic for addressing aspects of affective communication as an integral part of identity (and identification) positioning processes (Depperman, 2015), which helps us to move beyond essentialist accounts of emotion and identity. These concepts are presented in more detail in Chapter 3, along with the analytical framework of mourning as narrative that can guide the investigation of the changing forms of mourning and participation in death-related practices and rituals, witnessing, and testimony.

Notes

1. The terms *tradition, modern,* and *network* are put in scare quotes to highlight that these are socially constructed notions; they make part of *grand narratives* of modernity and post-modernity, which are beyond the scope of this discussion (for a discussion of the language ideologies in the construction of tradition and modernity, see Bauman and Briggs, 2003; also see van Dijk, 2006; Castells, 1996, on 'network societies').
2. Note also that there is some variation in the definition of the two terms in British versus American English, especially depending on whether they are followed by an object or objects (transitive verbs) or not (intransitive verbs): in British English, uses of *grieve* as a transitive verb meaning "to inflict injury, hardship, or sorrow on" are recorded as obsolete, whereas in American English, similar meanings are recorded for these uses, which are still in use.

3. Note, however, that in the original title in German, *Trauer und Melancholie,* the word *trauer* can refer both to the affect of grief and its outward manifestation.
4. Note that 'tellability' is often used interchangeably with the terms 'reportability' and 'storyability/narratability'.
5. For a critical commentary on the term 'mediatization', see Deacon and Stanyer (2014) and Corner (2018).
6. For more information about the Death Online Research Network, see: https://cc.au.dk/en/research/research-programmes/cultural-transformations/cultures-and-practices-of-death-and-dying/dorn/.
7. *The Guardian.* 2015. Sheryl Sandberg on husband's death: I have lived 20 years in these 30 days. *The Guardian,* June 3. Available at: www.theguardian.com/technology/2015/jun/03/sheryl-sandberg-facebook-death-david-goldberg. Accessed: 22 July 2019.

References

Abu-Lughod, L. (2000) Modern subjects: Egyptian Melodrama and postcolonial difference. In Mitchell, T. (Ed.), *Questions of Modernity.* Minneapolis: University of Minnesota Press, pp. 87–114.

Al-Bundawi, Z.E.S. (2018) *Sacred texts and identity construction in the Cardiff Muslim community.* Unpublished PhD Thesis. Cardiff University.

Ariès, P. (1981) *The Hour of Our Death.* London: Penguin.

Barnes, J. (2014) *Levels of Life.* London: Vintage.

Baroni, R. (2013) Tellability. In Hühn, P., J. Pier, W. Schmid, and J. Schönert (Eds.), *The Living Handbook of Narratology.* Available at: https://wikis.sub.uni-hamburg.de/lhn/index.php/Tellability.

Bauman, R. and C.L. Briggs (1990) Poetics and performance as critical perspectives on language and social life. *Annual Review of Anthropology* 19: 59–88.

Bauman, R. and C.L. Briggs (2003) *Voices of Modernity: Language Ideologies and the Politics of Inequality.* Cambridge: Cambridge University Press.

Baym, N. and D. boyd (2012) Socially mediated publicness: An introduction. *Journal of Broadcasting & Electronic Media* 56 (3): 320–329.

Becker, E. (1973) *The Denial of Death.* New York: Free Press.

Bell, J., L. Bailey, and D. Kennedy (2015) "We do it to keep him alive": Bereaved individuals' experiences of online suicide memorials and continuing bonds. *Mortality* 20 (4): 375–389.

Belshaw, J. and D. Purvey (2009) *Private Grief, Public Mourning: The Rise of the Roadside Shrine in British Columbia.* Vancouver: Anvil Press.

Bourdeloie, H. and M. Julier-Costes (2016) Deathlogging: Social life beyond the Grave: The post-mortem uses of social networking sites. In Selke, S. (Ed.), *Lifelogging: Digital Self-Tracking and Lifelogging: Between Disruptive Technology and Cultural Transformation.* New York: Springer, pp. 129–149.

boyd, D. and N. Ellison (2007) Social network sites: Definition, history and scholarship. *Journal of Computer: Mediated Communication* 13 (1): 210–230.

Briggs, C. (1992) "Since I am a woman, I will chastise my relatives": Gender, reported speech, and the (re)production of social relations in Warao ritual wailing. *American Ethnologist* 19 (2): 337–361.

Brubaker, J.R., G.R. Hayes, and P. Dourish (2013) Beyond the Grave: Facebook as a site for the expansion of death and mourning. *The Information Society* 29: 152–163.

Butler, J. (2004) *Precarious Life: The Powers of Mourning and Violence*. London: Verso.

Cable, D. (1996) Grief counseling for survivors of traumatic loss. In K. Doka (Ed.), *Living with Grief and Sudden Loss: Suicide, Homicide, Accident, Heart Attack and Stroke*. Washington, DC: Taylor& Francis, pp. 117–127.

Castells, M. (1996) *The Rise of the Network Society, The Information Age: Economy, Society and Culture, Vol. 1*. Oxford: Blackwell.

Corner, J. (2018) "Mediatisation": Media theory's word of the decade. *Media Theory*, May 21. Available at: http://mediatheoryjournal.org/john-corner-mediatization/.

Cumiskey, M.K. and L. Hjorth (2017) *Haunting Hands: Mobile Media Practices and Loss*. Oxford: Oxford University Press.

Darlymple, T. (2007) The dianafication of modern life. *Encyclopaedia Britannica Blog*. Available at: http://blogs.britannica.com/2007/08/the-dianafication-of-modern-life/. Accessed: 29 July 2019.

Deacon, D. and J. Stanyer (2014) Mediatization: Key concept or conceptual bandwagon? *Media, Culture & Society* 36 (7): 1032–1044.

Depperman, A. (2015) Positioning. In A. De Fina and A. Georgakopoulou (Eds.), *The Handbook of Narrative Analysis*. Hoboken, NJ: Wiley Blackwell, pp. 369–387.

de la Bretèque, E. (2013) *Paroles mélodisées. Récits épiques et lamentations chez les Yézidis d'Arménie*. Paris: Classiques Garnier.

de Vries, B. and P. Roberts (2004) Introduction to special issue. *Omega: The Journal of Death and Dying* 49 (1): 1–3.

Doka, K.J. (2009) Disenfranchised grief. *Bereavement Care* 18 (3): 37–39.

Feld, S. and A.A. Fox (1994) Music and language. *Annual Review of Anthropology* 23: 25–53.

Foley, W.A. (1997) *Anthropological Linguistics: An Introduction*. Malden, MA: Blackwell Publishers.

Freud, S. (1917) Mourning and Melancholia. *The Standard Edition of the Complete Psychological Works of Sigmund Freud*. Volume XIV (1914–1916): On the History of the Psycho-Analytic Movement, Papers on Metapsychology and Other Works, pp. 237–258.

Gal, S. (2008) Language ideologies compared. *Linguistic Anthropology* 15 (1): 23–37.

Gary, J.M. and L. Remolino (2000) *Coping with Loss and Grief through Online Support Groups: ERIC/CASS Digest*. Greensboro, NC: ERIC Counseling and Student Services Clearinghouse.

Giaxoglou, K. (2008) *Maniat laments as narratives: Forms and norms of entextualisation*. Unpublished PhD Thesis. King's College London.

Giaxoglou, K. (2017) Reflections on internet research ethics from language-based research on web-based mourning: Revisiting the private/public distinction as a language ideology of differentiation. *Applied Linguistics Review* 8 (2–3): 229–250.

Giaxoglou, K. (2019) Trajectories of treasured texts: Laments as narratives. In Falconi, E.A. and K.E. Graber (Eds.), *Storytelling as Narrative Practice: Ethnographic Approaches to the Tales We Well*. Leiden and Boston: Brill.

Giaxoglou, K. and K. Döveling (2018) Mediatization of emotion on social media: Forms and norms in digital mourning practices. *Social Media + Society* 4 (1): 1–4.

Giaxoglou, K., K. Döveling, and S. Pitsillides (2017) Networked emotions: Interdisciplinary perspectives on sharing loss online. *Journal of Broadcasting & Electronic Media* 61 (1): 1–10.

Gibbs, M., J. Meese, M. Arnold, B. Nansen, and M. Carter (2015) #Funeral and Instagram: Death, social media and platform vernacular. *Information Communication and Society* 18 (3): 255–268.

Giddens, A. (1990) *The Consequences of Modernity*. Stanford: Stanford University Press.

Goffman, E. (1959) *The Presentation of Self in Everyday Life*. Garden City, NY: Doubleday.

Gorer, G. (1955) The pornography of death. In Gorer, G. (Ed.), *Death, Grief, and Mourning*. New York: Doubleday, pp. 192–199.

Hegland, M. (1997) Mixed blessing: The Majles-Shi'a women's rituals of mourning in North-West Pakistan. In Brink, J. and J. Mencher (Eds.), *Mixed Blessings: Gender and Religious Fundamentalism Cross-Culturally*. London and New York: Routledge, pp. 179–196.

Hensley, L. (2012) Bereavement in online communities: Sources of and support for disenfranchised grief. In Sofka, C., I.N. Cupit, and K.R. Gilbert (Eds.), *Dying, Death, and Grief in an Online Universe: For Counselors and Educators*. New York: Springer Publishing Company, pp. 119–135.

Hjorth, L. and K.Y. Kim (2012) Mobile intimacy in the age of affective mobile media. *Feminist Media Studies* 12 (4): 477–484.

Holst-Warhaft, G. (1992) *Dangerous Voices: Women's Laments and Greek Literature*. Oxon: Routledge.

Jakoby, N. and S. Reiser (2013) Grief 2.0. exploring virtual cemeteries. In Benski, T. and E. Fisher (Eds.), *Emotions & the Internet*. London and New York: Routledge, pp. 62–69.

Jones, R. and C.A. Haffner (2012) *Understanding Digital Literacies: A Practical Introduction*. London: Routledge.

Julliard, V. and N. Quemener (2018) Garder les morts vivants. Dispositifs, pratiques, hommages. *Réseaux*, Juillet–Août: 11–20.

Jupp, P. and T. Walter (1999) The healthy society: 1918–98. In Jupp, C.P. and C. Gittings (Eds.), *Death in England: An Illustrated History*. Manchester: Manchester University Press, pp. 256–283.

Kasket, E. (2012) Continuing bonds in the age of social networking: Facebook as a modern-day medium. *Bereavement Care* 31 (2): 62–69.

Klass, D., P.R. Silverman, and S.L. Nickman (Eds.) (1996) *Continuing Bonds: New Understandings of Grief*. Bristol, PA and London: Taylor & Francis.

Klastrup, K. (2015) "I didn't know here, but . . .": Parasocial mourning of mediated deaths on Facebook RIP pages. *New Review of Hypermedia and Multimedia* 21 (1–2): 146–164.

Kübler-Ross, E. and D. Kessler (2005) *On Grief and Grieving: Finding the Meaning of Grief through the Five Stages of Loss*. London and New York: Simon & Schuster.

Labov, W. (2013) *The Language of Life and Death*. Cambridge: Cambridge University Press.

Labov, W. and J. Waletzky (1997 [1967]) Narrative analysis: Oral versions of personal experience. *Journal of Narrative and Life History* (Special Issue: Three Decades of Narrative Analysis) 7 (1–4): 3–38.

Lutz, C. (1982) The domain of emotion words on Ifaluk. *American Ethnologist* 9 (1): 113–128.

Lynn, C. and A. Rath (2012) GriefNet: Creating and maintaining an internet bereavement community. In Sofka, C., I.N. Cupit, and K.R. Gilbert (Eds.), *Dying, Death, and Grief in an Online Universe: For Counselors and Educators*. New York: Springer Publishing Company.

Madianou, M. and D. Miller (2013) Polymedia: Towards a new theory of digital media in interpersonal communication. *International Journal of Cultural Studies* 16 (2): 169–187.

Marwick, A. and N.B. Ellison (2012) "There isn't wifi in heaven!" Negotiating visibility on Facebook memorial pages. *Journal of Broadcasting & Electronic Media* 56 (3): 378–400.

Mazzoleni, G. and W. Schulz (1999) Mediatization of politics: A challenge for democracy? *Political Communication* 16 (3): 247–261.

Meese, J., M. Gibbs, M. Carter, M. Arnold, B. Nansen, and T. Kohn (2015) Selfies at funerals: Mourning and presencing on social media platforms. *International Journal of Communication* 9: 1818–1831.

Norrick, N.R. (2005) The dark side of tellability. *Narrative Inquiry* 15 (2): 323–343.

Ochs, E. and L. Capps (2001) *Living Narrative: Creating Lives in Everyday Storytelling*. Cambridge, MA: Harvard University Press.

Papacharissi, Z. (2012) Without you, I'm nothing: Performances of the self on Twitter. *International Journal of Communication* 6 (18).

Parkes, C.M., P. Laungani, and B. Young (1997) *Death and Bereavement across Cultures*. London: Psychology Press.

Phillips, W. and R.M. Milner (2017) *The Ambivalent Internet: Mischief, Oddity, and Antagonism Online*. Malden, MA: Polity Press.

Refslund Christensen, D. and S. Gotved (2015) Online memorial culture: An introduction. *New Review of Hypermedia and Multimedia* 21 (1–2): 1–9.

Refslund Christensen, D., Y. Hård af Segerstad, D. Kasperowski, and K. Sandvik (2017) Bereaved parents' online grief communities: De-tabooing practices or relation-building grief-ghettos? *Journal of Broadcasting & Electronic Media* 61 (1): 58–72.

Refslund Christensen, D. and K. Sandvik (2014) *Mediating and Remediating Death*. London: Routledge.

Roberts, P. (2006) From my space to our space: The functions of web memorials in bereavement. *The Forum* 32 (4): 1–3.

Roberts, P. and L.A. Vidal (2000) Perpetual care in cyberspace: A portrait of memorials on the web. *Omega: The Journal of Death and Dying* 40 (4): 521–546.

Rosenblatt, P.C. (2015) Grief in small scale societies. In Murray Parkes, C., P. Laungani, and B. Young (Eds.), *Death and Bereavement across Cultures*. 2nd ed. Hove: Routledge, pp. 23–41.

Rymes, B. and A.R. Leone (2014) Citizen sociolinguistics: A new media methodology for understanding language and social life. *Working Papers in Educational Linguistics* 29 (2): 25–43.

Seremetakis, N. (1991) *The Last Word: Women, Death, and Divination in Inner Mani*. Chicago: University of Chicago Press.

Shear, M.K. (2012) Grief and mourning gone awry: Pathway and course of complicated grief. *Dialogues in Clinical Neuroscience* 14 (2): 119–128.

Shuman, A. (2015) Story ownership and entitlement. In De Fina, A. and A. Georgakopoulou (Eds.), *The Handbook of Narrative Analysis*. Hoboken, NJ: John Wiley & Sons, pp. 38–56.

Sofka. C. (1997) Social support "internetworks", caskets for sale, and more: Thanatology and the information superhighway. *Death Studies* 21 (6): 553–574.

Sofka, C., I.N. Cupit, and K.R. Gilbert (Eds.) (2012) *Dying, Death, and Grief in an Online Universe: For Counselors and Educators*. New York: Springer Publishing Company.

Stage, C. (2017) *Networked Cancer: Affect, Narrative, and Measurement*. London: Palgrave.

Stroebe, M. and H. Schut (1999) The dual process model of coping with bereavement: Rationale and description. *Death Studies* 23 (3): 197–224.

Thompson, J.B. (2005) The new visibility. *Theory, Culture & Society* 22 (6): 31–51.

Turkle, S. (2011) *Alone Together: Why We Expect More from Technology and Less from Each Other*. New York: Basic Books.

Urban. G. (1988) Ritual wailing in Amerindian Brazil. *American Anthropologist* 90 (2): 385–400.

Urban, G. (2001) *Metaculture: How Culture Moves through the World*. Minnesota: University of Minnesota Press.

van Dijk, J. (2006) *The Network Society: Social Aspects of New Media*. 2nd ed. London: SAGE Publications.

Walter, T. (1991) Modern death: Taboo or not taboo? *Sociology* 25 (2): 293–310.

Walter, T. (2008) From cathedral to supermarket: Mourning, silence and solidarity. *The Sociological Review* 49 (4): 494–511.

Walter, T. (2014) The revival of death: Two decades on. *End of Life Studies* [Academic Blog]. Available at: http://endoflifestudies.academicblogs.co.uk. Accessed: 5 Jan. 2019.

Walter, T., R. Hourizi, W. Moncur, and S. Pitsillides (2011) Does the internet change how we die and mourn? *Omega: Journal of Death Dying* 49 (1): 57–76.

Wilce, J. (2009a) *Language and Emotion*. Cambridge: Cambridge University Press.

Wilce, J. (2009b) *Crying Shame: Metaculture, Modernity, and the Exaggerated Death of Lament*. Malden, MA: Wiley-Blackwell.

Willerslev, R., D. Refslund Christensen, and L. Meinert (2013) Introduction. In Refslund Christensen, D. and R. Willerslev (Eds.), *Taming Time, Timing Death: Social Technologies and Ritual*. London and New York: Routledge.

Worden, J.W. (1983) *Grief Counselling and Grief Therapy*. London: Tavistock.

Media Sources

Age UK [Website]. *Let's talk about death and dying*. Available at: www.ageuk. org.uk/information-advice/health-wellbeing/relationships-family/end-of-life-issues/talking-death-dying/. Accessed: 20 Aug. 2018.

BBC (2018) Call to end "taboo" of talking about death. *BBC* [Health], Feb. 26. Available at: www.bbc.co.uk/news/health-43169284. Accessed: 20 Aug. 2018.

BBC Radio 4 (2016–2017) *We need to talk about death*. Series 1 & 2. Available at: www.bbc.co.uk/programmes/b09kgksn/episodes/player. Accessed: 20 Aug. 2018.

Death Café [Website]. Available at: http://deathcafe.com/deathcafes/.

Dying Matters. *Let's talk about it* [Website]. Available at: www.dyingmatters.org/overview/about-us. Accessed: 20 Aug. 2018.

The Guardian (O'Hara, M.) (2017) Interview: BJ Miller: Death and dying continues to be seen as a big taboo. *The Guardian [Health]*, May 9. Available at: www.theguardian.com/society/2017/may/09/death-dying-big-taboo-bj-miller. Accessed: 20 Aug. 2018.

Marie Curie Blog (2017) *Help us break the taboo around death*. Oct. Available at: www.mariecurie.org.uk/blog/taboo-death/167432. Accessed: 20 Aug. 2018.

The Telegraph (2018) The taboo of talking about death. *The Telegraph* [Financial Solutions], Mar. 12. Available at: www.telegraph.co.uk/financial-services/retirement-solutions/funeral-plans/talking-about-death/. Accessed: 20 Aug. 2018.

3 A Small Stories Approach to Social Media Mourning

Introduction

This chapter presents the key ingredients of the narrative approach to the study of mourning in social media used in this book. It overviews definitions and approaches to narrative in terms of its key turns and focuses on the small story research paradigm, with special reference to the relevance of these turns for the study of health/illness narratives. It then moves on to present the analytical framework developed for the study of *mourning as small stories*, which draws on aspects of the empirical framework of sharing proposed by Androutsopoulos (2014), and *small story* research insights, methods, and heuristics (Georgakopoulou, 2015). The proposed framework offers a vocabulary and a multi-level matrix for the study of sharing life and death as *death-writing of the moment*, intimately connected to salient forms of broadcasting the self online as life-writing of the moment (Georgakopoulou, 2017a) and the creation and dissemination of *shared stories* (Page, 2018). This framework guides the empirical study of small stories attending to how different types of social-media afforded stories project different types of identity positioning (Bamberg, 1997; De Fina et al., 2006). Special attention is paid to *affective positioning*, which is introduced here as a concept for the analysis of affect as an integral part of narrative performance. The chapter also presents the research questions and the data used in this book.

Narrative

The Pervasiveness of Narrative

The term 'narrative' is used profusely, often interchangeably with the term 'story'. While for everyday language users, both these terms refer to an account of personal experience mainly about something that's happened in the past, for many literary scholars, a story is used to describe a fictional account, with a beginning, middle, and end, which follows a plotline. These different understandings of the term point to a fundamental distinction between *experiential* and *fictional* narrative, which accounts for a large part of the different realizations and functions of narrative.

In the public domain, stories are subject to a range of uses and applications. Since at least the 1990s, business and marketing 'gurus' have been celebrating stories as a powerful way of communicating a brand's presence, authenticating its identity, and captivating audiences' attention and desire, drawing on archetypal plots (see Booker, 2004; Adweek, 2012, Oct. 3). Narrative has also proved to be a productive format in contemporary political discourse, where politicians use stories to communicate their 'message' (Silverstein and Lempert, 2012) and to brand and authenticate their personas, by appealing to voters' 'appetite' for storytelling and story-consumption (Mayer, 2014; Seargeant, 2020). Furthermore, in psychology and in some corners of medical practice, stories occupy a central place as accounts of symptoms describing and often sustaining a patient's illness. These type of stories – also known as *illness or health narratives* and *pathographies* in their written form – are mobilized as a resource for giving voice to the suffering patient (Coles, 1989; Frank, 1995).

Dating back to at least the 1950s, illness narratives taking disease, death, or grief as their main point of departure have indeed emerged as a distinct publishing phenomenon among the diverse body of memoirs and other forms of life-writing and autobiography (Hawkins, 1993). In the past twenty years, the popularity of this kind of transgressive narrative has been steadily growing from literary accounts of the illness and dying of close ones, such as Philip Roth's *Patrimony: A True Story* (1991), John Bayley's *Iris: A Memoir of Iris Murdoch* (1993), and Joan Didion's *The Year of Magical Thinking* (2005), to grief memoirs, such as Julian Barnes's genre-defying account of coping with the loss of his wife (Barnes, 2013). This growth has been attributed to the identity-based social and political movements calling for the voicing of the personal as political as much as to the media's injunction to tell one's 'real life' story, which has turned the confessional into a trait of contemporary culture with an intense focus on the autobiographical 'I' (Gilmore, 2001, p. 17). The advent of social media seems to have revitalized this auto/biographical urge and energy (Cappello, 2014).

The pervasiveness of stories and narratives in social life noted so far foregrounds its socio-cultural significance and its complexity. This is further attested in the inclusion of the term *narrative* in the vocabulary of culture and society, both in its original compilation by philosopher and critic Raymond Williams in 1976 and in its revised edition in 2005 (Bennett et al., 2005). The vocabulary includes *keywords*, which are recognized as central to culture and whose use mixes interlocking, contemporary senses, that often lead to confusion in public debate (Durant, 2006, p. 4). In the revised edition, narrative is defined as "a story, told by a narrator about events which may be factual, fictional, or mythical"; its common association with myth has led to it taking on negative connotations that allude to its contrast to fact, history, and science and its invocation of modern senses of *imagination, creativity,* and *fiction* (Bennett et al., 2005, p. 230). The relevance of the term in cultural politics, in debates about history, and in feminist and post-colonial theory is also noted, traced in Lyotard's influential notion of *grand narratives*. This notion refers to the metadiscourses or metanarratives that weave the fabric of modernity based on claims of universal truth (ibid, p. 230). Understandings of 'narrative' and 'story' as generally dominant or potentially dominant ideas or ideologies, tropes, and metaphors are frequently encountered and very much taken for granted in writings in media and cultural studies (De Fina and Georgakopoulou, 2012, p. 143).

In recent years, attention has been drawn to the sharing of stories or storytelling as a branding tool and a capitalist commodity. Christian Salmon, in particular, has investigated the mechanics of "a storytelling machine", which immerses individuals in an affect-driven universe of filtered perceptions, ideas, and selected frames for interpreting the world (Salmon, 2010). Georgakopoulou (2019) has been looking, in particular, at the mismatches between the rhetorics of social media companies about 'stories' as a platform feature and the actual affordances available to users.

Given the wide range of meanings that *narrative* can encompass, it is important to delimit its definitional scope and provide the necessary background to the empirical framework developed to address the research questions raised in this book.

Narrative Turns

The development of the study of narrative is often described in consecutive *turns* or *waves* (see De Fina and Georgakopoulou, 2012; Hyvärinen, 2010) and their associated views of narrative as: (i) *experience, epistemology, and method*, (ii) *text*, (iii) *performance*, (iv) *practice*, and more recently (v) *small stories*. Each of these turns, which are not necessarily mutually exclusive but can overlap in various ways, are discussed in what follows, drawing attention to key aspects relevant to the concerns of this book, in particular *illness narratives* and *affect*.

The Turn to Narrative Experience

The narrative turn in the social sciences in the late 1970s and early to mid-'80s was a major epistemological shift, part of a wider movement to qualitative approaches concerned with matters of interpretation and the creation of meaning. Narrative, and in particular autobiographical narrative, became established as *a way of knowing*, a kind of thought different to logical thought, which involves the *transformation* of "the primary qualities of direct experience into the secondary qualities of higher knowledge" (Bruner, 1991, p. 69, 2004 [1986]). By *transformation* is understood, here, the sequencing of events over time and their placement in a meaningful context, endowing them with *exceptionality* (Bruner, 1991, p. 71). The view of narrative as a mode of knowing and thinking prompted systematic, qualitative explorations of human action and behaviour using life stories, interviews, and case studies as narrative occasions and as a method of inquiry (Riessman, 2008, p. 23; Andrews et al., 2013, p. 3). In this research tradition, known as *narrative inquiry*, narrative is mainly understood as a reflective mode focused on events that happened at some point in the past.

Narrative inquiry recognized the power of narrative "for expressing suffering and experiences" (Frank, 1995, p. 51) and helped to establish a central place for illness narratives in Western medical practice, training, and interdisciplinary research. Illness narratives have since been mobilized as part of a general surge against medical dominance (Bury, 2001) towards more patient-centred approaches to medicine and more systematic and sustained intersections between medicine, literature, and the arts and humanities, represented, for example, in the interdisciplinary field of medical humanities.

Illness narratives form a particular kind of testimony in which patients are positioned as witnesses to their illness and their transformation. For this reason, approaches to illness narratives have highlighted their inextricable connection to time (cf. Ricoeur, 1984) as experienced in the 'unfolding' of (chronic) illness, which is viewed as a major instance of "biographical disruption" (Bury, 2001, 264).

The study of illness narratives as a distinct experiential genre worthy of attention took place in the context of the broader anti-positivist turn in the social sciences and humanities. The increased interest in this type of narratives turned affective experientiality into a privileged domain of narrative inquiry research as the hallmark of a storyteller's authenticity and entitlement to voice. Nonetheless, approaches to the study of affect remained relatively under-developed in this research tradition until later turns.

The Turn to Linguistic Structure

The linguistic turn to narrative, which developed in the midst of the 'narrative turn' in the social sciences, probed more systematically into the structure of personal experience narratives and their functions and called attention to stories' emotional elements as integral to their constitution.

This influential turn, which has left its mark on the study of narrative in sociolinguistics and discourse (see Bamberg, 1997; De Fina and Georgakopoulou, 2012; Johnstone, 2016), emerged out of the examination of oral stories of personal experience told in response to the question: *Were you ever in a situation where you thought you were in serious danger of getting killed? Where you said to yourself 'This is it?'* These accounts were elicited by the sociolinguist William Labov as part of his study on how people speak in an unselfconscious, natural manner. Even though stories were not the main focus of Labov's research, their remarkably clear and well-defined structure led to important insights into the linguistic creativity involved in transforming the raw material of experience into a story. For Labov (Labov and Waletzky, 1997 [1967]; Labov, 1972), narrative is "one of many ways of reporting past events that have entered into the biography of the narrator" (Labov, 2006, p. 37).

A defining aspect of the structure of an oral story of personal experience is *temporal juncture* between two independent clauses: a change in the order of the clauses produces a change in the interpretation of the order of the referenced events in past time. Ordering clauses in ways that construct temporal (and causal) relations between them is, then, how narrators organize their experience into a story, which consist of discrete though interrelated parts. Typically, a fully developed story begins with an **abstract**, which summarizes what the story is about and serves as a preface to it (e.g. *I remember when . . .* , *'You won't believe what happened; Did I ever tell you about my first-ever flight? . . .*); an **orientation**, which provides information on persons, place, time, and behaviour involved (e.g. *We were driving back*); the **complicating action** which reports the main event(s) around which the story revolves, answering the question *and then what happened?* (e.g. *and the car got spinning on ice*); an **evaluation** section, which identifies the point of the story, answering the question *so what?* Evaluation can be expressed more or less directly. For example, a narrator may step out of the story and make an explicit statement about how the recounted events made them feel (e.g. *This was so scary!*) or transmit that feeling to the audience by showing the impact of the event (e.g. *I was shaking like a leaf!*; Labov and Waletzky, 1997 [1967]). The story can end with a **resolution** that relates how the complication was solved (e.g. *and then we headed back home*) and a **coda**, which returns the listener to the present time (e.g. *I've never been on a plane ever since*).

Not all stories need to be fully developed and feature all of these units. The parts that are essential to a story are the complicating action,[1] i.e. the reporting of a main event or action, and the evaluation, which assesses the main event(s) or action(s) in the interest of the teller. In his later work, Labov (1972) clarified that evaluation is often pervasive to the narrative and can be expressed through the addition of (i) extra detail (e.g. *it just started snowing/just this real light wet snow/and the ground wasn't froze yet*), (ii) suspension of the action via paraphrase or repetition (e.g. *I opened the door /I opened the door slowly*), (iii) 'intensifiers' such as quantifiers (e.g. *it tasted sooo good*), (iv) elements that compare what did happen with what did not happen, could have happened, or might happen (e.g. *it could have been me on that plane*), (v) 'correlatives' that indicate what was occurring simultaneously; and (vi) 'explicatives' that are appended to narrative or evaluative clauses (Johnstone, 2016, p. 546).

Labov's model of narrative has proved useful to the study of personal narratives of health and illness. As Harvey and Kotyeko note (2013), the 'what is said' about the narrated events should not be overlooked (pp. 80–81). They cite McKay and Bonner's (2002) study of women's illness narratives published in a lifestyle magazine as affirming the significance of the evaluation section of these narratives for tellers' construction of their identities as sufferers. The category of evaluation remains influential, given that it foregrounds the centrality of affective elements in the making up of a story and provides a possible entry point into their systematic study. And yet personal experience stories, and in particular illness stories, do not always follow a clear, temporal development and do not, thus, easily fit Labov's model.

Labov's approach to narrative leaves little space for the consideration of the interactional and performance aspects of storytelling and aspects of audience engagement, despite acknowledging that some conversational work is required for the initiation of a narrative (Labov, 2004, p. 38).

The Turn to Performance

Research by conversation and discourse analysts has extended the study of narrative to investigations of narrative-in-interaction and its use as an identity resource (see Goodwin, 1986, 2015; Georgakopoulou, 1996; Norrick, 2000; Schiffrin, 1996). In addition, linguistic anthropologists have uncovered the performative aspects of storytelling events, recognizing that telling a story does not only involve the report of a reportable event or a compelling topic, but that it also entails the narrator's responsibility to an audience for a display of communicative competence; it is, in other words, a *performance* (Bauman, 1986). This recognition has led to the identification of the specific evaluation devices that skilled storytellers routinely use to involve their audiences, also known as *performative cues* or *involvement devices*. These include, for example, repetition, which adds a sense of rhythm to the telling, the use of reporting expressions ('and he said'), and direct speech through which the words of the main story characters are reconstructed (also known as *constructed speech*; Tannen, 1986). The use of involvement devices not only adds intensity and drama to the story's telling, but it also helps to engage the audience in the story-world by turning listeners into witnesses to what was said and done. In addition, all these devices function as cues, which signal to listeners that the discourse activity unfolding in front of them is a storytelling performance. The recognition of the performative dimensions of stories has been central in establishing narrative as an arena for identity performance (Bamberg, 1997) as well as for the performance of affect.

The linguistic turn to narrative has put forward a view of narrative as a formally patterned *text,* or as *a text in context,* pointing further to the transformation of the basic referential uses of language and the links between form and function (Bauman, 1986, p. 292).

The Turn to Practice

In the approaches reviewed so far, the stories selected for analysis encompass a particular type of stories amenable to this type of textual or (con) textual analysis, leaving out a rich array of discourse activities in everyday life that show a narrative orientation to the world.

Ochs and Capps (2001) called attention to these left-out "living narratives" of our life, which are central to the creation of self and community. Attending to the heterogeneous and inconsistent nature of narrative as a genre as much as an activity which is constantly in flux, narratives can be collaboratively told by more than one teller, opening up opportunities for exploring the meaning and importance of events, happenings, and feelings (p. 19). Ochs and Capps have shown how grammar and narrative structure are used as a resource for creating and recreating emotions, actions, and events; in some cases, as for example in the case of agoraphobic individuals, reiterating narratives and scenarios ends up not only describing a certain emotional experience but also maintaining the teller's sense of being locked in it (Capps and Ochs, 1997).

Ochs and Capps (2001) point to the open-endedness of stories and their configuration along a set of dimensions, namely: *tellership,* relating to whether there is one or more teller; *tellability,* referring to the extent to which an account is considered to be worth telling; *embeddedness,* that is whether and how a story is embedded in other contexts (e.g. as part of a conversation); *linearity,* relating to whether and how events are temporally and causally ordered; and finally, *moral stance,* which draws attention to the teller's (and characters') stances to the telling.

This dimensional approach to narrative opened the way for the consideration of stories that do not readily fit the *typical* types of personal experience stories, i.e. those fully fledged stories, often elicited in the context of interviews – also known as 'big stories' – that largely fall on one end of the continuum of dimensional narrativity, i.e. "one active teller, highly tellable account, relatively detached from surrounding talk and activity, linear temporal and causal organisation, and certain, constant moral stance" (Ochs and Capps, 2001, p. 20). The extension of the domain of narrative study to atypical stories has pointed to the importance of moving beyond the study of illness narratives as 'big' stories, which showcase stable meanings and a constant moral stance, and look out for the stories where the affective experience of illness is embodied in the storytelling performance, where meaning and identity positions are in flux. These investigations form part of an attempt to provide narrative insights into "the messier business of living and telling" (Georgakopoulou, 2007, p. 154).

The Turn to Small Stories

The need to encompass a wider range of stories than 'big stories' gave the impetus to the research paradigm of 'small stories', which marked a compelling turn away from narrative as text or text-in-context to narrative as social practice embedded in other activities. Small stories are studied through an ethnographic focus on speech events, which emerge out of specific *ways of telling, sites,* and *tellers.* As Georgakopoulou (2017a) explains "ways of (story)telling capture socio-culturally shaped and partly conventionalised themes and styles of telling (ranging from generic framing devices to modes of emplotment) that are, in turn, seen as modes of acting, inter-acting, producing, and dynamically receiving text, revealing of a rhetorical stance and orientation to the world" (p. 22). Despite the fact that small stories are often pitted against big stories, the two approaches can be seen as complementary. Both perspectives, for example, acknowledge that narrative constitutes a powerful mode for communicating the teller's experience from a particular angle, even if that evaluative angle is more or less in negotiation. Each approach is, however, directed to slightly different aspects of narrativity in relation to linguistic versus its social and interactional functions.

The importance of the small stories research paradigm lies in that it calls for the revisiting of the basic dimensions of narrativity, including *narrative temporality* and *structure*, proposing concrete connections with process of *identities* and *positioning*. In what follows, I summarize three key aspects at the heart of the small stories turn as these relate to the analytical framework used in this study:

1. Small stories research extends the traditional focus on temporality as a defining criterion of narrative to the study *of time and place as interactional resources in the act of storytelling,* drawing on Bakhtin's notion of chronotope as what "makes narrative events concrete" (Bakhtin, 1981; Georgakopoulou, 2007, p. 13; see also Georgakopoulou, 2015).
2. Small stories research is grounded in views of narrative as talk-in-interaction, as dialogic, intertextual, and recontextualizable, and as consisting of a multitude of genres. It draws attention to narrative structure as *sequential* and *emergent, temporalized, variable,* and *potentially fragmented* (Georgakopoulou, 2007, p. 86).
3. In small stories research, narrative identities are "invoked and traced both as roles and types of participation and as ways of telling and style" (Georgakopoulou, 2007, p. 152). They are, thus, closely linked to processes of *positioning*, which offers a powerful metaphor of

identities as ways of locating oneself and others (ibid, p. 124). Narrative identities are also closely linked to *emplotment* (Ricoeur, 1984) – the interpretive act of arranging events by forging meaningful connections between them from the narrator's present vantage point.

This paradigm has now become a mainstay in narrative analysis in sociolinguistics and digital communication as an umbrella paradigm, which can encompass a variety of discourse activities and fleeting moments that show a narrative orientation to the world (Bamberg and Georgakopoulou, 2008). Despite its widespread recognition as the state-of-the-art approach to narrative, there is still ample scope for the systematic operationalization of its key theoretical and methodological principles in specific domains of social activity. The flexibility of the small stories research paradigm makes it an apt approach for the study of personal stories of illness, death, and mourning in social media, which do not always present a clear or fixed line of narrative development.

Sharing Small Stories Online

The small stories paradigm pre-figured the emergence of stories shaped by – and shaping – new media technologies of communication (Georgakopoulou, 2015). On social media sites, people engage in storytelling activities enabled – as much as restricted – by the affordances of these platforms, which relate to the different kinds of things, meanings, relationships, thoughts, and social identities that technologies make easier or more difficult to 'do' (Jones and Hafner, 2012, pp. 5–7).

A consistent finding in language-based research on digital stories is their departure from the so-called 'typical' or 'big' stories, which had been privileged as an object of inquiry (De Fina and Georgakopoulou, 2012, p. 121). As Hoffman and Eisenlauer (2010) note, digital stories are characterized by a certain fragmentation of themes and perspectives, a versatile access to the narration, a lack of closure, and semiotic flexibility as a result of medium-enabled features. Page (2012, p. 3) has also pointed to the 'smallness', fleetingness, situatedness, and story-life fragmentary form of digital storying in the case of Facebook updates, where sharers update networked 'friends' on what they have had for dinner or report affectively significant life events, such as accounts of illness. 'Breaking news', in particular, has been recurrently identified as a type of small stories, focused on the here and now, which dominates everyday story practices in social media contexts (Georgakopoulou, 2013b).

More recently, the study of different types of shared stories, defined by Ruth Page as *a retelling, produced by many tellers, across iterative textual segments, which promotes shared attitudes between its tellers*, has also pointed to the need for encompassing the extended interactions, which participate in larger-scale public discussions in relation to matters of public concern (Page, 2018). In this expanded landscape of stories, small stories are found to also incorporate retrospection alongside recency and the here and now, which has been posited as the typical temporality mode of breaking news stories.

Stories online are not, however, restricted to or solely fixed to social media contexts but move between the online and offline (Georgakopoulou, 2013a). Specific connections between the two have been shown in blended ethnographies of online and offline interaction; for example, Facebook users report their perception of the platform as a space for interaction and expression, feeding off and impacting broader patterns of social relations (Tagg et al., 2017). Digital stories enact the potential of narrative to get lifted from its original context (*decontextualization*) and be relocated in a new one (*recontextualization*) via local text and meaning-making mechanisms (*entextualization*), acquiring new meanings in the process (see Bauman and Briggs, 1990). Transportability and reiterativity (with changes) emerge as distinctive characteristics of digital stories, echoing the way stories are shared among peers in face-to-face interaction (Georgakopoulou, 2007); in some respect also, these 'new' storytelling formats echo the way oral stories are shared from mouth to mouth in 'traditional societies', serving as a special type of social 'glue' (see Chapter 2).

The proliferation of this type of stories as the main mode of interaction and connection online has arguably brought about a significant shift. The long-held understanding of the self and personal experience as narrative typical of the first narrative turn has been giving way to a new understanding of *personal experience as sharing*, whereby personal experience is constituted, understood, and constructed in and through particular practices of broadcasting – and curating – significant moments with networked audiences (lately this conceptualization of personal experience is shifting to an orientation to 'not-sharing' as a claim to a self-disciplined 'return' to real life propounded by social media users[2]).

According to Nicholas John "ours is an age of sharing", and sharing is a metaphor we live by (2017, p. 5); it forms "a complex and contradictory set of practices and meanings through which we can read and make sense of large swathes of contemporary society; it is also a normative yardstick by which we evaluate the way we live" (John, 2017, p. 157). This explains why the metaphor of sharing remains powerful even at a time when not-sharing is emerging as a growing trend. In practical terms, sharing refers to self-expression and the entextualization of self, i.e. the construction of the self through text that is written, spoken, and/or visual (e.g. messages, videos, images).

Shared Stories and Participation

Telling stories is not only an integral part of the constitution and performance of "the networked self" (Papacharissi, 2017, p. 5) but also a key form of public and networked participation affording "the ability to represent the world around us using a shared infrastructure" (Couldry, 2008, p. 374). People can show alignment with or distancing from others and, by doing so, negotiate social connections and relations with others. Public participation online is part of processes of subject formation, given that by taking a position, subjects inflect dominant ideologies, and its study, then, can point to modes of online connectedness and the creation of collective identities.

Studies seeking to connect the two areas of networked performance have drawn attention to the importance of narrative. Often, though, the terms 'narrative' or 'stories' have been used rather loosely to refer, for instance, to "stories people tell about themselves on these platforms" or "stories people tell about themselves, others, and events they experience on these platforms" (Papacharissi, 2017, p. 4). Despite a shared interest of scholars in 'new' and dynamic theorizations of communication, self, and participation, there seems to be a gap between large parts of media and cultural studies and socio-linguistic research in digital communication, when it comes to delimiting and focusing on stories as an object of study. In the former, 'stories' tend to encompass 'personal experience stories' or meta-discourses, while in the latter, their definition is grounded in existing and emerging epistemologies of narrative summarized earlier in this chapter.

Narrative could, thus, be a productive point of cross-fertilization between the different fields concerned with digital storytelling, facilitating the synthesis of consistent findings and clarifying processes of mediation and mediatization, modes of subjectivation, and collectivization of experience and identities. Mediated narrative analysis (Page, 2018), in particular, which combines qualitative and quantitative methods, especially corpus methods, can be instrumental to this cross-disciplinary bridging. Page calls attention to the mediation of stories shared on a large scale as a form of interaction, mediated by the people who produce, consume and reproduce them, as well as by various technological resources and by their various socio-cultural contexts. In this respect, this approach echoes concerns raised in studies of earlier phases of mediation, for example TV mediation, as for instance questions about how the spectator is constituted as a public subject.

Chouliaraki's "analytics of mediation" has specifically focused on the mediation of suffering, which consists of three dimensions: (i) *the politics of pity* – how the relationship between the spectator and the suffered is constructed through a variety of media on TV; (ii) *the management of space-time* – the ways in which mediation manages spectators' distance from or proximity to the scene of suffering; (iii) *the management of agency*, which relates to the resolution of the spectators' incapacity to act on distant suffering (Chouliaraki, 2006, p. 46). These dimensions are also relevant to the exploration of the constitution and storying of different types of participation as networked publics and are discussed in more detail in Chapter 6.

The interest in the mediation of stories focused on how shared stories create enduring habits of exchange, archiving, commentary, and reinterpretation, on wider spatial and social scales than otherwise possible (Couldry, 2008, p. 388) also needs to be supplemented by a focus on mediatization. Mediatization considers the embedding of standardized media formats in particular areas of contemporary life. Such processes also extend to social media, referring to the re-presentation of core elements of cultural or social activities through social media forms (see also Chapter 1). In other words, an approach to sharing stories online needs to consider the media and social media practices of production, circulation, and reception as part of mediated narrative analysis. It also needs to attend to the conditions for representability of aspects of social life on and via social media, which determine the broader valence and visibility of shared stories.

The remainder of this chapter synthesizes these insights into stories in the proposed analytic framework for the study of sharing illness, death, and mourning as small stories in social media.

Sharing Illness, Death, and Mourning as Small Stories

Despite the growing body of work on small stories online, there has been surprisingly little attention paid, so far, to small stories of illness, death, and mourning. Furthermore, while 'sharing' has become part of the vocabulary for talking about online communication, its use does not always acknowledge the complex meanings it has accrued since the 2000s and has not always been systematically embedded in empirical analyses.

As pointed out in the previous section, sharing online involves the broadcasting of important life events and everyday happenings, stances to news, political views, feelings, and thoughts. In addition to life events, illness, death, and grief also become shareable online variously connected to offline related practices and norms. Death is shared in the form of breaking news of death and reactions to such news, posts of deathversary wishes, the broadcasting of funeral selfies, or the curation of video diaries (vlogs) of living with terminal illness. This type of sharing can be seen as an extension of what Georgakopoulou describes as the sharing and updating of the self as *life-writing of the moment* ("Ego Media", 2018), which extends earlier understandings of narrative as predominantly relating to a reflective sequencing of past events.

In this study, sharing illness, death, and mourning is approached as small stories, i.e. as "discourse engagements that engender specific social moments [which show a narrative orientation] and integrally connect with what gets done on particular occasions and in particular settings" (Georgakopoulou, 2007, p. 148). Applying the key theoretical principles of small stories to the analysis of an emerging mode of *death-writing of the moment*, this book shows how death 'opens up' to different types of shared stories of mourning, which end up reconfiguring (self)-witnessing to death, dying, and grief. A small stories approach allows the examination of stories' multi-semioticity, (cross)contextual, emergent, and participatory potential of these shared stories (Georgakopoulou, 2015).

The empirical study of the storying practices in this book draws on the empirical framework proposed by Androutsopoulos (2014), which recognizes the constitutive semiotic activity of sharing as worthy of empirical study. This framework foregrounds the participatory character of social media that involves the user's entextualization of self while addressing a knowing audience made up of diverse people existing on an online domain of sociability. In the context of social media, entextualization further involves the use of visual and audio resources that can result in assemblages of texts, pictures, videos, comments, and likes that become an integral part of the sharing and are termed *vernacular spectacles* (Androutsopoulos, 2010).

The empirical framework of sharing online as entextualization involves three inter-related stages:[3]

   i. *selecting*: what the sharer chooses to broadcast to their networked audience
   ii. *styling*: how the sharer entextualizes their selected significant moments, and
   iii. *negotiating*: how the audience engages with what is being shared.

In this framework, moments are understood as single communicative acts, which entextualize an event that is of importance to a participant and their network of 'friends' and which relate to the background knowledge and the linguistic resources that members of the networked audience have in common with the sharer (Androutsopoulos, 2014, p. 15).

In mediated narrative analysis (Page, 2018), the empirical analysis of sharing specifically focuses on the examination of shared stories online on three different levels, each analyzed along different aspects of their typical characteristics:

   i. sharing as a form of telling a story;
   ii. sharing as a form of dissemination;
   iii. sharing as the 'familiar' values and socio-cultural myths indexed or presupposed through the unfolding story or the social meanings and effects that emerge from these modes of sharing.

In this book, sharing small stories of mourning is analyzed on the levels listed next, which are taken as heuristics for the study of the different case studies:

   i. *Sharing as selecting*: this level attends to the particular types of death picked out as worthy of shared mourning and the particular kinds of moments of mourning judged as relevant and appropriate entex-tualizables. It also includes attention to the choice of platforms considered most appropriate for such displays and the platform-specific affordances (e.g. text, images, hashtags, videos, etc.) drawn upon in shaping the shared content.

ii. *Sharing as storying*: at this level, the focus is on how selected events and moments are configured as stories (*emplotment*) over multiple turns or aggregating posts. This level is concerned with clarifying the types of small stories and dimensions of their temporality associated with sharing death and mourning online.

iii. *Sharing as positioning*: at this level, the way shared moments are negotiated with networked audiences is examined, with a focus on the different types of identity and affective positioning they make available. This level allows the analysis to move beyond the focus on the moment to the uptake of the stories and the social meanings they are associated with.

This combined framework allows us to ask in turn (i) whose life and death is selected as reportable, shareable, and grievable, (ii) how different types of death and mourning are emplotted in different types of small stories, (iii) how death and mourning are shared online, and (iv) what the networked uptake of shared small stories of mourning is. The next section will explain in more detail the level of small stories as positioning, (selectively) reviewing key approaches to positioning.

Small Stories and Positioning

Sharing a moment with and for a networked audience does not simply involve the selection, storying, and dissemination of a significant event or the expression of thoughts and feelings. It involves acts of positioning, locating social and affective selves as participants in an interaction or discourse and as social beings producing one another in terms of roles and relationships of proximity or distance.

The concept of positioning has been traced back to Foucault's notion of 'subject positions' relating to formation of subjects within domains of discourses, which highlight the production and reproduction of the status, power, legitimate knowledge, and practices people have access to (Foucault, 1969). The concept was picked up in social constructionist approaches after its critical use in explorations of gender issues and inequality. This use led to the revisiting of the idea of positions in social-cultural psychology as making part of limiting action or act repertoires (Harré and Moghaddam, 2003, p. 5). Positioning has been, since, woven into theories of identity in social psychology[4] focused on the role of communication in shaping identity. These theories contributed a discourse-based, interactional approach to selves and identities, which attended to the importance of rights and duties in the organization and management of social action (Davies and Harré, 1990; Harré and van Langerhove, 1998; Harré and Moghaddam, 2003).[5]

The notion of *position* was initially theorized as a 'triangle' made up of (i) speech and other acts, i.e. socially meaningful and significant verbal or non-verbal action, (ii) the story line understood as social episodes which unfold in already established patterns of development and expressed as socio-categorial relationships, either dual, e.g. 'doctor/patient' or triple, e.g. 'doctor/nurse/patient', and (iii) social acts embedded in jointly produced story-lines as "determinate speech acts" (Harré and Moghaddam, 2003, p. 6). In this theorization of positioning, it is recognized that social actors can project several positions at once or may interpret their own or others' positions differently, thereby attesting to the multi-layered, dynamic, and ambiguous nature of such acts (Depperman, 2013). As Depperman (2013, p. 6) notes, however, despite its dynamic and interaction-oriented direction, this theory of positioning has not considered the sequential nature of social interaction and narrative, given that it was not based on empirical data. More recent scholarship on positioning has shown that positions emerge in the context of complex performances: they are multi-layered, dynamic, and often ambiguous, with social actors projecting a number of different, sometimes conflicting positions and potentially having their positions interpreted by others differently than they had intended (Depperman, 2013). The complexity of projected positions reveals the different identity dilemmas that social actors navigate around (i) *continuity and change*, (ii) *uniqueness and conformity*, and (iii) *agency and construction* (Bamberg, 2015).

Empirical approaches to positioning, which developed out of observations about the importance of evaluation and the display of emotional stances (Bamberg, 1997), have led to the revision of the conceptualization of positioning as emergent in and through three interrelated levels of narrative interaction (Bamberg, 1997; De Fina, 2013; Georgakopoulou, 2007). These are summarized as follows:

Positioning Level 1: this is the level of the story or taleworld,[6] i.e. the representation of characters through their description and evaluation in event sequences. At this level, the analyst asks, 'How are the characters positioned to one another within the reported events?'

Positioning Level 2: the level of interaction or storyrealm, i.e. the interactional uses and rhetorical functions that the aspects of the story construction serve. At this level the analyst asks, 'How does the speaker position him/herself to the audience?'

Positioning Level 3: the level of the self, i.e. the establishment of a sense of self. At this level, the analyst asks, 'How do narrators position themselves to themselves? How do tellers address the question "Who am I?"'

The third level of positioning has been extended to include the consideration of how the narrator projects a sense of self with regard to dominant discourses or master narratives and establishes themselves as a particular kind of person (Bamberg and Georgakopoulou, 2008, pp. 385–391). It has also raised discussions around the nature of identity as stable and continuous or as changing and fluid. Georgakopoulou (2013b) approaches positioning "as a process of situated snapshots of aspects of a teller's self with built in contingency and iterativity" (p. 106) that surface in the close connections between types of positioning and types of stories told in specific sites. Positioning analysis is not only a productive and flexible framework for the study of identity. As I argue, positioning can also be useful for studying affect as an integral part of internal and narrative activity.

Affective Positioning

Although affect has been acknowledged as a privileged window to experience and as a constitutive element of story making in more or less constant articulations (e.g. taking the form of a separate evaluative section in a story or the expression of a moral stance in flux), its study remains largely in the margins of narrative analysis. And yet attention to the way in which affect is created, negotiated, and sedimented in different contexts is currently called for, given the centre-stage that emotions occupy in digital cultures of participation and sharing.

In these emerging social contexts, emotions are experienced and (re)presented in *mediated* ways, i.e. transmitted and communicated via different media. They are also *mediatized*, that is submitted to or becoming dependent on the media and their logic (Hjarvard, 2008, p. 113) and *social-mediatized*, i.e. intertwined with social media affordances and logics (Georgakopoulou and Giaxoglou, 2018). Despite the growing body of work on *networked[7] emotion* (Benski and Fisher, 2014; Tettegah, 2016; Giaxoglou et al., 2017), the role of social media in amplifying emotional reactions to events (Sumiala et al., 2018) around affective publics (Papacharissi, 2015), the interrelationship between emotion and politics (Demertzis, 2013), and the increasing metrification of networked affect (Stage, 2017), there are still open questions about how emotion is used as a resource for sharing social life online as well as about how such uses are related to practices of storying and positioning. This gap motivates the extension of identity positioning to affective positioning.

'Affective positioning' is a term which has not attracted systematic attention in theorizations of positioning or affect so far. Carter and McCarthy (1999) have used the term to refer to an aspect of interpersonal grammar that is concerned with the production of interpersonal meanings emergent in interaction. Such meanings depend on "how the speaker cares to position the subject, event and (possible) agents and circumstances relative to judgments about perceived responsibility and involvement of the participants, the inclusion of essential information, and affective factors, such as distaste, humour, amazement etc. reflecting the speaker's reaction to the event" (idem, p. 154). Carter and McCarthy also acknowledge that affective positioning can be more or less socio-culturally conditioned and call for an interpretive approach rather than a probabilistic or predictive one; they have, however, restricted its scope to its linguistic study, leaving aside aspects of its embedding to interactional and narrative activities.

It is argued, here, that an empirical framework for the study of affective positioning is needed to address the dilemmas social actors face when they find themselves in a (story)telling situation in which they are expected to produce and authenticate their emotional experience. The dilemmas they face in such situations include, for example, the uniqueness and representativeness of the shared emotional experience, the audience's identification or distancing from the represented experience, and the emotional control or loss of control social actors are shown to have over the situation they are talking about and their projected emotional self, which also displays their alignment or disalignment with master discourses of affect.

Affective positioning is defined, here, as the use of linguistic and discourse cues for modulating degrees of distance from or proximity to events and characters, audiences, and the self. It is proposed that it can be empirically examined at the three levels posited for the study of identity positioning – taleworld, storyrealm, and teller – attending more specifically to:

Level 1: direct and indirect evaluations about events and characters as falling into particular types of events and characters (e.g. 'tragic' events, 'suffering' characters);

Level 2: affective stances that project particular kinds of relationships with story recipients as intimate, proximal, or distant and which invite particular kinds of reactions, for example 'support', 'empathy', or 'solidarity';

Level 3: the projection of particular types of an affective self, e.g. as 'sad', 'happy', more or less 'in control' of a situation, which inflect as much as they are inflected by broader sociocultural norms of emotional displays.

Affective positioning can be considered to be an integral part of narrative identity positioning, given that the questions of 'who I am' or 'how I want my interlocutors to see me' and 'how I situate myself in social roles and grouping' (see Bamberg, 2012) implicate affective meaning significance; they depend to a large extent on the way social actors assess events and themselves in relation in them and in relation to their interlocutors and their own sense of self. Narrative identity and affective positioning analysis at the different levels outlined is partly linguistically oriented, as will be explained in the next section.

Positioning Cues

Positioning analysis attends to language in its concern with the identification of precise language and narrative choices and strategies mobilized by tellers to project and negotiate different kinds of identity and affective positions. These choices or strategies have been termed *positioning cues* (Georgakopoulou, 2013b). The fact that these choices can be recognized as cues by an analyst attests to the interdiscursive chains they make part of. The reiteration of their use in social interactions in association with social positions explains how such forms accumulate social meanings and become recognizable indexes. This idea resonates with Wortham's approach to positioning – inspired by Bakhtin – as the ways of speaking which "index social positions, contexts, assessments, and ideological stances, and which have become associated with linguistic choices by previous social usage". In this respect, positioning cues are also types of entextualization markers, i.e. linguistic cues that point to the local context but also to invoked contexts, past and future, that are revealing of processes of narrative and identity sedimentation. Wortham proposes five types of linguistic cues used to position the teller and the audience interactionally: (i) reference and predication, (ii) metapragmatic descriptors (e.g. verbs of saying), (iii) quotation, (iv) evaluative indexicals, and (iv) epistemic modalization (Wortham, 2001, pp. 70–75). In addition to the linguistic and paralinguistic cues, Lucius-Hoene and Depperman (2004) have also suggested different kinds of temporal and interactive sources of positioning (Depperman, 2015, pp. 377–380).

In the present study, the analysis of positioning draws on the aforedescribed types of positioning cues as heuristics. It is suggested, however, that it is also important to clarify such cues empirically rather than postulate them in advance. Importantly, positioning cues include linguistic and paralinguistic cues but also narrative strategies for temporalizing, emplotting and updating, reiterating, and sedimenting narrative identities and affective positions as *ways of telling* and as *types of participation*. Among the linguistic cues of interest in my examination of positionings in small stories of mourning, deixis is particularly important, as it brings together linguistic, interactional and narrative types of positioning cues and can shed light into different types of affective positionings relating to *proximity* or *distance* at different levels.

Deixis as Positioning Cues

Deixis refers to the use of linguistic expressions that establish the speaker in relation to other aspects of context, namely in relation to the hearer(s) (*person deixis*), space (*spatial deixis*), and time (*temporal deixis*). In English, for example, there is a set of indexical expressions, such as 'I', 'here', 'today', 'tomorrow', whose reference shifts, depending on the context in which they are uttered. Tellers use deixis strategically to create positions for themselves and others as speakers and addressees and emplace themselves and others as close or distant from centred locations. Deixis is also used to show the teller's orientation to events as past, present, or future (Toolan, 1999). The three dimensions of person, space, and time are the most commonly discussed deictic domains and are crucial in the interpretation of any utterance. They are also known as the *deictic center* of linguistic events.

There are two main types of deictics: static and dynamic deictics. Static deictics point at an entity, e.g. in English *here* (space), *then* (time), and *we* (person). Dynamic deictics point at movement in space (*hithe*r), developments in the course of time (*from now on*), or events that take place between persons ('*I-you*'; Zuniga, 1998 cited in Zuniga, 2006, pp. 30–31). Local deixis can be further classified in terms of binary distinctions that separate between persons (e.g. 'we' as separate from 'them') in person deixis or between places (e.g. 'here' as separate from 'not-here'; 'near' and 'far') in place deixis (van Peer and Graf, 2002). In addition to local deixis, there is also social and discourse deixis, in which spatial parameters like *proximal* or *distal* are used to structure aspects of the social space indexed.

Approaches to time and space, which attend to aspects of context pointed at by the deictic referent – in other words, their indexical uses – are of utmost relevance to the analysis of positioning, given that they point beyond the referential level of deixis to the social embedding of the deictic field across interactional contexts (Hanks, 2005). As he notes (2005, p. 193), "to perform an act of deictic reference is to take up a position in the deictic field", which can be summarized as "an articulation of several logically ordered layers" (ibid, p. 210). Extending this claim to the field of discourse and narrative studies, time and place are not just background material used to anchor tellings but interactional resources used by tellers (and co-tellers) which allow positionings at multiple levels (Georgakopoulou, 2003, 2007).

In addition to deixis, stance and its related concepts of alignment and affiliation are also important aspects of positioning processes (Depperman, 2013). By taking a stance, one can assign value to objects of interest, position social actors with respect to those objects, calibrate alignment between stancetakers, and invoke presupposed systems of sociocultural value (Du Bois, 2007, p. 140). Stance processes mobilize and deploy sociocultural value invoked in the evaluative act with a focus on a precise target that gets selected as salient. Acts of stancetaking in interaction are not solely speaker-centred language phenomena. They are sequential in that the act of taking a stance often becomes a target for the next speaker's stance. For addressing the sequentiality of stancetaking, the concepts of 'alignment' and 'affiliation', developed in conversation analysis, have proved particularly useful: alignment addresses how participants position themselves vis-à-vis each other in joint activities, while affiliation has to do with sharing evaluative stances (Depperman, 2013, p. 11). These concepts will also be drawn upon, where appropriate, to analyze identity and affective positionings in sharing mourning online.

Positioning is, thus, a framework apt for capturing both stable and fluid aspects of biographical identity construction in their situated and emergent (co-)construction. In addition to its biographical dimension, it is proposed here that positioning is also useful for capturing aspects of affective subjectivities relevant to engagement with news and global events. In summary, mourning in social media is approached as small stories associated with specific types of identity and affective positioning with a view to shed light into digitally afforded practices of self making as mediatized performance and participation.

Research Methods

The Case Studies

The case studies selected for the analysis of small stories of mourning in social media cover different types of death events, involving mass or individual death or dying. These events have attracted increased media and social media attention and illustrate the mobilization of affordances of different social media platforms, namely Twitter, Facebook, and YouTube. They are all examples of highly visible or *spectacular death* and dying, which showcase key dimensions of practices of public (or semi-public) sharing online, and the way that this is shaped by – as much as shaping – existing media frames, social media, and narrative affordances. The selection of wide-ranging case studies seeks to capture aspects of remediation and emergence in phenomena of digital mourning practices and at the same time sketch the distinctive characteristics of small stories of mourning in specific contexts.

Case Study 1

The first case study looks at an emergent phenomenon whereby patients diagnosed with terminal conditions create their own legacy and conditions for collective mourning and remembrance, by publicly documenting their experience of dying. Based on the examination of the vlog of Charlotte Eades from Brighton, UK, which has attracted a lot of media attention and is also listed among the ten top cancer vlogs, I illustrate the vlogger's affective positioning at different levels to her illness, her audience, and her own self. The vlog counts a total of 112 videos, plus three final updates posted by her mother on behalf of the vlogger reporting on her last days and passing. Her mother and brother (Alex and Miles Eades) have been maintaining the vlog ever since, using it as a remembrance site and a forum for a charity raising funds for research into and awareness raising of the rare form of glioblastoma multiform that afflicted her (www.charlottesbag.com).

Case Study 2

This case study shifts the focus to the study of Facebook memorial groups created to remember a friend. The group selected for study was created in May 2012 as a tribute to the sudden and tragic loss of a young adult (henceforth referred to as David) in a U.S. city. The administrators of the group are six of the closest friends of the deceased. The medium-sized group brings together more than one thousand (1,000) members including schoolmates and acquaintances of the deceased from the local community (e.g. school, Christian Baptist community). At the time of writing, the group has accumulated 526 logs of 29,136 words, the first posted one day after the event of death in May 2012 and the most recent on February 16, 2018. The analysis of small stories of mourning in this Facebook group draws attention to aspects of collectivization of grief affording mourners positions of intimate, everyday witnessing and remembering.

Case Study 3

This case study focuses on small stories of mourning relating to highly mediatized mass death as a result of the attack at the offices of satirical magazine *Charlie Hebdo* in Paris on January 7, 2015. The attack left twelve people dead, among whom were eight employees including five well-known cartoonists-journalists, a guest at the offices, a maintenance worker, and two police officers. From January 7 to January 9, seventeen people were killed in the offices of the magazine *Charlie Hebdo*, a kosher grocery store, and the Paris suburb of Montrouge (CNN, 2018). Journalists immediately started covering the events in live reports appearing on television, radio, news blogs, and Twitter. At 12:52 p.m. (local time), French designer Joachim Roncin posted via his Twitter account a logo using the masthead of the magazine featuring the words 'Je Suis Charlie'. Seven minutes later, the logo was retweeted by Twitter user Thierry Puget, who further added the hashtag '#JeSuisCharlie'. This has since been used more than 5 million times on Twitter alone (ABC News, 2015).

The case study examines practices of small storying in the live blog on the *Charlie Hebdo* attacks by *The Guardian* updated by Claire Phipps and Alexandra Topping (in London) and Tom McCarthy (in New York), which was launched at 11:20 on the day of the event and ended on the same day a couple of minutes after midnight. It also analyzes practices of sharing as small stories and positioning in uses of the shared hashtag #JeSuisCharlie on Twitter. This case study illustrates how mourning is collectivized and mobilized for symbolic functions at a global scale as hashtag stories of mourning, associated with specific types of affective participation positions for witnessing death in mediated proximity.

Case Study 4

The final case study is also concerned with the collectivizing functions and symbolic dimensions of mourning, this time in the case of the death of a migrant child. The focus, here, is on the death of three-year-old Alan Kurdi, who drowned in the course of a risky migrant journey to Europe in the early hours of September 2, 2015. His image showing his lifeless body on the shore became viral on social media on September 3, 2015, in association with a series of hashtags either unique to the specifics of this event, such as #kiyiyavuraninsanlik (trans. *humanity washed ashore*), #JeSuisAylan, or already existing hashtags relating to the refugee crisis, such as #RefugeesWelcome. This case study calls attention to uses of multimodal resources in the small storying of mourning, mainly on Twitter, making the death of the 'Other' visible as a form of witnessing death at a distance.

Remix Research Methods

Among the advantages of the eclectic approach taken here are that the analysis is not restricted to a single individual, group, site, or type and encompasses instead an array of mourning activities, some of which might not even – at first sight – be viewed as mourning. The cultural or linguistic context is not pre-determined; rather, its importance and relevance are determined by sharers. This eclectic mix of data is motivated by the need to show shared aspects of digital mourning phenomena, connecting different practices to social-media practices of writing, broadcasting, and sharing the affective self and broader sociocultural ideologies of affect and communication. This selection also serves to illustrate a flexible framework of sharing as small stories and affective positioning that can be adapted to the examination of different phenomena.

Importantly, this is an attempt to combine a creative, almost experimental approach with systematic robust empirical methods to reflect the processes driving creativities online, which is more in line with the vernacular creativities attested online. The approach taken in this book is inspired by Markham (2013), who posits the importance of remix methods driven by the process of *play, borrowing, (reflective) interrogating, generating,* and *moving* as well as *being moved* by what we encounter in our research journeys. She further notes the importance of adopting a reiterative practice of collecting, selecting, dissecting, (tr)reading and (th)reading together data and findings, moving back and forth in a non-positivist[8] engagement with "writing culture". Remix methods have been adapted in small story research especially in studies concerned with digitally afforded emplotment (see Georgakopoulou and Giaxoglou, 2018).

In this study, I have drawn on data collected following what Roland Barthes in his selection of photographs describes as a principle of *advenience* or adventure, making his selection of a picture for discussion depending on the attraction that image had for him and its potential for animating the viewer (Barthes, 2000, p. 20). Each case study raised further questions and gave the impetus for looking at the next one (even though the case studies are not presented here in the chronological order in which they were selected and analyzed).

My starting point for this research 'adventure' has been the selection of key events that have 'animated' not only me but also others, as evident by their posting, sharing, and resharing, or liking related posts. A starting point for identifying and selecting key events for analysis has been the notion of "media event" and its reconceptualization in a global age as "spectacular media event" that Kellner defines as "certain situated, thickened, centering performances of mediated communication that are focused on a specific thematic core, cross different media products and reach a wide and diverse multiplicity of audiences and participants" (22). In this book, spectacular media events refer to *social media events* or *'spectacles'* around which networked audiences band and disband into affective publics (see Papacharissi, 2014).

These are just selections among an array of sites, groups, pages, hashtags that I have browsed, looked at, or hung around as part of 'guerilla ethnography' rather than a full-fledged or blended ethnography. By 'guerilla ethnography', I refer to an alternative to the highly systematic type of ethnography used as a method in the social sciences and qualitative research. It is based on the basic principle of 'observation', making the familiar strange and the strange familiar, synthesizing different types of sources, reports, self-reflections as a guide for interpretation and a critical reading of contemporary reality. Guerilla ethnography has proved useful in observing behaviour in public settings, for example eating and drinking in a pub or a restaurant or travelling on public transport, as it helps to point to patterned behaviours and social norms in the everyday (Mariampolski, 2005, p. 47). In this study, guerrilla ethnography is also informed by a discourse-centred online ethnography angle (Androutsopoulos, 2008), which meant that I followed more closely key conversations unfolding on a single platform, e.g. Twitter or Facebook, as well as across platforms.

My use of this type of ethnography has meant that I've spent time browsing and 'hanging out' in pages, groups, hashtags, Facebook updates trying to gain a sense of emerging norms, users' habits, and trends. It has also involved me visiting offline memorials, talking to people or letting people talk to me about their stories of grief and attitudes to displays of mourning online and offline, alongside reading media articles, analyses, interdisciplinary research on death online from different angles, while reflecting on my own losses. All these have inevitably fed into how I see the material I'm studying and what I see as important aspects of the phenomenon worthy of study; in other words, they are part of my own positioning vis-à-vis the stories and their tellers.

Ethics in Digital Research

Ethics decisions in this study were guided by the assessment of the risks posed by the type of data and research questions. In the field of internet research, studies are situated on a continuum ranging from *low* to *high risk* for human subjects (Page et al., 2014; Buchanan, 2011). The dimensions of risks are summarized in Table 3.1:

Table 3.1 Dimensions of ethical risk in online research

Aspects of Research	Low Risk	High Risk
1 Types of data	Large scale or 'big' data obtained via computerized programmes (e.g. Java, API protocols)	'Small' data obtained via ethnographic observation methods, interviews, surveys, online ethnographies
2 Methodology	Quantitative	Qualitative
3 Site/Platform	Sites/platforms with privacy settings (e.g. Facebook)	Sites/platforms without privacy settings (e.g. early days of MySpace)
4 Research focus	Focus on large-scale trends Focus on discourse patterns	Focus on persons and their lives

The study is positioned towards the high-risk end of the continuum with respect to the type of data ('small' data) and method (qualitative) and towards the low-risk end of the continuum with respect to the privacy settings (public posts) and research focus (i.e. text- and discourse-focused). In other words, the study can be described as a *medium-risk* study.

As I have suggested elsewhere (Giaxoglou, 2017b), there is a need to add an extra dimension to the ones outlined: participants' own perceptions of the site as public/private (or as in between the two). To do that, close attention is paid to participants' discourse-stylistic preferences and the kinds of orientations to both known and new audiences as they manifest in the data (see also Mackenzie, 2017). In cases that involve sharing of sensitive or potentially sensitive information, such an approach is arguably preferable to generic informed consent forms (Markham and Buchanan, 2012). In digital contexts, it has been acknowledged, for example, that research on social media can be ethically responsible without consent in some cases, provided that the interests of those involved may be safeguarded in other ways (Elgesem, 2002). Informed consent for collecting and analyzing social media material is not needed if ethics principles for social media data are seen as an extension of mass media ethics principles, where mediated personal data is defined as 'information relating to an identifiable living individual' (ESRC, 2015, p. 23), unless 'the information contained in the personal data has been made public as a result of steps deliberately taken by the data subject' (UK Data Protection Act 1998; see Spilioti, 2017, p. 3).

The material for the case studies selected for analysis all concern public data in the sense that they have been drawn from public or semi-public sites. However, as Bolander and Locher (2014) have pointed out, the sensitivity of topics counts as an important factor in "assessing the publicness of a communicative space" – even seemingly non-sensitive topics can also raise ethical concerns "if they are embedded in discourse activities that are face threatening" (Spilioti, 2017, p. 11). Emotional disclosures can be sensitive topics, so due attention has been paid to the way the data are represented and discussed across the case studies in line with an *iterative* (Spilioti, 2017), *re-ethicizing* (Georgakopoulou, 2017c), or *process approach* to research ethics (Page et al., 2014), which calls for reflection on ethical issues and conundrums as an integral part of the project, giving consideration to the different aspects and stages of the project throughout its development. Each stage and analytic framework address slightly different research questions relating to the content, discourse, and language patterns of practices of mourning and raises slightly different ethical concerns.

In the first case study of the vlog, ethics issues around the public–private conundrum are further complicated by the fact that its creator has passed away. This means that the reproduction or discussion of her content impacts her post-mortem identity and legacy as well as on her bereaved family's attitudes to the public vlog. The fact, however, that the vlog is being still maintained by her family, who post their own content and also release previously unpublished and unedited footage, suggests their positive alignment to the public broadcasting of the vlogger's life with illness. The vlog has become for them a resource for coping with their loss, helping them to turn their loved one's death into a force for inspiration and charity action. My analysis and discussion of the vlog are very much aligned to this aim, seeking to bring further visibility to the vlog and the fundraising effort it is now part of, as a way of showing respect to the vlogger and her family and affirming the vlogger's legacy. During the analysis of the vlog, the reproduction of some of the later videos in which the deterioration of the young adult was visible raised further ethical challenges, given the risk of sensationalizing the vlogger's illness, despite the fact that these videos are mobilized for the public good, to raise funds for research into the rare cancer she suffered from.

To address this conundrum, I have opted for using verbal transcripts with added detail about non-verbal features but not to reproduce images. Still, as Page notes (2017), reflecting on her own study of cancer blogs, ethics issues are bound to change with the passing of time, including, for example, the potential of harm in the case of the erasure of the personal stories online and their maintenance (even if in the form of extracts) in an academic publication. At the same time, such maintenance may in some cases be considered a valuable archival practice.

In the second case study of the Facebook memorial group, its semi-publicness has ensured me access to a group whose members were previously unknown to me. The focus of the posts on expressions of grief for a friend makes these posts sensitive in nature. For this reason, memorial posts reproduced in the discussion were selected for their typical patterning with a concern about observable linguistic and discourse patterns. Posts were anonymized by removing all references to names, geographical locations, or other possible identifiers. Similarly to the vlog, my approach to this group has been an approach which has sought to reproduce the orientation of its users towards the amplification of the deceased young adult's legacy and impact (see also Giaxoglou, 2017b).

In the third case study, posts featuring the hashtag #JeSuisCharlie were drawn from Twitter. The hashtag is an indicator of the users' aim for increased visibility, so these posts are considered public. Even though some of these deal with politically contested issues of identity, especially in the context of Twitter threads, an attempt has been made to protect the anonymity of the users whose posts have been reproduced in the chapter.

In the fourth case, posts resharing and commenting on the image of Alan Kurdi raise important issues of the ethics of representation of controversial images of the death of a child (Giaxoglou and Spilioti, 2018). The controversies surrounding the publication of the image are discussed in more detail in Chapter 7. In light of these issues, the image of the dead body of the three-year-old has not been reproduced in full and instead has been only verbally described. This ethical decision seeks to ensure that the uncritical reproduction of the image that could reinforce a broader kind of co-opting cosmopolitan emotion is avoided.

In summary, across the different case studies, the guiding ethical principle has been to consider individual posts as taking their meaning in and through the multiple posts alongside which they feature and the orientation of sharers towards the performance of a public self as a condition for their selection for analysis. I have sought to safeguard the privacy of sharers by anonymizing posts and, where necessary, redacting references to names, places, or any other potential identifiers of individuals, places, and events. I have not, however, anonymized posts by public figures, especially when these have also been reproduced in the media and can be considered to be in the public domain. It is hoped that my commitment to a respectful treatment of the people whose posts or stories I'm bringing up and talking about is ultimately acknowledged by them as part of a well-intended attempt to showcase the narrative complexity of displays of mourning online and challenge common criticisms that see it as 'fake grief' or as 'trivializing mourning'.

The consideration of ethics for this study raises important questions about existing understandings and distinctions between private/public. As I have argued elsewhere (Giaxoglou, 2017b), the categories private/public are often understood in contrastive terms, despite the fact that they are, in fact, linguistic shifters, whose meaning is locally and culturally dependent (see Gal, 2008).

Conclusion

This chapter presented a small stories approach to the study of digital mourning. The analytical framework presented here offers a vocabulary and a multi-level matrix for the study of different types of online shared reactions to dying, death, and mourning as *small stories of mourning*. These modes of sharing are argued to extend salient forms of broadcasting the self online as *life-writing of the moment* (Georgakopoulou, 2017b) into an emerging mode of *death-writing of the moment* and attest to shifts from the narrative constitution of the self to the formation of self as sharing. The empirical study of small stories is called for by attending to different levels of sharing (*selecting, storying, and positioning*), whose analysis can point to the association of specific types of stories with different kinds of identity positioning. Special attention is paid to acts of positioning that relate to modulations of temporal, spatial, and social relations indexing intimacy, proximity, or distance at different levels: the affective characterization of the taleworld, the emotional investment to projected relationships with the audience (storyrealm), and projections of the affective self, which are inflected by and inflecting different kinds of emotion ideologies. These acts of positioning are encompassed here by the term *affective positioning* and are to be studied as part of positioning analysis through the identification of linguistic and narrative positioning cues. The chapter also presented the data and methods, guiding the selection of the different cases for analysis. The empirical framework of sharing as small stories and the concept of affective positioning will be illustrated in the analyses presented in the ensuing chapters addressing the following research questions:

1. How are dying, death, and mourning narrativized for sharing?
2. How (and why) are dying, death, and mourning mobilized across different contexts as resources for the construction of identities and affective positions and stances?

Addressing these questions will shed light into the specific narrative, affective, and technological conditions that render a death event or the experience of mourning tellable and shareable with and for others in specific online contexts.

Notes

1. Labov (2006, p. 38) also later revised the category of complicating action, turning his attention to the cognitive process of narrative pre-construction that can pinpoint how a narrator selects an initial event, termed *the most reportable event*, and then takes steps backward in time to explain how and why this event came about, presenting, for example, earlier events that stand in a causal relation to it (e.g. "I fell and I broke my leg"). As he clarifies "if the event is reportable, it does not happen every day, as a product of every-day activities ("I got up this morning.")" (ibid, p. 37).
2. For example, *Medium* blogger Chris Marchie calls on others to "live your life, not theirs", but he also confesses to still feeling jittery when it comes to experiencing events without sharing them.
3. See also Giaxoglou (2009, p. 420) for a suggested empirical framework for the analysis of entextualization of verbal art in terms of the interrelated practices of: "(a) selection and organization of collectables: the specific choices on what to include in notes or in a collection indicating what is considered as worthy of being extracted and collected, (b) extraction practices: the practices relevant to the process of decontextualization, namely the circumstances of the encounter between the collector and the informant where the artefact is being 'originally' entextualized, (c) resetting practices: the practices relevant to the process of its recontextualization(s), in this case the transfer of the extracted material to the new context of the written page, and (d) editing practices: the practices relevant to the process of entextualization, i.e. the set of transcription choices and linguistic interventions on the collected vernacular forms, which qualify certain forms as entextualizables and others as non-entextualizables."
4. Wendy Hollway, Jonathan Potter and Margaret Wetherell, Rom Harré and Bronwyn Davies as well as sociologist Luk Van Langenhove have all been variously involved in weaving positioning into a theory of identity.
5. For a review of the concept and theory of positioning, see also De Fina and Georgakopoulou (2012), Page (2018), Depperman (2013), and Harré (2012).
6. The distinction between the taleworld and the storyrealm goes back to Young (1987); see also De Fina (2016).
7. 'Networked' practices refer both to "being networked, i.e. digitally connected to other individuals and groups", and "being in the network, i.e. embedded in the global digital mediascape of the web" (Androutsopoulos, 2015, p. 18).
8. Markham (2013) observes that "even when defined as a non-positivist process, procedures still retain linear and compartmentalized foundations. One begins with a phenomenon that informs one's research questions, which in turn inform particular strategies for data collection, analysis, and interpretation. Various stages are described as separate moments, and findings are written up at the end".

References

ABC News (2015) Charlie Hebdo shooting: #JeSuisCharlie tweeted more than five million times. *ABC News*, Jan. 10. Available at: https://www.abc.net.au/news/2015-01-10/jesuischarlie-tweeted-more-than-five-million-times/6010004. Accessed: 20 Jan. 2019.

Adweek (Nudd, T.) (2012) 7 types of stories: Which one is your brand telling? *Adweek*, Oct. 3. Available at: www.adweek.com/brand-marketing/7-basic-types-stories-which-one-your-brand-telling-144164/. Accessed: 10 Nov. 2018.

Andrews, M., C. Squires, and M. Tamboukou (2013) *Doing Narrative Research*. 2nd ed. Thousand Oaks, CA: Sage Publications.

Androutsopoulos, J. (2008) Discourse-centred online ethnography. *Language@ Internet 5* (Special issue on Data and Methods in Computer-Mediated Discourse Analysis), Article 8.

Androutsopoulos, J. (2010) Localizing the global on the participatory web. In Coupland, N. (Ed.), *The Handbook of Language and Globalization*. Malden, MA: Wiley-Blackwell.

Androutsopoulos, J. (2014) Moments of sharing: Entextualization and linguistic repertoires in social networking. *Journal of Pragmatics* (Special Issue: The Pragmatics of Textual Participation in the Social Media) 73: 4–18.

Androutsopoulos, J (2015) Networked multilingualism: Some language practices on Facebook and their implications. *International Journal of Bilingualism* 19 (2): 185–205.

Bakhtin, M. (1981) Forms of time and of the chronotope in the novel: Notes towards a historical poetics. In Holquist, M. (Ed.), C. Emerson and M. Holquist (Trans.), *The Dialogic Imagination*. Austin, TX: University of Texas Press, pp. 84–258.

Bamberg, M. (1997) Positioning between structure and performance. *Journal of Narrative and Life History* (Special Issue: Three Decades of Narrative Analysis) 7 (1–4): 335–342.

Bamberg, M. (2012) Narrative practice and identity navigation. In Holstein, J. and J. Gubrium (Eds.), *Varieties of Narrative Analysis*. London: SAGE, pp. 99–125.

Bamberg, M. (2015) Who am I? Narration and its contribution to self and identity. In B. Gough (Ed.), *Qualitative Research in Psychology, Volume III: Methodologies 1-From Experiential to Constructionist Approaches*. Los Angeles, London, and New Delhi: Sage Publications, pp. 233–256.

Bamberg, M. and A. Georgakopoulou (2008) Small stories as new perspectives in narrative and identity analysis. *Text & Talk* 28: 337–396.

Barnes, J. (2013) *Levels of Life*. London: Jonathan Cape.

Barthes, R. (2000) *Camera Lucida*. London: Vintage Publishing.

Bauman, R. (1986) *Story, Performance and Event*. Cambridge: Cambridge University Press.

Bauman, R. and C. Briggs (1990) Poetics and performance as critical perspectives on language and social life. *Annual Review of Anthropology* 19: 59–88.

Bennett, T., L. Grossberg, and M. Morris (2005) *New Keywords: A Revised Vocabulary of Culture and Society*. Malden, MA: Blackwell Publishing.

Benski, T. and E. Fisher (Eds.) (2014) *Internet and Emotions*. New York and London: Routledge.

Bolander, B. and M. Locher (2014) Doing sociolinguistic research on computer-mediated data: A review of four methodological issues. *Discourse, Context, and Media* 3: 14–26.

Booker, C. (2004) *The Seven Basic Plots: Why We Tell Stories*. London and New York: Continuum.

Bruner, J. (1991) Self-making and world-making. *The Journal of Aesthetic Education* (Special Issue: More Ways of Worldmaking) 25 (1): 67–78.

Bruner, J. (2004 [1986]) Life as narrative. *Social Research* 71 (3): 691–710.

Buchanan, E.A. (2011) Internet research ethics: Past, present, and future. In Consalvo, M. and Ch. Ess (Eds.), *The Handbook of Internet Studies*. Malden, MA: Wiley-Blackwell.

Bury, M. (2001) Illness narratives: Fact or fiction? *Sociology of Health & Illness* 23 (3): 263–285.

Cappello, M. (2014) Wending artifice. In DiBattista, M. and E. Wittman (Eds.), *The Cambridge Companion to Autobiography*. Cambridge: Cambridge University Press, pp. 237–252.

Capps, L. and E. Ochs (1997) *Constructing Panic: The Discourse of Agoraphobia*. Cambridge, MA and London, England: Harvard University Press.

Carter, R. and M. McCarthy (1999) The English get-passive in spoken discourse: Description and implications for an interpersonal grammar. *English Language and Linguistics* 3 (1): 41–58.

Chouliaraki, L. (2006) *The Spectatorship of Suffering*. London: Sage Publications.

Coles, R. (1989) *The Call of Stories: Teaching and the Moral Imagination*. Boston: Peter Davison.

Couldry, N. (2008) Mediatization or mediation? Alternative understandings of the emergent space of digital storytelling. *New Media & Society* 10 (3): 373–391.

CNN (2018) 2015 Charlie Hebdo attacks fast facts. *CNN Library*, Dec. 24. Available at: https://edition.cnn.com/2015/01/21/europe/2015-paris-terror-attacksfast-facts/index.html. Accessed: 20 Jan. 2019.

Davies, B. and R. Harré (1990) Positioning: The discursive production of selves. *Journal for the Theory of Social Behaviour* 20 (1): 43–63.

De Fina, A. (2013) *Identity in Narrative: A Study of Immigrant Discourse*. Amsterdam: Benjamins Publishing.

De Fina, A. (2016) Storytelling and audience reactions in social media. *Language in Society* 45 (4): 473–498.

De Fina, A. and A. Georgakopoulou (2012) *Analyzing Narrative: Discourse and Sociolinguistic Perspectives*. Cambridge: Cambridge University Press.

De Fina, A., D. Schiffrin and M. Bamberg (2006) Discourse and identity. *Journal of Pragmatics* 39 (7): 1324–1328.

Demertzis, N. (Ed.) (2013) *Emotions in Politics: The Affect Dimension in Political Tension*. London: Palgrave Macmillan.

Depperman, A. (2013) Editorial: Positioning in Narrative Interaction. *Narrative Inquiry* 23 (1): 1–15.

Depperman, A. (2015) Positioning. In De Fina, A. and A. Georgakopoulou (Eds.), *The Handbook of Narrative Analysis*. Malden, MA: Blackwell Publishing, pp. 369–388.

Du Bois, J. (2007) The stance triangle. In Englebertson, R. (Eds.), *Stancetaking in Discourse: Subjectivity, Evaluation, Interaction*. Amsterdam and Philadelphia: John Benjamins Publishing Company, pp. 139–182.

Durant, A. (2006) Raymond William's keywords: Investigating meanings "offered, felt for, tested, confirmed, asserted, qualified, changed". *Critical Inquiry* 48 (4): 1–26.

Elgesem, D. (2002) What is special about the ethical issues in online research? *Ethics and Information Technology* 4 (3): 195–203.

ESRC (2015) *Framework for research ethics*. Available at: https://esrc.ukri.org/funding/guidance-for-applicants/research-ethics/. Accessed: 10 April 2020.

Foucault, M. (1969) *L'archeologie du savoir*. Paris, France: Gallimard.

Frank, A.W. (1995) *The Wounded Storyteller: Body, Illness, and Ethics.* Chicago: Chicago University Press.

Gal, S. (2008) Language ideologies compared. *Linguistic Anthropology* 15 (1): 23–37.

Georgakopoulou, A. (1996) *Narrative Performances: A Study of Modern Greek Storytelling.* Amsterdam: John Benjamins Publishing Company.

Georgakopoulou, A. (2003) Plotting the "right place" and the "right time": Place and time as interactional resources in narrative. *Narrative Inquiry* 13 (2): 413–432.

Georgakopoulou, A. (2007) *Small Stories, Interaction and Identities.* Amsterdam and Philadelphia: John Benjamins Publishing Company.

Georgakopoulou, A. (2013a) Storytelling on the go: Breaking news stories as a travelling narrative genre. In Hatavara, M., L.-C. Hydé, and M. Hyvärinen (Eds.), *The Travelling Concepts of Narrative.* Amsterdam and Philadelphia: John Benjamins Publishing Company.

Georgakopoulou, A. (2013b) Building iterativity into positioning analysis: A practice-based approach to small stories and self. *Narrative Inquiry* 23 (1): 89–110.

Georgakopoulou, A. (2015) Small stories research: Methods-analysis-outreach. In De Fina, A. and A. Georgakopoulou (Eds.), *The Handbook of Narrative Analysis.* Malden, MA: Wiley Blackwell, pp. 178–193.

Georgakopoulou, A. (2017a) Narrative/life of the moment: From telling a story to taking a narrative stance. In Schiff, B., E. McKim, and S. Patron (Eds.), *Life and Narrative: The Risks and Responsibilities of Storying Experience.* Oxford: Oxford University Press, pp. 29–52.

Georgakopoulou, A. (2017b) Sharing the moment as small stories: The interplay between practices & affordances in the social media-curation of lives. *Narrative Inquiry* 27 (2): 311–333.

Georgakopoulou, A. (2017c) "Whose context collapse?": Ethical clashes in the study of language and social media in context. *Applied Linguistics Review* 8 (2–3): 169–191.

Georgakopoulou, A. (2019) Designing stories on social media: A corpus-assisted critical perspective on the mismatches of story-curation. *Linguistics and Education.* https://doi.org/10.1016/j.linged.2019.05.003.

Georgakopoulou, A. and K. Giaxoglou (2018) Emplotment in the social mediatization of the economy: The poly-storying of economist Yanis Varoufakis. *Language@Internet* 16, Article 6: 1–15.

Giaxoglou, K. (2009) Entextualizing vernacular forms in a Maniat village: Features of orthopraxy in local folklore practice. *Pragmatics* 19 (3): 419–434.

Giaxoglou, K. (2017a) Storying leaks for sharing: The case of leaking the "Moscovici draft" on Twitter. *Discourse, Context & Media* (Special Issue: The Digital Agora of Social Media) 19: 22–30.

Giaxoglou, K. (2017b) Reflections on internet research ethics from language-based research on web-based mourning: Revisiting the private/public distinction as a language ideology of differentiation. *Applied Linguistics Review* 8 (2–3): 229–250.

Giaxoglou, K., K. Döveling, and S. Pitsillides (2017). Networked emotions: Interdisciplinary perspectives on sharing loss online. *Journal of Broadcasting & Electronic Media* 61 (1): 1–10.

Giaxoglou, K. and T. Spilioti (2018) Mediatizing death and suffering: Rescripting visual stories of the refugee crisis as distant witnessing and mourning. In Burger, M., J. Thornborrow, and R. Fitzerald (Eds.), *Discourse des réseaux sociaux: enjeux publics, politiques et médiatiques.* Brussels: De Boeck.

Gilmore, L. (2001) *The Limits of Autobiography: Trauma and Testimony*. Ithaca, NY: Cornell University Press.

Goodwin, C. (1986) Audience diversity, participation and interpretation. *Text* 6 (3): 283–316.

Goodwin, C. (2015) Narrative as talk-in-interaction. In De Fina, A. and A. Georgakopoulou (Eds.), *The Handbook of Narrative Analysis*. London: John Wiley & Sons, pp. 195–218.

Hanks, W. (2005) Explorations in the deictic field. *Current Anthropology* 46 (2): 191–220.

Harré, R. (2012) Positioning theory: Moral dimensions of social-cultural psychology. In Valsiner, J. (Ed.), *Oxford Library of Psychology. The Oxford Handbook of Culture and Psychology*. Oxford: Oxford University Press, pp. 191–206.

Harré, R. and F.M. Moghaddam (2003) *The Self and Others: Positioning Individuals and Groups in Personal, Political, and Cultural Contexts*. Westport, CT, and London: Praeger.

Harré, R. and L. van Langerhove (1998) *Positioning Theory: Moral Contexts of International Theory*. Malden, MA: Wiley Blackwell.

Harvey, K. and N. Kotyeko (2013) *Exploring Health Communication: Language in Action*. London and New York: Routledge.

Hawkins, A.H. (1993) *Reconstructing Illness. Studies in Pathography*. West Lafayette, IN: Purdue University Press.

Hjarvard, S. (2008) The mediatization of society: A theory of the media as agents of social and cultural change. *Nordicon Review* 29 (2): 105–134.

Hoffman, C.R. and V. Eisenlauer (2010) Once upon a blog . . . Storytelling in weblogs. In C.R. Hoffman (Ed.), *Narrative Revisited: Telling a Story in the Age of New Media*. Amsterdam: John Benjamins Publishing Company, pp. 79–108.

Hyvärinen, M. (2010) Revisiting the narrative turns. *Life Writing* 7 (1): 69–82.

John, N. (2017) *The Age of Sharing*. Cambridge, UK, and Malden, MA: Polity Press.

Johnstone, B. (2016) "Oral versions of personal experience": Labovian narrative analysis and its uptake. *Journal of Sociolinguistics* (Special Issue: Labov and Sociolinguistics: Fifty Years of Language in Social Context) 20 (4): 542–560.

Jones, R. and C.A. Hafner (2012) *Understanding Digital Literacies: A Practical Introduction*. Oxon and New York: Routledge.

Labov, W. (1972) *Language in the Inner City*. Philadelphia: University of Pennsylvania Press.

Labov, W. (2004) Ordinary events. In Fought, C. (Ed.), *Sociolinguistic Variation: Critical Reflections*. Oxford: Oxford University Press, pp. 31–43.

Labov, W. (2006) Narrative pre-construction. *Narrative Inquiry* 16 (1): 37–45.

Labov, W. and J. Waletzky (1997 [1967]) Narrative analysis: Oral versions of personal experience. *Journal of Narrative and Life History* (Special Issue: Three Decades of Narrative Analysis) 7 (1–4): 3–38.

Lucius-Hoene, G. and A. Depperman (2004) Narrative identity empiricized: A dialogical and positioning approach to autobiographical research interviews. *Narrative Inquiry* 10 (91): 199–222.

Mackenzie, J. (2017) Identifying informational norms in Mumsnet Talk: A reflexive-linguistic approach to internet research ethics. *Applied Linguistics Review* 8 (2–3): 293–314.

Mariampolski, H. (2005) *Ethnography for Marketers: A Guide to Consumer Immersion*. Thousand Oaks: Sage Publications.

Markham, A. (2013) Looking under methods: An experiment in play. *Blog Post*, Feb. 27. Available at: https://annettemarkham.com/2013/02/looking-below-methods-to-find-remix-practices-an-experiment-in-play/. Accessed: 15 Jan. 2019.

Markham, A. and E. Buchanan (2012) *Ethical decision-making and internet research: Recommendations from the AOIR ethics working committee (version 2.0)*. Available at:www.aoir.org/reports/ethics2.pdf.

Mayer, F.W. (2014) *Narrative Politics: Stories and Collective Action.* Oxford: Oxford University Press.

McKay, S. and F. Bonner (2002) Evaluating illness in women's magazines. *Journal of Language and Social Psychology* 21 (1): 53–67.

Norrick, N.R. (2000) *Conversational Narrative: Storytelling in Everyday Talk.* Amsterdam: John Benjamins Publishing Company.

Ochs, E. and L. Capps (2001) *Living Narrative: Creating Lives in Everyday Storytelling.* Cambridge, MA: Harvard University Press.

Page, R. (2012) *Stories and Social Media: Identities and Interaction.* London and New York: Routledge.

Page, R. (2017) Ethics revisited: Rights, responsibilities and relationships in online research. *Applied Linguistics Review* 8 (2–3): 315–319.

Page, R. (2018) *Narratives Online: Shared Stories in Social Media.* Cambridge: Cambridge University Press.

Page, R., D. Barton, J.W. Unger, and M. Zappavigna (2014) *Researching Language and Social Media: A Student Guide.* London and New York: Routledge.

Papacharissi, Z. (2014) *Affective Publics.* Oxford: Oxford University Press.

Papacharissi, Z. (Ed.) (2017) *A Networked Self, and Platforms, Stories, Connections.* London and New York: Routledge.

Ricoeur, P. (1984) *Time and Narrative.* Volume 1 (Trans. by K. McLaughlin and D. Pellauer). Chicago: University of Chicago Press.

Riessman, C.K. (1990) Strategic uses of narrative in the presentation of self and illness. *Social Science and Medicine* 30: 1195–1200.

Riessman, C.K. (2008) *Narrative Methods for the Human Sciences.* Thousand Oaks, CA: Sage Publications.

Salmon, C. (2010) *Storytelling: Bewitching the Modern Mind* (Trans. by D. Macey). London and New York: Verso.

Schiffrin, D. (1996) Narrative as self-portrait: Sociolinguistic constructions of identity. *Language in Society* 25 (2): 167–203.

Seargeant, P. (2020) *The Art of Political Storytelling: Why Stories Win Votes in Post-truth Politics.* London: Bloomsbury Academic.

Silverstein, M. and M. Lempert (2012) *Creatures of Politics: Media, Message and the American Presidency.* Bloomington: Indiana University Press.

Spilioti, T. (2017) Media convergence and publicness: Towards a modular and iterative approach to online research ethics. *Applied Linguistics Review* 8 (2–3): 191–191.

Stage, C. (2017) *Networked Cancer: Affect, Narrative, and Measurement.* London: Palgrave.

Sumiala, J., K. Valaskivi, M. Tikka, and J. Huhtamäki (2018) *Hybrid Media Events: The Charlie Hebdo Attacks and Global Circulation of Terrorist Violence.* Bingley: Emerald.

Tagg, C., P. Seargeant, and A.A. Brown (2017) *Taking Offence on Social Media: Conviviality and Communication on Facebook.* London: Palgrave Macmillan.

Tannen, D. (1986) *That's Not What I Meant! How Conversational Style Makes or Breaks Relationships*. New York: Ballantine.

Tettegah, S.Y. (Ed.) (2016) *Emotions, Technology, and Social Media*. Amsterdam: Academic Press.

Toolan, M. (1999) New work on deixis in narrative. In Grunzeig, W. and A. Solbach (Eds.), *Transcending Boundaries: Narratology in Context*. Tübingen: Gunter Narr Verbal Fubingen.

van Peer, W. and E. Graf (2002) Spatial language in Stephen King's IT. In Semino, E. and Culpeper, in cognitive linguistics: Language and cognition, Semino and Culpeper, J. (Eds.), *Cognitive Stylistics: Language and Cognition in Text Analysis*. Amsterdam: John Benjamins Publishing Company.

Wortham, S. (2001) *Counseling and Development Series: Narratives in Action: A Strategy for Research and Analysis*. New York: Teachers College Press.

Young, K.G. (1987) *Taleworlds and Storyrealms: The Phenomenology of Narrative*. Dordrecht: Martinus Nijhoff.

Zuniga, F. (2006) *Deixis and Alignment*. Amsterdam: John Benjamins Publishing Company.

4 Small Stories of Illness and Dying on YouTube

Introduction

This chapter considers small stories of mourning in the context of an emerging mode of *death-writing of the moment*, which involves uses of online broadcasting media for self-documenting, updating, and curating moments of life with – and despite – terminal illness as it unfolds. Taking the position of a personal story-teller, young adults are sharing their unique life-changing experience for and with intimate publics and, in the process end up shaping, more or less consciously, their own post-mortem legacy.

Focusing on the examination of video blogging (also known as vlogging) on cancer, I will discuss how these *live-writing* practices extend existing forms of autobiographical writing on illness in an emerging mode of telling, sharing, and visualizing the (terminal) *illness narrative* online. More specifically, I draw attention to how selecting, storying, and positioning affordances are drawn upon in a selected vlog, illustrating motivational forms of death-writing of the moment and their typical types of small storying and affective positioning.

I start by overviewing vlogging practices relating to the cancer experience and the literature on illness narratives. I then move on to discuss the case of a vlog, analyzing the selection, storying, and positioning practices and showing how illness is mobilized in the form of small stories for affective positioning at multiple levels. This mode of sharing small stories of illness and dying helps to increase value, visibility, and empathic affiliation around largely commodified idea(l)s of 'authentic' life sharing, motivation, and inspiration.

Vlogging on Cancer

Vlogging has been attracting increased media interest (Testa, 2016; *The Guardian*, 2017) and is becoming the topic of study from different disciplinary angles, bringing to the fore, for instance, interactional-narrative practices of biographizing mothers and the potential of vlogging for small and poly-storying practices (Hoejholt, 2015). One of the main sites for vlogging has been YouTube, which developed from an amateur broadcasting site to a highly professionalized and industrialized business (Hou, 2018). YouTube currently offers its users or 'creators' quick-start guides and courses through its Academy, helping them to learn how to 'share your stories with the world', 'pursue your creative passion', and 'set up your channel' (YouTube Lesson, 2019).[1]

Research on vlogging predictors of popularity has pointed out the importance of the vlogger's age, with the younger having an advantage over the older ones, even when the content is similar (Borghol et al., 2012). With respect to gender, even though men are reported to post more vlogs than women (58% males to 33% females), female vloggers are more likely to vlog about personal matters when compared to men, who are said to prefer to vlog about technology and entertainment (Molyneaux et al., 2008). This finding echoes earlier insights on blogging about cancer, which suggested that cancer blogs were mostly created by young females using a narrative and emotionally revealing style, while male vloggers were found to prefer a more information-based style, even when it came to talking about their illness experience (e.g. talking about medication regimes; Chen, 2012). High numbers of views have been found to correlate with highly edited, active vlogs, i.e. where the vlogger is moving rather than standing stationary in front of the camera, talking at a fast pace, and looking to the camera while speaking (Biel and Gatica-Perez, 2010). The strongly interactional character of vlogs is reflected in their description as "conversational video-blogs", which have evolved from a format of "chat from your bedroom" to highly creative forms of user-generated video content (Biel and Gatica-Perez, 2010, n.p.).

Yet their study, so far, has mainly focused on their function as 'new' ego-spaces and a 'new' form of self-expression. According to Griffith and Papacharissi (2010), vlogs can be used as (i) diaries, (ii) media for identity expression (*I vlog, therefore I am*), and (iii) a means to indulge in narcissism in the sense that they talk about their self, interests, and concerns and at the same time need and see, attention from others. Despite the apparent self-centredness of vlogs, they can turn into immensely popular channels, attracting millions of subscribers by broadcasting light-hearted, entertaining, and intimate content.

The particular form this content takes depends on the type and aims of the videos posted. For example, García-Rapp's study (2016) has categorized beauty gurus' videos into *commercial-oriented videos*, which includes beauty 'know-how' videos, and *community-oriented videos*, which are shared and curated as vlogs recorded in a user's bedroom with the user talking directly to the camera. More recently, YouTube videos focus on 'slices of life', where "YouTubers take the camera with them (almost) everywhere they go and document their daily lives" (Hou, 2018, p. 9).

These vloggers push the boundaries of celebrity image making, which has been characterized by extraordinariness, perfection, glamour, and distance (Senft, 2008; Turner, 2004), to the performance of ordinariness, intimacy, and equality, with its distinctive industrial and cultural logic (Hou, 2018, pp. 2–3). The rising centrality of ordinariness, intimacy, and equality in pursuit of increased YouTube views seems to have also motivated the mobilization of illness as a resource for creating and affirming a sense of authenticity. This is a "staged authenticity", in the sense that it is based on the interactive representation of the intimate and private self and the adoption of affiliative techniques to show equality and commonality with fans (Hou, 2018, p. 15).

Uses of YouTube and other video sites, such as TikTok, for example, as sites for different types of death-writing of the moment has been little explored so far, despite their growing popularity, especially among young adults (a search for 'my cancer story' videos on Google, for example, brings up 37,000,000 results at the time of writing) and the media attention that such practices have attracted as human-interest stories (*The Sun*, 2018; Vice, 2018; *Marie Claire*, 2018). For example, Talia Joy Castellano (taliajoy18) from Orlando, Florida, became an internet celebrity, attracting more than a million followers with her beauty videos, makeup tutorials, and updates on her hospital treatments for neuroblastoma. She even appeared on *The Ellen DeGeneres Show* and became the face for CoverGirl cosmetics ads before passing away in 2013, just a month before her fourteenth birthday. More recently, South Korean beauty vlogger Dawn Lee hit the headlines when her cancer journey vlog went viral, attracting almost 4 million views (BBC, 2019).

Sharing stories and experiences of ill health has been found to be helpful for peer support (Liu et al., 2013, p. 49) and often proves to be a much-needed boost for people who have to spend extended periods of their time in hospital, experiencing boredom, social isolation, and a sense of lack of control over their own lives. In the case of young adults, vlogs have become a site for reconfiguring the cancer experience within a growing subculture of online support communities. The articulation of these personal stories is often characterized by a raunchy sense of humour and sarcasm (Iannarino, 2018), while in some cases it is driven by the contemplation of death (Sànchez-Querubín and van Laarhoven, 2019).

Narrating events that involve biographical disruption brought about by illness – particularly chronic or terminal – is seemingly a far cry from the broadcasting of events that focus on the mundane, trivial, and light-hearted flow of everyday life. For many vloggers, however, this 'transgression' into more serious and 'ugly' content is justified by the hope that this content could help others in a similar situation, as Korean vlogger Dawn Lee explains (BBC, 2019). In addition, broadcasting short videos as one goes through the many ups and downs of illness can be a distracting and fun activity, despite the high demands that the maintenance of such a vlog often places on a vlogger.

Despite the increasing popularity of these vlogs, questions about how (and why) (ill)-health vloggers adapt social media to share their stories has received scant attention so far.

Illness Narratives

The study of illness narratives has pointed out their various uses as resources for (i) bearing witness to the experience of illness (*testimonial narratives*), (ii) resisting the rational modalities of the medical system, (iii) putting forward healing, spiritual, and holistic alternatives to medical treatments (Hawkins, 1993). Illness narratives have been found to be useful in helping to create trust and empathetic relationships between patients and medical carers (Kleinman, 1989; Halpern, 2001) and have proved particularly beneficial for patients, especially for those who have to adjust to living with a chronic condition, helping them to reinforce their coping strategies (Cheshire and Ziebland, 2005, p. 40). Importantly, their central role in patients' identity work echoes widely recognized narrative functions (Riessman, 1990) of bridging "discontinuities between a person's idealized sense of who they are and the restrictions that an illness imposes on what a person can do and the kind of person they can be in reality" (Cheshire and Ziebland, 2005, p. 26). These narratives help the 'wounded storyteller' (Frank, 1995) to make sense of changes in their health status and their changing identity while also allowing them to reclaim a sense of control over these important life shifts (Sharf et al., 2011, p. 42).

As Shapiro (2011) notes, however, a patient's story is rarely just a story, and it's certainly not devoid of social and cultural mediation. Illness narratives are the result of conscious and unconscious representations and performances of intricate personal motives and dominant metanarrative influences. Such metanarrative influences become evident in the plot templates that have been argued to variously guide their crafting in specific social and cultural formations. According to Frank (1995, p. 101), these plot templates include:

  i. the *restitution* narrative, which is oriented to the conclusion of illness and recovery from it, the ultimate victory over illness, an individual's reintegration into society and return to the normalcy of everyday life; in this plot type, uses of military and combative metaphors abound;
                              (Smith and Sparkes, 2004, p. 68; Halperin, 2017)

 ii. the *quest* narrative, which focuses on the temporal enactment of the illness experience and an individual's transformation over time;
iii. the *chaos* narrative, an anti-narrative that highlights the interruptions caused by illness.

To the plot templates, the plot of the illness experience as "a modern adventure story constructed around recovery and healing" has been added by Langellier and Peterson (2006, p. 190). This plot type is especially relevant to accounts of the cancer experience. Narrative templates are, of course, subject to change and index popular ways of talking about illness mainly in the Western world, where research in illness narratives has also been burgeoning.

Illness narratives have been studied in the context of approaches that view them as "in whole or part retrospective narratives, written or told from a relatively secure vantage point of recovery or remission, where threat of recurrence is closed off, even if incompletely" (Langellier and Peterson, 2006, p. 190). These approaches are couched in narrative inquiry views of life-writing or autobiography as "a retrospective narrative that undertakes to tell the author's own life, or a substantial part of it, seeking (at least in its classic version) to reconstruct his/her personal development within a given historical, social and cultural framework" (Schwalm, 2014, n.p.).

Despite the uniformity implied by the collective designation of these narratives as *illness narratives*, these tend to vary, depending on a number of factors, including, for example, the gender and age of the storyteller, the type of illness, and the social and cultural context in which they are told.

As a special form of autobiographical writing, illness narratives can be viewed not as an autonomous act of self-reflection but as a form of social action (Kohli, 1981: 505–16, Sloterdijk 1978: 21 cited in Schwalm, 2014, n.p.). As such, the tendency to over-celebrate illness narratives as a transparent window to personal experience, while neglecting aspects of their socially based performative dimensions, has been addressed as a criticism to the privileging of illness narratives as a resource for giving voice to a sufferer's experience (Atkinson, 2017).

More recently, research has started to investigate the uses of illness narratives as resources for gaining value and visibility in, for example, blogs (Stage, 2017), calling for further studies that look at these dimensions in image-based social media, such as vlogs and Instagram, as well as for the critical evaluation of existing narrative approaches to health (Harvey and Kotyeko, 2013, p. 92). In addition, applied linguists working in the area of health communication have foregrounded the usefulness of existing discourse analytic frameworks for moving away from essentialist and medically instituted notions of identity, including the identity of 'patient', and shift attention to situated performances of identity in everyday digital interactions (Kotyeko and Hunt, 2018, p. 1).

In light of these considerations, adapting a small stories lens to the study of emerging modes of telling the illness story in social media is well suited for bringing to the fore their performative, multi-semiotic, and participatory dimensions as well as the different types of affective positioning for staging experientiality and managing connectedness with intimate publics. The examination of a cancer vlog in this chapter also helps to bring to the fore practices of death-writing of the moment that make it possible for tellers of disruptive personal experience to negotiate dilemmas relating to the production and authentication of experientiality in the context of the performance of emotion for personal publics. As it is argued here, these dilemmas include the negotiation of the degree of *uniqueness and representativeness of the shared personal experience*, the call for *audience identification with or distancing from the teller*, and the teller's *level of emotional control or loss of control* on recounted situations and the projected self. In the remainder of this chapter, I will turn to the close examination of a single vlog selected and coded for an analysis of selecting, storying, and positioning. Details of the vlog are provided in the next section.

The Case Study: Charlotte's Journey

The vlog selected for study was launched in June 2014 by a young adult, Charlotte Eades, from Brighton, UK. Charlotte had been diagnosed with a rare form of brain cancer (glioblastoma multiforme) in July 2013, when she was sixteen, which ultimately claimed her life in February 2016, three years later, when she was nineteen.

Charlotte was selected to be the face of a CLIC Sargent's campaign (see the short film on her story, *I'm Still Here*,[2] 2015) and was interviewed on BBC news the same year (June 13, 2015;[3] see also video on vlog July 22, 2015). Her vlog is featured among the top ten cancer vlogs[4] and has attracted extensive media attention, especially after her death, when tributes for the "inspirational vlogger who used video to 'open up' dialogue about illness" poured in (BBC, 2016; *The Telegraph*, 2016; *The Guardian*, 2016). Her lasting popularity is attested to not only in the growing number of subscribers to her vlog (27,997) and the number of views of her videos (7,374,534; see Table 4.1) but also in the high level of support being raised by the charity for research in glioblastoma multiforme that was created in her honour by her family. The charity is called Charlotte's Bag after Charlotte's passion for handbags.[5] More recent tributes attesting to her legacy to this day include the Brighton & Hove council's decision to name Bus No. 27 (the bus Charlotte was using before she became too ill to travel) in her honour[6] in February 2019.

Table 4.1 YouTube user summary

Uploads	Subscribers	Video Views	Country	Channel Type	User Created
212	28,189	7,430,987	GB	People	June 14, 2014

Source: Socialblade.com; July 5, 2019.

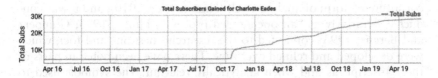

Figure 4.1 Total subscribers for Charlotte Eades' YouTube channel
Source: Socialblade.com; July 5, 2019.

The number of subscribers to the vlog has reached 28,189, with new viewers gained in late October 2017 (see Figure 4.1). This boost in subscriptions may have been motivated by the release of a Channel 4 documentary *Fighting Cancer: My Online Diary*, featuring Charlotte among three extraordinary young people with cancer who share their experiences online.[7]

The vlog counts 112 videos posted by Charlotte herself and three additional updates posted by her mother on behalf of her, where she updates viewers on the vlogger's last days and, ultimately, her passing. After her death, Charlotte's mother, Alex Eades, her brother Miles, and her cat, Nala, have been keeping the vlog active, having broadcast, at the time of writing, a total of 100 videos. Through their sustained and regular video-sharing activity, the channel is currently maintained as a live memorial for Charlotte, reinforcing her legacy as an inspirational figure and as the 'face' of the charity created in her honour, Charlotte's Bag.

Coding the Vlog

The vlog has been coded for content types, narrative organization, identity, and affective positioning. The coding for narrative organization has been based on the identification of major shifts or *turning points*, which signal a break in the vlogger's journey with cancer and hence in her affective experience, storying, and sense of self. The videos which mark a major turning point in Charlotte's story (four in total) were transcribed, using the voice recording Voice Typing on Google Docs.[8] This was done by watching and listening to each video, using earphones, and speaking out what the vlogger was saying while the tool transcribed what was said into a Google Doc, then edited to ensure accuracy. This form of *revoicing* the vlogger's words turned the process of transcription into an *embodied* activity, allowing an intimate and empathic engagement with the vlogger as part of my research ethics design for dealing with the sensitive nature of these videos.[9]

The second stage of transcription, which involved the selection of specific verbal and non-verbal aspects of the video, such as self-repairs, rate of speech, pauses, gestures, head movements, and eye-gaze for capturing, constituted a form of analysis itself (Hammersley, 2010), and it was conducted iteratively as "an open-ended process" (Ehlich, 1993; Gumperz and Berenz, 1993) connected to the research questions and foci, which were developed and refined over time. These have been noted in parts of the transcript, as and when analytically relevant. The symbols used to represent verbal and non-verbal elements have been adapted from Jefferson's notation system (2004) and Ochs' notation system for visual transcripts (1979, p. 62; see Table 4.4). Points in the video where editing is obvious are marked as [cuts] and are taken to signal a change to a new section in the transcript. For each video, visual elements, such as snapshots of the vlogger's facial expression at the start- and end-points of each video, head movements and gestures, the vlogger's distance from the camera, and the background to the video, have been noted as part of analyzing these videos as multimodal data. However, the screenshots are not reproduced but described when relevant, due to ethical concerns relating to extracting and recontextualizing parts of sensitive data without the consent of the vlogger.

The units of analysis used for representing the vlogger's speech are ethnopoetic lines (Hymes, 2003), which are short clauses consisting of at least one main verb and making up a small meaning unit, often marked by a pause. Larger narrative sections identified on the basis of linguistic markers that signal a shift in topic, deixis (temporal, spatial, personal), or tense have been used to segment the video and are labelled in the transcript as *opening, main plotline, evaluation* (internal and external), and *coda* on the basis of linguistic markers. The categories of evaluation and coda are drawn from Labov's model of personal experience stories (1972), which has proved highly influential, especially with regards to the analysis of the affective and interactional elements of the narrative (see Chapter 3).

The small story approach to the analysis of these videos called for the coding of different story elements and connections between them, including main events (happenings or moments), the temporality in which they are articulated (retrospective, real-time, or prospective), and evaluations and stances expressed about them. In addition, aspects of identity and affective positioning have been identified at the three interrelated levels of the *taleworld*, the *storyrealm*, and the *outside world* (see De Fina, 2016). The analysis of identity positioning has focused more specifically on the vlogger's metalinguistic statements about the vlog provided in descriptions of her channel and videos. Affective positioning has been examined with respect to the three levels presented as follows:

Level 1 (*Taleworld*): evaluations of the illness thematized as the main topic or focus of the story or other focalized moments and events;

discourse strategies signalling the uniqueness versus representativeness of the personal experience shared.

Level 2 (*Storyrealm*): the vlogger's inter-personal and inter-affective orientation to her viewers, shaped by modulations of different degrees of proximity to or distance from her viewers, inviting them to identify with her personal experience or distance themselves from it (and the sharer).

Level 3 (*Outside World*): positioning to the projected affective self, evident in modulations of proximity to or distance from the illness experience and uses of verbal and non-verbal cues for displaying emotional control, in alignment or disalignment to existing plot types of illness narratives and social discourses of affect.

Affective positioning is studied as an integral part of self-representational strategies for staging authenticity in this vlog and includes not only verbal but also non-verbal visual cues. More specifically, the analysis of positioning has relied on the coding for a range of positioning cues established through iterative examination of the data. These include references (or not) to the illness (Level 1), metacommunicative frames used at the opening and the closing of the video (i.e. sections of the story where the teller explicitly focuses on the message; Level 2), and explicit references to the self as well as affect markers (e.g. uses of the personal pronoun 'I', uses of evaluative adjectives, visual markers of affect such as head movements and so on; Level 3).

The comments to each video have also been coded for the time of their posting (around the time of the video's broadcast or after the passing of the vlogger) as well as thematically to assist with the investigation of the participation modes made available by the vlogger's small storying practices.

The remainder of this chapter presents the analysis, guided by the following questions:

i. How does the vlogger plot her experience of living with – and despite – a rare form of illness, drawing on the visual affordances of online broadcasting media?

ii. How does the vlogger position herself to others, herself, and her illness in and through her storying practices?

iii. What does vlogging on illness tell us about the way in which illness, dying, and mourning are mediatized online?

The analysis starts with the examination of the vlogger's projected identity positioning and selection practices and then moves on to consider the storying practices emergent in the vlog and their associated types of affective positioning.

Storying and Positioning

Identity Positioning

The emplotment of life with and despite cancer is based on the chrono-topic configuration of experience into a story and relies on the selection of events or moments to be (re)presented. This ultimately depends on what the teller (and her audience) consider worth telling, storying, and sharing. The vlogger's views on what types of content are considered worthy for sharing on her vlog become evident in the metalinguistic spaces available on the YouTube platform, i.e. the spaces for general descriptions of the vlog and individual videos, as well as in the specific metalinguistic affordances drawn upon to make content visible and searchable, for example the videos' titles and tags. These metacomments reveal the vlogger's choices of identity positioning and are discussed in this section.

The vlog is named after the vlogger's full name, 'Charlotte Eades'. Using one's real name is one possibility among others for new vlogs, provided that the name is a short and memorable name, so that it can be easily retrieved via an online search (according to online guides for new vloggers). The choice of not including the C-word at all in the channel's title is notable, given that there are plenty of popular YouTube vlogs entitled 'My Cancer Story'. The selected naming strategy allows the vlogger to take some distance from other illness vlogs but also from the identity of a cancer patient. Instead, this vlogger opts for creating a 'me-channel', which is purported to be about who she is and what she loves. This is stated more clearly in the opening page of the channel, where the vlogger provides the following brief description:

> I'm here to show others that everyone is beautiful. I'd like to be an inspiration to all. Please subscribe!"

Her identity positioning as an aspiring influencer who wants her life to be an inspiration to others is further reaffirmed during her interview on BBC news[10] (June 13, 2015), where the vlogger makes it clear that she doesn't want to be known as the girl with cancer but as a spokesperson for young people with cancer and anybody else. She thus aligns herself with *cancer advocates* who can speak up for those who can't, helping people to navigate the difficult landscape of life with cancer. Given the central role that cancer advocates have in contemporary cancer charities, such as *Stand up to Cancer*, acting as one offers increased opportunities for connecting with the cancer community. It also provides a forward-looking frame for approaching illness in a positive way and as a resource for motivational action.

In the launching vlog post, dated June 14, 2014, the vlogger explains further her reasons for creating the vlog and for selecting different types of content for her videos:

I've been wanting to make a youtube channel for ages now to discuss the cancer but also discuss things like beauty and fashion because these are really the things I love about life but I found that when I had the cancer I wanted some advice videos (.)[11] there aren't many about it on youtube so I'm here to be the sort of ((smiles)) guru of cancer if you like and answer questions about hair loss, medication, socializing, friendship, all things that cancer affects but, most of all, the daily life.

In the launching video of the vlog, Charlotte draws explicitly on her chronological age as an identity resource, presenting herself as "a teen-ager with a twist". References to chronological age or life stages have been found to be central in reflections of individuals diagnosed with can-cer (Pecchioni, 2012, p. 764) and can serve as cues to patients' position-ing to their illness, story-recipients, and their own self. The chronological organization of the illness experience presents particular types of chal-lenges for young adults, faced with a major disruption in their unfold-ing life story. In this case, the vlogger's intertwining of chronological age and health status at the start of the vlog prefigures the centrality of this tension that emerges in later videos. The next section turns to the closer examination of selection practices in the vlog.

Selecting Content for Sharing

The coding[12] of all videos for themes has pointed to the organization of the vlog around the following four types of content:

i. *cancer*: clips that offer advice relating to cancer or updates on cancer treatments;
ii. *fashion*: updates and reviews on fashion items, such as handbags, clothing, shoes, and makeup;
iii. *entrepreneurial*: clips with explicit promotional functions (e.g. char-ity fundraising), which also include videos using popular YouTube videos aimed to promote viewer engagement (e.g. Tag videos, Q&A; Printsome, 2018) and finally,
iv. *personal*: clips where the vlogger makes her thoughts or feelings about a particular moment or event into the main topic of the video.

As the word-cloud of the vlog post titles shows (see Figure 4.2), where the larger-size font indicates the frequency of the use of the word, in this vlog, cancer is just one topic among different kinds of reviews, updates, look-books, and favourite YouTube-style videos.

Selected types of content in this vlog were found to oscillate in an extremely well-balanced way between fashion- and cancer-focused videos, entrepreneurial, and personal videos. Fashion videos and cancer-focused

Figure 4.2 Word-cloud of vlog content

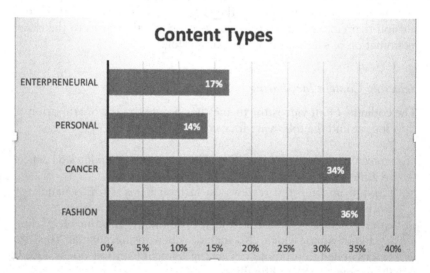

Figure 4.3 Types of content and distribution in the vlog

videos make up the majority of the vlog's content (36% and 34%, respectively). In some cases, they are brought together, as in the case of a video on "Cancer and Cosmetics/Beauty". Videos related to entrepreneurial activity were found to slightly outnumber personal videos (17% versus 14%; see Figure 4.3).

Fashion and entrepreneurial videos indicate the driving of content selection by and for the YouTube community. Their design draws on typical YouTube templates such as 'Closet confidential', 'What's in my bag', 'Shop Haul', and 'Outfit of the day' for fashion videos or audience engagement video-formats, such as 'Tag', where significant others or guests also appear on the video and answers to questions from subscribers (e.g. 'Sibling TAG', 'Things that I love'). The high number of this type of videos indicates the vlogger's orientation and interdiscursive connection to YouTube beauty and fashion influencers, reproducing popular conversational templates for engaging subscribers and building fan loyalty that goes beyond addressing exclusively a community of young cancer sufferers. Adopting an inclusive orientation to her intended audience helps increase the potential for her vlog's visibility. This vlog design also serves as a way of negotiating the tensions between her ideal or anticipated life as a teenager and her lived experience by explicitly positioning her among other (vlogging) teenagers rather than among other cancer patients. In his study of cancer blogs, Stage (2017) argues that such blogs constitute sites for new entrepreneurial patient practices, which challenge dominant constructions of illness and patient identities. Based on the content selections just described, it seems that this is also the case for this vlog.

The content categories echo the tips and guidance for vlogging like a pro(fessional) available on online courses offered by the You Tube Creator Academy (2019), which summarize the key elements that can make a vlog successful and appealing to viewers, foregrounding in particular the importance of 'authenticity'. Creators are expected to be "their authentic selves on camera", aspiring not just to gain an audience, i.e. a group of listeners, but to create a community of 'friends' following them from video to video. In order to 'do authenticity', vloggers are encouraged to be "conversational" and to post (i) on personal topics, offering a peek into their life, (ii) personal views on general topics, such as travel, product reviews, or tutorials, and (iii) do their best to respond to comments, preferably on camera or in the comments, to build fan loyalty.

Implicit in this guidance is that users upload videos with the intention to achieve large numbers of views and economic rewards. This is also reflected in the interface design, which invites more audience-centric users and interactive usage (Burgess and Green, 2018). For example, beauty vloggers' authenticity and trustworthiness are constructed in three main types of content: tutorials, consumer reviews, and consumption exhibitions, whose value can be leveraged for commercial messages. These types of videos are accompanied by conventional titles, topics, and tags – for instance, 'monthly favourites', 'beauty/fashion haul', or '20-dollar challenge" that can be easily searched for, retrieved, and recognised by viewers (Hou, 2018, pp. 8–10). In the case of illness vlogs, as illustrated here, the selection of fashion-related topics is part of the vlogger's strategies of distancing herself from the identity of a cancer patient and instead aligning herself to her identity as a teenage vlogger, an influencer akin to beauty influencers or a "cancer guru" seeking to engage others' attention and be an inspiration to them. In the vlog, this identity is most strongly projected in the series "Cancer and . . ." (included in the vlog's playlist), which most clearly display the vlogger's intention to raise awareness about life with cancer.

In most of the broadcast videos, the vlogger faces the screen on her computer in a 'talking head' pose (i.e. upper torso up), with the exception of videos in which she is modelling clothes or shoes, which require her to also show her upper or lower body. The videos are produced in-house mostly by Charlotte, using a small handheld camera on a tripod. The coding of videos for location shows a preference for shooting the videos in her bedroom, with the exception of entrepreneurial videos, which include guests, or some fashion videos that require a different space configuration for showcasing outfits. The choice of the teenager's bedroom as the main background to the videos is a key strategy of staging authenticity and an integral part of her attempt to forge an intimate relationship with her viewers. Viewers are invited into Charlotte's personal space and called upon to take up positions of affectively engaged 'confidants' to her thoughts and feelings, recipients of advice, or supporters, even after she's gone.

Overall, the videos in this vlog are characterized by (i) *inclusivity*, addressing not only cancer patients but anyone who may be interested in finding out about this particular kind of illness experience; (ii) *interactivity*, embedding opportunities for audience participation via commenting; and (iii) *interdiscursivity*, creating connections with the vlogging practices of popular young adults on YouTube and claiming a visible place among them.

A similar upbeat style and a preference for mixed-content selections is also attested in the vlog after it is appropriated by members of her family following the vlogger's death. In this new phase, which starts with the video entitled "A quick update and our plans for the future" (March 6, 2016), the vlogger's mother and brother share moments from their journey with Charlotte and her cancer ("Cancer and the Emotional Rollercoaster", March 27, 2016) or from their daily life coping with grief ("Cancer, death and grief", June 5, 2016). They also post Q&A videos answering questions from viewers and upload videos that reveal known ("Charlotte's handbag collection!"; June 1, 2016) and unknown facets of Charlotte ("Things about Charlotte that you may not have known & update"; Dec. 3, 2017), including 'unedited' found footage on calendar-important dates such as her birthday, deathversary, or Christmas ("Happy 21st Charlotte"; February 18, 2018). Their vlog activity also includes updates on their own everyday life, for example updates on Miles's university studies ("Charlotte bringing us some good news!"; August 7, 2018) and updates on the charity, including awards received in acknowledgment of their efforts and social impact.

This co-creation and curation of content by members of her family that extends beyond her death is particularly interesting in light of research findings suggesting that cancer survivors or bereaved relatives of cancer bloggers often enter a "tellability crisis" once the main purpose of their blog ceases to exist and the readers' expectations cease to align with the needs of the survivor (or their relatives) to move on (Stage, 2017). Many of the bloggers who survive their illness resort to closing down the blog and move on to other platforms to continue with their personal life sharing, while it is often the case that the relatives of bloggers who didn't survive are unsure what to do with the accounts of their loved ones. Charlotte Eades's vlog offers a different example of a vlog which continues after her death as a live memorial and forum for the charity created in her honour. In fact, this new phase results in almost doubling the number of subscriptions to the channel and further enhancing the visibility of the vlogger's story, while interlaying a new voice into the vlogger's echoing voice. As Alex Eades noted in a tweet posted via the official Charlotte's BAG account (July 4, 2019), "I'm now Charlotte's voice".[13]

The videos on Charlotte's channel have been attracting millions of views and thousands of comments (see Table 4.2). In particular, videos after the vlogger's death, i.e. after February 2016, and videos documenting the last period of her life make it to the top of this list. Videos posted at the earlier days of the vlog were found to be less popular, with the exception of two videos: Charlotte's welcome video launching the channel ("Welcome to My Channel"; June 14, 2014) and a video with YouTube celebrity Marcus Butler as part of a "Stand Up to Cancer" creative fundraising campaign ("Stand Up to Cancer with Marcus Butler"; October 17, 2015). This trend suggests that story viewability on this channel doesn't follow the temporal unfolding of the story as it is being broadcast, but it is instead driven by drama and climactic intensity. This preference for sensational content could also account for the popularity of videos from the last phase of the vlogger's illness trajectory and unedited footage videos ("The unedited footage we found when Charlotte passed away"; "Happy 21st Charlotte"; "Unedited and unseen footage from Charlotte"; see Table 4.2) broadcast after the vlogger's death as 'new memories' by her family. This preference attests to the audience's desire to take a peek into the vlogger's intimate and backstage realm. Video views also suggest the popularity of compilation videos ("Brain cancer: Dying to Live"; "Living to Die in 4:42"; "Stand Up to Cancer with Marcus Butler"; see Table 4.2), which make it easier for viewers to piece together the vlogger's life story as they navigate the channel.

The list of the most-viewed clips has served as a starting point for the analysis presented in the remainder of this chapter, guiding the selection of the videos for closer examination and analysis discussed in the next section.

Table 4.2 22 Most-viewed videos

Date	Video title	Views	Rating %*	Comments
2017–09–02	Brain cancer: Dying to Live, Living to Die in 4:42 minutes	2.2M	98.5%	5K
2017–02–24	This unedited footage we found after Charlotte passed . . .	1.5M	98.5%	2K
2016–02–25	Thank you all – 1997–2016	182.5K	99.2%	84
2016–02–19	Update –February 19	140.7K	98.1%	212
2017–03–05	Charlotte's last few days at home	128.1K	98.9%	0
2016–01–06	The Medication Isn't Working . . .	125.5K	99%	86
2016–02–04	World Cancer Day!!	121.8K	99.3%	124
2014–06–14	Welcome to my channel I Charlotte Eades	113.8K	99.7%	115
2016–02–11	Update – February 11	98.0K	99.4%	70
2016–01–19	Still here!	94.6K	99.5%	103
2015–01–19	Update	92.6K	98.6%	104
2015–09–09	Bad News I Charlotte Eades	80.5K	99.4%	143
2016–01–12	Update I Charlotte Eades	74.3K	97.3%	116
2017–01–15	Terminal diagnosis	74.6K	99.3%	91
2016–01–23	Me Again!	73.1K	97.9%	108
2017–03–12	Glioblastoma finally won	59.1K	99.4%	207
2018–02–18	Happy 21st Charlotte xx	52.2K	98.5%	128
2015–11–01	How I'm Doing/Cancer Update	47.6K	99.4%	52
2015–12–28	Fed Up . . .	43.4K	98.8%	30
2015–10–17	Stand Up To Cancer 2015 With Marcus Butler I Charlotte Eades	36.6K	99.5%	174
2016–03–06	A Quick Update and Our Plans for the Future	35.0K	98.7%	50
2017–05–07	Unedited and unseen footage from Charlotte	33.6K	99.3%	63

Source: Socialblade.com; July 5, 2019.

*The rating percentage metric is derived from the number of likes and dislikes of this specific video.

Emergent Narrativity

The analysis of narrativity and participation in the vlog pointed out that emplotment on the vlog emerges at two interrelated levels:

i.   The first level refers to the post-factum accumulation of clips on the YouTube channel which makes up the 'big story' of Charlotte's journey. This story is constructed retrospectively after the vlogger's passing and affords multiple points of entry for individual viewers, depending on when they access the vlog and which clips they choose to view;

ii.   The second level covers the individual videos, which range in duration from 00:28 min. (minimum) to 12:33 min. maximum and (re)present the vlogger's selected moments of her life with and despite her illness.

The coding of key turning points that cumulatively make up Charlotte's story has revealed three main parts in which the vlog is organized. These three parts have been labelled using the vlogger's lexical choices in the video or the title: (i) *'teenager with a twist'*, (ii) *'bad news'*, and (iii) *'fed up'* (see Figure 4.4).

The largest part of the vlog deals with everyday aspects of living with the diagnosis as a 'teenager with a twist' before the turning point of the 'bad news', when news about the growth of the tumour is announced. The section 'fed up' covers the last period of her illness, where cancer treatment results in a visible transformation in her appearance and the vlogger's ability to walk and talk. These difficulties also make vlogging more difficult and, as it will be shown, mark a liminal phase in the vlogger's affective positioning to the illness, her viewers, and her own self.

The remainder of this chapter will look in more detail at aspects of emplotment and affective positioning in the vlog.

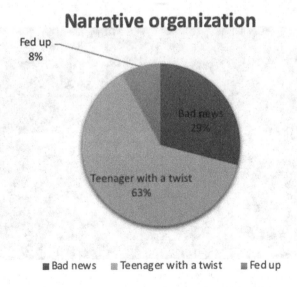

Narrative organization

Fed up
8%

Bad news
29%

Teenager with a twist
63%

■ Bad news   ■ Teenager with a twist   ■ Fed up

Figure 4.4 Narrative organization of the vlog

The 'Big' Story of Charlotte's Journey

The first level of the emplotment of living with dying, i.e. the post-factum level, which refers to the vlogger's life-story as it emerges cumulatively across the vlog, is best illustrated by the most-viewed video, entitled "Brain Cancer: Dying to Live, Living to Die in 4:42 minutes" (September 2, 2017). The video was created by the vlogger's family after her passing has, so far, attracted more than 2 million views and 5 million comments.

The video is a compilation of selected moments shared by the vlogger across different videos, from the launch of the channel to the vlogger's last days, woven together into a temporally sequenced verbal and visual narration. By imposing narrative order to the vlogger's video sharing, this tribute video creates a 'big' story of her journey and allows viewers to peek into the ins and outs of Charlotte's life with and despite cancer in just 4:42 minutes.

The starting point of the video is the launch video, in which the vlogger introduces herself as a teenager with cancer. This is followed by narrative text (Image 4.1), which explicitly anchors the vlogger's video in calendar time and provides a starting point for the unfolding of Charlotte's life story.

Temporal and spatial anchors are used throughout the strips of narrative text (see parts in bold in narrative text below) for configuring the vlogger's illness experience into a retrospective mode of narration, i.e. a mode of 'big' storying constructed by looking back from the main event of the vlogger's death through key moments and critical turning points of her journey.

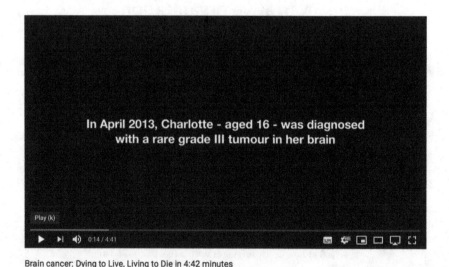

Brain cancer: Dying to Live, Living to Die in 4:42 minutes

2,251,390 views   47K   712   SHARE   SAVE   ...

Image 4.1 "Brain Cancer: Dying to Live, Living to Die in 4:42 minutes": screenshot of narrative text

Narrative text used to weave together selected video snippets from Charlotte's sharing:

1.

In April 2013 Charlotte aged 16 was diagnosed with a rare grade 3 tumour in her brain.

2.

In 2014 Charlotte started a YouTube channel where she also discussed fashion beauty and her beloved handbags.

3.

Charlotte had severe anxiety in school, but cancer and YouTube transformed her confidence.

4.

Over two years Charlotte uploaded 112 videos and was viewed over 1 million times.

5.

but in September 2015 everything changed . . .

6.

Charlotte was diagnosed with a new tumour in her brain, a grade four glioblastoma multiform, known as the terminator.

7.

Charlotte's decline was rapid, but she kept the camera recording.

8.

Charlotte died on 24 February 2016, aged 19.

5000 people under the age of 14 die every year from glioblastoma Yet only 1% of cancer research funding goes into brain tumour research **We can change this www.charlottesbag.com**

Key moments selected for inclusion have been predominantly drawn from the vlogger's fashion-focused videos and are part of the thread of videos about being 'a teenager with a twist'. In terms of plot type, this 'big' story is akin to typical narratives of illness and dying of 'quest': based on a combination of good and bad moments, the video tells the story of how cancer transformed a girl suffering from severe anxiety at school into a confident young woman vlogging about fashion, her beloved handbags, and her battle with cancer. This is a tribute story celebrating Charlotte's life and at the same time mobilizing her illness story to raise awareness about the rare form of brain cancer that afflicted her. This broader, 'entrepreneurial' aim is foregrounded in the closing line of the video story: "We can change this – www. Charlottesbag.com".

While the 'big' story of Charlotte's story woven by others after her passing is (re)presented as a retrospective account of quest, the vlogger's flow of sharing in the vlog is characterized by overlapping aspects of both a 'quest' and a 'chaos' life story of illness and dying emplotted in a mix of retrospective and real-time modes of storying.

Small Storying the Illness Experience

The study of emergent narrativity at the level of the individual videos broadcast by the vlogger has been based on the analysis of three videos, documenting key moments or turning points in the overall thematic and narrative development of the vlog from a post-factum point of view (see Table 4.3).

Table 4.3 Turning points in the narrative development of the vlog

Video title & Description	Date broadcast	'Big story' section	Duration/ Word Count	Views	Comments
When things aren't going to plan "I look so awful in this video and I apologise for not editing it one bit. Please remember my message and share it with other".	27/10/2014	Teenager with a twist	05:43	11,270	43
			916 w.		
Bad News "Hi guys, I am very scared at the moment, I don't know whether this leaves me. All I can say is please subscribe as it adds a smile to my face. Lots of love. Charlotte xx"	09/09/2015	Bad news	07:24	77,465	91
			361 w.		
Fed Up (No description)	28/12/2016	Fed Up	01:04	35,498	49
			124 w.		
Unedited footage "Share, please"	24/02/2017	Fed Up	08:05	1,154,023	1948
			1316 w.		

Each video has been analyzed for its mode of emplotment and its associated types of affective positioning, bringing to the fore the way small storying of life with – and despite – illness changes over the course of the vlog, reflecting the vlogger's dynamic trajectory with cancer.

The first video, "When things aren't going to plan" (October 27, 2014), illustrates a mode of a retrospective narration temporally organized around the past and covering the lived time since the cancer diagnosis to the present moment (see Extract 1A). The vlogger focuses on "a few problems" (l. 22) she's been having "recently" (l. 21) with "dealing with things" and "feeling normal" and shares with her viewers the struggle of negotiating tensions between the ideal life plot of a 'normal' teenager and her lived experience, which has been disrupted by the cancer.

As shown in Extract 1A,[14] this aspect of her personal experience with cancer is plotted as a *recount* of the impact that cancer has had on her everyday life since the diagnosis, with a focus on the present moment of sharing ("I have cancer", l. 26; "I can't drive for two years", l. 27; "it's extremely difficult to get a job", l. 29;" I don't really get to socialise", l. 32). The report-like listing of the everyday difficulties in the life of the vlogger featuring little explicit evaluation echoes the story genres of blogging on illness (Page, 2011). Evaluation is limited to assessments of the practical and social consequences of cancer viewed as a disruption to "normal" life (l. 25), everyday life activities, such as driving (l. 27) and plans for the future (l. 29).

Extract 1A

20. I for some reason
21. I've been having a few problems recently
22. with dealing with things
23. and feeling normal
24. Umm I will quickly go through this:
25. the first reason why I don't feel normal
26. is because I have cancer (.)
27. the second reason being I can't drive for two years because I had a seizure last year (.)
28. the third reason being
29. it's extremely difficult to get a job
30. which I'm sure a lot of you can relate to
31. and the third reason being
32. that I don't (_) really get to socialise that much.

The recount of the vlogger's difficulties is used for affectively positioning herself to the illness, the viewers, and herself. The illness experience is framed as an experience which potentially resonates with viewers (l. 30), constructing it as a unique experience, which is more broadly representative of human experience in moments of crisis. As shown in the following extract from the multimodal transcript, the vlogger pays particular attention to the management of her relationship with viewers (see Extract 1B, Table 4.4). The video has a clear opening and closing, where the vlogger provides orientating details about the process of making and the motivation for shooting this video. She offers, more specifically, details about the decision to film the video in "the space of ten minutes" (l. 4), which is taken to justify the natural look of the vlogger (not wearing any makeup, l. 5–6) and the low-quality sound (l. 135) and she explains that her aim is to "get the message out there" (l. 12). The vlogger's explicit orientation to her viewers seems to be further reinforced by a shift in the position of her head, from the viewer's right-hand side, which seems to be the base position for the vlogger, to the viewer's left. Shifts in head positions are argued to mark the launch or closing of the vlogger's broadcasting mode.

Table 4.4 Transcript of the opening (00:00–00:22) and the closing of the video "When things aren't going to plan" (05:13–05:41)

Extract 1B

Time	Line	Verbal
00:00	0	n/a
00:03	1	Hi everybody
	2	I am **back today** with a (.) really sudden video
	3	which I decided to film
	4	in the space of about 10 minutes (.)
	5	I'm not wearing any makeup
	6	uhm I've just come out of the bath
	7	it's a Sunday evening
	8	but while I was in the bath
	9	I had a thought
	10	and I really wanted
	11	to share it with everybody
00:22	12	and get the message out there
		[. . .]
		[. . .]
05:13	133	anyway
	134	I will film another video soon
	135	I'm sorry for the crappy quality
	136	you may have realised from the viewfinder
	137	But please just remember to stay true to yourself
	138	and sometimes you can be your own worst enemy
	139	but you all can do it
	140	and please just share this video
	141	remember to speak to someone
	142	don't ever hold things in
05:41	143	thank you for watching

Extract 1B

Video title: ***When things aren't going to plan***
Date: 27/10/2014
Duration: 05:42
Location: Charlotte's bedroom [Aspects of background: Lightly lit room]

Openings and closings in this video, and the vlog more generally, serve as metacommunicative devices, which frame it as part of an ongoing series created for the sake of viewers. They are not just an audience-involvement device but an integral part of the (re)presentation of the illness experience. These frames are used as authenticating strategies for affirming the spontaneity of content creation on the vlog and for projecting an intimate relationship between the vlogger and her viewers. These strategies, coupled with her bodily proximity to the camera, contribute to her affective positioning as one of intimacy with her viewers, constructed as a personal public.

In addition to the opening and closing metacommunicative frames, the vlogger also uses the pronoun 'you' ("but please just remember", l. 137), fashioning her experience into a small story that opens up the space for her followers to share in her struggles and also to intimate their own stories of difficult situations in the comments space. By explicitly orienting to her followers through the use of the second-person personal pronoun ('you'), the vlogger projects herself as an inspirational teenager, strong, positive, and in control of what's happening even "when things are not going to plan". This identity position is enacted through the emplotment of cancer 'troubles', helping her to construct an affective position at a relative distance from the difficult emotions she's feeling and self-present at the frontstage as being in control of her emotions.

Additional aspects of the vlogger's affective positioning to herself are evident in the paralinguistic features in the part of the video which immediately follows the opening and brackets the main part of the sharing. A selection of these features is annotated in the multi-modal transcript[15] that follows (see Transcript Key, Table 4.5; Transcript, Table 4.6).

Table 4.5 Transcript key

/	Utterance/ethnopoetic line boundary
(.3)	Pause length placed before utterance; utterances separated by significant pauses are placed on separate lines
-	Self-interruption; placed at point of interruption (example: some-all of it/)

(Continued)

Table 4.5 (Continued)

.	low fall
?	high rise
!	exclamatory utterance
CAPITAL LETTERS	increased volume
_____	emphasis (e.g. I want <u>that</u> one)
:::	lengthened syllable (each: = one beat)
-h	Audible in-breath
h	Audible out-breath
↓	Upward eye-gaze
↑	Downward eye-gaze
→	Right-directed eye-gaze
⊙	Centred & focused eye-gaze
}	Eyes frown
(())	Gestures
>	Head tilted to the right
<	Head tilted to the left
[. . .]	Omitted text

Table 4.6 Transcript: Multimodal transcript of video "When things aren't going to plan" (00:42–00:55)

Time	Line	Verbal
00:42	1	-h I (.) < ⬅
00:43	2	for some reason: > (.) ➡
	3	>I've been having< ➡
00:46	4	a few-h (.) problems. (.)
	5	recently.
	6	with (.) ➡
	7	dealing with things and (.)
00:52	8	feeling: (.) normal. (.)
	9	Umm ((slightly moves back))
00:55	10	I will ↑ quickly go through this

As shown in the multimodal transcript, this part of the video opens with the utterance of "I", which is paralinguistically marked by a range of features: it is fronted by an audible in-breath, its articulation is elongated over one second and followed by a short pause and a shift of the vlogger's head and gaze to the left. This combination of linguistic and paralinguistic cues brings attention to the affective 'I'. The over-laying of emotionality continues in the vlogger's utterance of the phrase "for some reason" with an elongated final consonant '-n', a slow down of her earlier quick pace and a return of her head to the neutral position (i.e. the right-hand side), which marks her being 'out of' broadcasting mode. The phrase "problems recently" (line 2) is uttered in a low pitch and a low fall, audibly marking the weight of these issues for the teller. The vlogger moves her head and body slightly closer to the camera when she utters "dealing with things" (line 7), while she utters each of the words in the phrase "and feeling [normal]" (line 8) almost separately, adding emphasis to the content. The move to the next part of the video is signalled by the discourse marker "uhm" and is accompanied by a slight move of her head back to her base head position and a change of affective "gear" to the quick-paced summary of the reasons for how she's feeling. The accumulation of para-linguistic features in this short section discussed here points to how the vlogger invests her sharing performances with emotion through 'small' acts of *embodied affective positioning*, which include short pauses, sound elongations, slight head movements, and speech pace, inviting viewers to empathically witness how she's feeling in the here and now.

Commenters to this video opt for displays of alignment to the vlog-ger, showing *ritual appreciation* (e.g. "Such a beautiful, inspirational girl! Good on you!"; "Great video I agree with you all the way"; cf. Geor-gakopoulou, 2016), with few cases of second stories (Georgakopoulou, 2007). The majority of the comment space in this case (69.7% of the comments) is taken up by posts shared after her passing. These are either expressed as direct addresses to Charlotte (e.g. "will keep your words in mind! RIP Charlotte") or as small acts of witnessing and validating her experience ("I'm always impressed of her confidence for things She is talking about. I don't know how many people fell in love with her. She is a good example. She did the best When she decided to create this You-Tube channel to inspire people"). This difference in the temporal anchor-ing of the comment responses is found in the comment space underneath other posts, too, and is a point of discussion, to which I will return to later in this chapter.

"Bad News": Breaking News of Illness

The second video, which marks the start of the second phase of the vlog, is centred around an important medical diagnosis event that happened on that day. The "bad news" is that the MRI scan showed that the tumour has grown, and the vlogger shares how she's feeling about it.

The emphasis of this cancer update is placed on the very recent past, documenting the vlogger's immediate reaction to the "bad news" and, more specifically, her fear about any kind of operation on her brain and her attempt to affirm her positive spirit and her belief that everything's going to be fine. Cancer is plotted here as a medical condition, linked to medical operations and treatments that are, on the one hand, scary and intrusive and, on the other hand, offer some hope of treatment and get-ting well.

The vlogger draws on the authentication strategies mentioned earlier, as evident in the opening and closing of the video, using metacommuni-cative frames that reaffirm her proximity with her viewers. The use of markers of authentication ("I know I look a bit different today I'm wear-ing no make-up and it's very late at night i didn't even look if the camera's

Table 4.7 Transcript: Multimodal transcript of part of video "Bad news" (00:14–02:43)

Time	Lines	Verbal
00:14	1	Uhm <u>today</u> ● I got som:e very bad news.
	2	uhmm ⬇
	3	A few weeks ago ⬇
	4	I was told that it looked like }
	5	something was: in my brain ((gestures))
	6	basically on the MRI scan
	7	some sort of aah you know <u>growth</u> ((gestures))
	8	there was some sort of ⬅
	9	and uhm (.) six weeks later <u>today</u> uhm
	10	>they needed to wait for six weeks
	11	just to see if it was anything
	12	and six weeks later < <u>today</u>
	13	it has grown from being
	14	3 or 4 millimetres to 3 centimetres ⁻ʰ
	15	which is obviously ◉
	16	you know (.)
	17	very- very scary ➡ uhm
	18	I'm very ◉ scared? ⬇
	19	Uhm and basically
	20	I don't know what to do now uhm (.)
	21	I was just got told this information
	22	literally a few hours ago and uhm
02:43		[. . .]

on or not") marks the post as a personal post. The vlogger positions her viewers as the centre of her concern ("but right now I just wanted to update you") and at the same time expresses her need of support ("please subscribe of course it would make me feel really great at the moment"). Negotiating her viewers and herself as at the centre of concern reveals her ongoing efforts to affectively position herself as being in control over this unwanted development of her illness.

As in the case of the video discussed in the previous section, in this case, too, the vlogger's affective positioning indexing the vlogger's emotional turmoil is evident in the accumulation of paralinguistic features at the point of announcing the main topic of the video (see Transcript 2).

As the multimodal transcript shows, the vlogger repeatedly uses emphasis in uttering "today" emphatically (l. 1; l. 9; l. 12) and also focuses her gaze to the centre point of the camera. She also uses emphasis when uttering the word 'growth' (l. 7), using gestures to mimic what the 'growth' looks like. Her utterances tend to end in a low fall (l. 2, l. 3), a lowering of her gaze, and an almost cracking voice. The only exception to this trend for low end uttering was noted in l. 18, where the phrase "I'm scared" ends in a high rise and a lowering of her gaze that could be seen as an affective performance strategy that further authenticates the sharing.

"Fed Up": Envisualizing Illness

The video "Fed up" makes part of the last phase of the vlog, which marks the final stage of the vlogger's cancer. These last videos are difficult to watch without feeling extremely sad and upset about the fast pace of her deterioration. In this short video, the vlogger focuses on her here and now and shares her anger, despair, and exhaustion over her illness experience, leading her to question when it will all end.

Emotion is centre-stage in this video, both verbally and non-verbally. The vlogger's awareness and self-conscious approach to her sharing are evident in the addition of text at the start of the video, where she apologizes for her slurred voice, as well as in the warning issued at the opening of the video that this is a 'down' video. Furthermore, the video features a high level of edits (three in total in a video which lasts 1:04).

The description of the physical marks and psychological repercussions of her state in this video is closely matched by her visible and audible transformation. The vlogger finds herself in a position of little control over the cancer and the way it has changed her. She acknowledges the tensions between expectations of jolliness for Christmastime and her low mood. And yet she still hangs on to her desire to share this change with her followers and continue with the broadcasts.

Even though this video features less extensive metacommunicative frames compared to other videos, it encodes affectivity in the most 'authentic' way, sparking strong waves of emotion from viewers. This is achieved by the vlogger's affective positioning through the offering of a glimpse of the 'backstage' of the illness, so far carefully safeguarded in the vlog. As she is becoming visibly transformed by the illness, the broadcasting self is also changing. This video illustrates how the envisualization of her illness becomes the ultimate affective marker of her illness experience and authenticating resource.

Even though there is no explicit call for support or engagement, supportive reactions to the post abound in the comment space, as illustrated in Examples 1–4:

Example 1

"Charlotte. Darling. You look amazing, beautiful as ever. I am sorry that you are not feeling too great. But chin up hun. We are here for you. Big hugs and a lot of kisses. [name] Xxx"

Example 2

"Stay strong beautiful ❤"

Example 3

"Oh sweet girl . . . she didn't need to apologize for slurring . . . poor thing. She suffered so much"

Example 4

"Two years ago today ☺ You're never forgotten Charlotte ☕".

In this comment-space, which has accumulated forty-nine comments, only six were posted after her death and are illustrated in Examples 5–8 below:

Example 5

"Man i still look at her videos even though she passed long ago 😭😭😢😢"

Example 6

"I wish I started watching her sooner :("

Example 7

"Im so heart broken . . . "

Example 8

"Nothing is really working or happening :(((this is unimaginable sad".

While a sense of being allowed in the vlogger's personal space is offered in the vlog, a great deal of care is also taken in safeguarding that space by carefully selecting, editing, and presenting each video, as part of Charlotte's "frontstage" or public self (Goffman, 1959), even when talking about her most intimate moments of her life with cancer. The "backstage" remains hidden – at least until later in the vlog. This negotiation of the frontstage and the backstage illustrates the vlogger's handling of the tensions surrounding the broadcasting of the self on YouTube but also the tellability of the transgressive experience of living with dying as a teenager. Difficult topics are broached in a 'safe' manner, i.e. in a way that viewers, but also the vlogger herself and her family, can handle and cope with, switching between a light and serious tone, introspection and sociability, feeling, thinking, and doing.

The Vlogger's 'Backstage'

The vlogger's backstage, as well as her video-making process, is revealed more starkly in the footage broadcast by her family after her death. In the case of the video "The unedited footage we found after Charlotte passed . . .", which attracted about 1.5 million views (see Table 4.2) and is longer (08:05 min) than the videos posted by the vlogger, the vlogger is sharing her raw experience of the illness. As Extract 4 shows, Charlotte uses adjectives of negative feelings not encountered in earlier posts, including 'rubbish', 'alien', and 'ugly':

Extract 4

I'm not feeling good I'm feeling particularly **rubbish** [. . .] but but yeah this kind of the life of a teenager with cancer [. . .] I just I just feel really **alien** I feel really **ugly** and I feel like if nobody could offer me anything (.) all I want is my life back I just want the cancer to go and I just want to be normal and I just I'm just I'm just going mad you know I can't do this I feel like I can't deal with this it's all too much and I'm just just you know I feel even though I'm 18 I feel like an elderly person in a young person's body I feel you know just **rubbish** all the time [. . .].

[emphasis added]

These more negative parts in this footage, which would have been most likely edited out to create a shorter and more upbeat video in line with YouTube broadcasting conventions, point to the use of self-recording as a form of diary writing and a necessary first step into crafting a story that can be shared with others after the appropriate editing and cuts.

Comments to the unedited footage video include a flurry of second stories, often lengthy ones, about viewers' own experiences with cancer, as shown in Example 9.

Example 9

"I lost my Dad to cancer 4 months ago. We took care of him at home. I can really relate to what she said about people romanticizing cancer. I don't know what I thought it would be like. Maybe sitting around and reminiscing with the person. Having some great talks. Remembering to tell them that you love them, which I did do a lot. But it's not that way at all. He was so very ill. It was horrible. It was just absolutely horrific to see someone I loved suffering like that. I said to one of the nurses who came in to check on him, 'This is no Norman Rockwell painting'. She said, "No. No it's not".

Commenters also offered expressions of sadness about her suffering and pain (see Example 10) or highlighted particularly emotional points in her videos (see Example 11).

Example 10

"who else started crying in this video?'; "The clear pain she's feeling is just really shocking. It's really hard to watch".

Example 11

"3:00–3:08 pain and sadness in her eyes are heartbreaking. i can't . . ."

Others commented on how her story inspired them in their life (see Example 12), offered metacomments on other users' behaviour (see Example 13), or expressed general views about cancer (see Example 14).

Example 12

"I was so moved by Charlotte, that I spoke to a loved one whom I had not spoken to in 4 years. We think we have all the time in the world, but the truth is, we don't"

Example 13

"the 245 dislikes, horrible"

Example 14

"This video is so raw and heartbreaking. This was Charlottes reality. She summed it up perfectly . . . . its absolutely shit".

Lastly, many viewers expressed regret for not having viewed the vlog while Charlotte was still alive to offer their support to her (see Example 15)

Example 15

"So damn sad I couldn't have offered any kind of encouragement of how BEAUTIFUL and AMAZING you were and still are. Rest in Peace. ❤".

The range of comment types shows how viewers – who are often people who've never met Charlotte before – pick up particular aspects of the emplotment of Charlotte's experience and her positioning to herself, her cancer, or her audience and reinforce it via their comments. This particular mode of participation afforded by vlogging practice is a testament to the extension of the impact of Charlotte's life to levels that she wouldn't have imagined. As her mother noted on a recent tweet, "I know you would not be able to believe a million people have viewed your story. M x" (December 11, 2018).

In the next sections, the observations made here about viewer comments are discussed more broadly in relation to the different types of positions that they reveal for viewers across the vlog.

Types of Participation

Commenters in the vlog were seen to take up positions of feeling supported and inspired by the vlogger but also positions of supporters when this was explicitly requested by the vlogger. They also participated in the story by expressing their appreciation of the vlogger as a beautiful, wise, brave, and strong person, showing ritual alignment commonly encountered in sequentially organized interactions online (see Georgakopoulou, 2016).

These different positions are found to be associated with the small storying type and the time of viewing the video – around the time of its broadcast or after the vlogger's passing. Comments to the videos discussed earlier were posted both near the time the video was first broadcast (58%) as immediate reactions but also at different points in time after the vlogger's passing (42%) as tributes. Notably, certain vlog videos prompted more tributes than immediate reactions, such as the video "When things aren't going to plan". Tributes were a lot less common in the video of Charlotte's expressing her feeling "fed up" where her illness was envisualized.

This difference in the distribution of posts suggests that the earlier videos in the vlog when the deterioration of the vlogger, and ultimately her passing, seem unforeseen are more amenable to serving as sites of mourning. Such videos, which register an image of the vlogger as the beautiful, vivacious teenager seeking to support and motivate others facing difficulties, invite viewers to align to her projected identity positioning. By doing so, they co-construct her legacy as an inspirational figure and heighten the emotional impact of her death through affective reactions of disbelief at her passing.

The video "Fed up", on the other hand, is a post that mainly prompts expressions of support from followers and is not commented on after her passing as much as other videos. It is suggested that this points to viewers' dis-preference for expressions of pity or explicit engagements with aspects of the visible suffering in the last stages of the vlogger's cancer.

An additional interesting aspect of the comments shared in reaction to the videos is the emphasis on viewing, watching, and re-watching Charlotte's story as an inspirational story rather than a concern with sharing it. This resonates with recent findings about increasingly popular collocations of the word 'story' with the verb 'view' (Georgakopoulou, 2019). The vlog – and in particular the comment space – arguably emerges as a site for mourning related to modes of *story viewing*: the available affective positions participants can take up depend on when they access the vlog – before or after the vlogger's passing – and on how they browse and select videos for watching. Displays of mourning tend to be particularly called for in the case of videos in which the likelihood of death is still unforeseeable, affording possibilities for admiring the vlogger's youth, beauty, and courage, and in videos where followers can show an alignment to the vlogger's projected identity positioning as an inspirational figure. This observation points to a shift towards story participation positions intimately related to modes of viewing, which deserve further attention in the analysis of mourning online and digital stories more broadly.

Shifts in Emplotment and Affective Positioning

The discussion of the key moments in Charlotte's vlog reflects key modes of emplotting the illness experience as a resource for identity and affective positioning at different levels.

The analysis showed how turning points in the vlogger's illness experience drive the emplotment of different aspects of that experience. As it was shown, with the passing of time and the development of the illness, this focus shifts from general aspects of the teenage experience which are not 'normal' for a teenager to more personal (and visible) aspects of the experience of being ill.

The emplotment of her experience in the key moments analyzed here was found to gradually change from approaching cancer as a distant challenge to envisaging cancer as a scary intruder and, ultimately, to documenting its alienating and ugly impact. Cancer is initially plotted as (i) a disruption and nuisance to everyday life, (ii) a medical condition that can be (hopefully) treated but which also implies intrusions and interventions to the sufferer's body, and ultimately (iii) an alienating and transformative experience. The shift in this emplotment is further marked by shifts in the use of personal pronouns. From the oscillation between 'I' and 'you' in the clip "When things aren't going to plan", the vlogger moves on to plotting herself as the experiencer of the story living through small changes and frustrations and ultimately being irrevocably transformed by them. Still, the emphasis of the vlogger throughout her broadcasts is firmly placed on living with and despite cancer. Motifs of love ("I am not dying, I am living, I am loving"), hope ("hope to be able to speak to you all again soon"), fight ("I am still fighting"), and life ("I am still here, I am fine") recur across the vlog.

Three main types of storying were identified, which varied depending on the temporal focus on (i) the past and its impact on the present, (ii) the very recent past, or (iii) the here and now of the vlogger. These different types of storying were found to be associated with different types of affective positioning that ranged from distant to intimate as the illness deteriorated. In addition, they revealed how the vlogger negotiated the dilemmas of portraying her experience as more broadly representative of human experience, being in control of emotions, and aligning to the injunction to stay positive in the face of adversity.

In sum, this vlog illustrates the strategies mobilized to relate a transgressive experience, in which, as Norrick (2005, p. 328) suggests, involves rejection risks: listeners may refuse to listen to it, or if they do, they may negatively judge the teller for the behaviour reported, resulting in the loss of face for the teller. Tellers take on those risks with a view to gain the listeners' support or admiration for the experience through modulations of intimacy: for example, self-disclosures can inspire similar self-disclosures or second stories and consolidate the teller as an inspiring and resilient figure.

In the vlogger's self-disclosures, emotional performances are carefully managed along the affordances of asynchronicity and video editing. As Georgalou (2019) has shown in her study of polymedia practices of emotional expression, these uses result in mixes of elements of instantaneity (emotional self now) and reflexivity (emotional self then), which make it difficult to draw a clear distinction between real-time and reflective emotional displays (see also Galasiński, 2004, p. 127). This insight points to the use of time as an emplotment resource for encoding emotion rather than as an anchor for the story and sheds light into the complex construction of 'authenticity' in self-broadcasting videos.

Summary

The examination of this single vlog suggests how emerging visual modes of sharing the illness experience depart from reflective, 'big' illness narratives and their collectivizing functions (see Hyden, 1997). Instead, they signal a shift to the hyper-personalization of the illness experience and open it up for public comment and varied forms of story participation. Unlike typical narratives of illness which thematize the hero's restitution, quest, or chaos, this visual mode of storying covers different phases in the experience of illness and offers an intimate peek into the flow of life disrupted by illness, mobilizing illness as a resource for affectively positioning the vlogger at different levels and across time as an inspirational figure and an influencer rather than as a 'wounded' storyteller (Frank, 1995).

Visual modes of illness narratives on YouTube vlogs suggest the emergence of a 'new' mode for the articulation and authentication of the experience of illness and dying, which marks a shift to young adults taking control of their post-mortem identity by engaging more or less consciously in ante-mortem and peri-mortem activities. Small visual stories transform the teenage experience of cancer as everyday moments for storying the self in the here and now while also integrating looking-forward and looking-back modes for sharing emotions. For a sufferer of a serious illness, sharing life is at the same time a form of sharing for life, archived as a lasting visual mark of life. These vlogs are, thus, not just a diary or a way for teenagers to connect to others; they are a way of making sense of the illness experience and of creating a sense of continued presence that extends beyond the vlogger's lifetime.

Viewers can follow the story as it unfolds or can look back on her story in reverse order – from its endpoint to its start – and build up their own version of it, selecting, for example, to view the most popular clips or browsing the video timeline. As participants, they are invited to validate the sufferer's experience, show appreciation for the vlogger, support her at difficult points in her illness trajectory, but also feel supported by her. Ultimately, they are invited to co-create the vlogger's legacy as an inspirational person gone too soon via tribute sharing in the comments space. In brief, the vlog emerges as a poly-storying site: a support-exchange hub, a source of inspiration, and a special type of impromptu online memorial, where new tributes co-exist with old messages of support and wishes for the individual's recovery.

The emphasis on the stories' visuality in the vlog raises new questions about the conditions that contribute to their popularity. The fact, for example, that the majority of these vloggers are young and female echoes long-held cultural obsessions with the dead female,[16] pointing to illness or health vlogs as sites in which cultural gender constructions are played out. There is, thus, plenty of scope for exploring further the social meanings of visual stories of illness.

Conclusion

The examination of this emerging practice of self-documentation on YouTube illustrates a particular form of death-writing of the moment before and around the time of death that can be described as *motivational*. The explicit aim of the users engaged in sharing such intimate and 'non-pretty' moments from their personal life is to inspire others and help them to cope with similar situations, raise awareness and public visibility of wider issues, and promote fundraising actions. Illness and dying are mobilized, here, as authenticating resources that assign credibility to the affective sharing.

Vlogging on illness illustrates a mode of visual storying, which attests to the wider turn to the visual on social media (Meese et al., 2015). In addition, it foregrounds the growing importance of story curation in online environments. The sharing of disruptive moments and transgressive stories makes visible 'ugly' aspects of life, even if this visibility is largely shaped by the norms of sharing on video platforms, which are characterized by high levels of careful editing. Each video illustrates different types of designed and embodied affective positioning, which changes over time, depending on the aspect of the illness experience focused on and the degree of proximity or distance the teller can (afford to) take from it.

Videos as small stories of illness invite the audience's participation via mainly viewing (as it is views which are the main metric of the vlog's popularity) and less so via commenting. As Georgakopoulou et al. (in press) note, these modes of participation call for the examination of technical and metrics in the potential they create for pre-positioning tellers and audiences.

This chapter has focused on a case of personalized, anticipatory mourning and memorialization organized around the shared, curated content of an individual sufferer, who has sought to take some control over her posthumous legacy. The next chapters turn to activities of collectivized mourning and memorialization, which afford positions of co-tellership in the storying of another person's life.

Notes

1. See YouTube Academy: https://creatoracademy.youtube.com/page/lesson/jump start?cid=bootcamp-foundations&hl=en-GB#strategies-zippy-link-2.
2. The full video is available here: www.youtube.com/watch?v=BnXap21lCzI.
3. The full video is available here: www.youtube.com/watch?v=L0Tz_xfgiv4.
4. The vlog is listed in the top ten cancer vlogs in the search results from Feedspot and Google, conducted in October 2018.
5. More information about the charity and details about donating can be found on: www.charlottesbag.com.
6. More information about this tribute is available here: http://history.buses. co.uk/history/fleethist/483ce.htm. (See also video *Charlotte's Bus!* March 17, 2019).
7. See also Miles Eades' video, Documentary is Out Tomorrow & a Big Thank you!, October 25, 2017.
8. Voice Typing is a feature that transcribes what you say directly into a Google Doc. Its use for video transcription relies on the speaker listening to the recording via earphones and speaking out loud as you listen, stopping or returning to the text at a later point to correct any misspellings.
9. For a more detailed discussion of embodied transcription as a creative method, see: Brooks, C. 2010. Embodied transcription: A creative method for using voice-recognition software. *The Qualitative Report* 15 (5): 1127–1242.
10. BBC News. 2015. Interview with Charlotte Eades, Saturday June 13. Available from: www.youtube.com/watch?v=L0Tz_xfgiv4. Accessed: 11 Sept. 2019.
11. In the transcripts of the videos the use of transcription symbols has been kept to a minimum and includes the use of '(.)' to indicate short pauses in the speech flow.
12. In cases when topics overlap, coding was based on what seemed to be the primary focus of the vlog post, taking into account the video's descriptions and/or tags.
13. Alex Eades (Charlotte's mother) was named Lorraine's Inspirational Woman of the Year in 2017 and awarded a Certificate of Honour in recognition of exceptional positive impact on society and as an inspiration to others from the British Citizen Awards on July 4, 2019.
14. In Extract 1, the line numbering, starts at line 20, reflecting where it occurs in the longer transcript.
15. In the multimodal transcript, line numbering starts from line 1, given the differential level of detail in this transcription; for numbering representing the place of this snippet in the longer transcript, see Extract 1.
16. The fascination with the death of young women is illustrated in the following quote by poet Edgar Allan Poe: "the death, then, of a beautiful woman is, unquestionably, the most poetical topic in the world" (Poe, E.A. 2006. The poetic principle. In Kennedy, J.G. (Ed.), *The Portable Poe*. New York: Penguin Group, 2006, 548). This fascination is felt to this day in popular literature and crime fiction.

References

Atkinson, P. (2017) Illness narratives revisited: The failure of narrative reduction-ism. *Sociological Research Online* 14 (5): 1–10.

BBC (2019) *Beauty vlogger Dawn Lee shares cancer treatment journey.* Aug. 6. Available at: www.bbc.co.uk/news/av/health-49212243/beauty-vlogger-dawn-lee-shares-cancer-treatment-journey. Accessed: 6 Aug. 2019.

Biel, J.I. and D. Gatica-Perez (2010) Vlogcast yourself: Nonverbal behavior and attention in social media. *International Conference on Multimodal Interfaces and the Workshop on Machine Learning for Multimodal Interaction,* ACM, Beijing, China, Nov. 8–12, n.p.

Borghol, Y., S. Ardon, N. Carlsson, D. Eager, and A. Mahanti (2012) The untold story of the clones: Content-agnostic factors that impact YouTube video popu-larity. *Proceedings of the 18th ACM SIGKDD International Conference on Knowledge Discovery and Data Mining,* ACM, Beijing, China, Aug. 12–16, pp. 1186–1194.

Burgess, J. and J. Green (2018) *YouTube: Online Video and Participatory Culture.* 2nd ed. Oxford, UK: Polity Press.

Bury, M. (2001) Illness narratives: Fact or fiction? *Sociology of Health & Illness* 23 (3): 263–285.

Chen, A.T. (2012) Exploring online support spaces: Using cluster analysis to examine breast cancer, diabetes and fibromyalgia support groups. *Patient Edu-cation Counselling* 87 (2): 250–257.

Cheshire, J. and S. Ziebland (2005) Narrative as a resource in accounts of the experience of illness. In Thornborrow, J. and J. Coates (Eds.), *The Sociolin-guistics of Narrative.* Amsterdam and Philadelphia: John Benjamins Publishing Company, pp. 17–41.

De Fina, A. (2016) Storytelling and audience reactions in social media. *Language in Society* 45 (4): 473–498.

Ehlich, K. (1993) HIAT – A transcription system for discourse data. In Edwards, J.A. and M.D. Lampert (Eds.). *Talking data: Transcription and coding in dis-course research.* Hillsdale, NJ: Lawrence Erlbaum, pp. 123–148.

Frank, A.W. (1995) *The Wounded Storyteller: Body, Illness, and Ethics.* Chicago: Chicago University Press.

Galasiński, D. (2004) *Men and the Language of Emotions.* London: Palgrave Macmillan.

García-Rapp, F. (2016) The digital media phenomenon of YouTube beauty gurus: The case of Bubzbeauty. *International Journal of Web Based Communities* 12 (4): 360–375.

Georgakopoulou, A. (2007) *Small Stories, Interaction and Identities.* Amsterdam: John Benjamins.

Georgakopoulou, A. (2015) Small stories research: Methods-analysis-outreach. In De Fina, A. and A. Georgakopoulou (Eds.), *Handbook of Narrative Analy-sis.* Hoboken, NJ: John Wiley & Sons, pp. 256–271.

Georgakopoulou, A. (2016) From narrating the self to posting self(ies): A small stories approach to selfies. *Open Linguistics* 2 (1): 300–317.

Georgakopoulou, A. (2017) Sharing the moment as small stories: The interplay between practices & affordances in the social media-curation of lives. *Narra-tive Inquiry* 27 (2): 311–333.

Georgakopoulou, A. (2019) Designing stories on social media: A corpus-assisted critical perspective on the mismatches of story-curation. *Linguistics and Education.* https://doi.org/10.1016/j.linged.2019.05.003.

Georgakopoulou, A., S. Iversen, and C. Stage (in press) *Quantified Stories: A Narrative Analysis of Metrics and Algorithms on Social Media.* London: Palgrave.

Georgalou, M. (2019) Taking stances on the Greek crisis: Evidence from Facebook interaction. *Internet Pragmatics* 2 (1): 136–161.

Goffman, E. (1959) *The Presentation of Self in Everyday Life.* Garden City, NY: Doubleday.

Griffith, M. and Z. Papacharissi (2010) Looking for you: An analysis of video blogs. *First Monday* 15: 1–4. Available at: http://journals.uic.edu/ojs/index.php/fm/article/view/2769/2430. Accessed: 31 Jan. 2019.

Gumperz, J. and N. Berenz (1993) Transcribing conversational exchanges. In Edwards, J.A. and M.D. Lampert (Eds.), *Talking Data: Transcription and Coding in Discourse Research.* Hillsdale, NJ: Lawrence Erlbaum and Associates, pp. 91–122.

Halperin, E.C. (2017) Military metaphors and the consequences of the language of cancer. *Practical Radiation Oncology* 7: 1–3.

Halpern, J. (2001) *From Detached Concern to Empathy: Humanizing Medical Practice.* Oxford: Oxford University Press.

Hammersley, M. (2010) Reproducing or constructing? Some questions about transcription in social research. *Qualitative Research* 10 (5): 553–569.

Harvey, K. and N. Kotyeko (2013) *Exploring Health Communication.* London and New York: Routledge.

Hawkins, A.H. (1993) *Reconstructing Illness. Studies in Pathography.* West Lafayette, IN: Purdue University Press.

Hoejholt, M. (2015) Narrating (M)others' Lives: A narrative interactional analysis of storytelling practices related to YouTube vloggers. PhD Project. http://www.ego-media.org/projects/broadcasting-onesself-a-narrative-analysis-of-vlogs-by-youtube-mommies/. Accessed: April 11, 2020.

Hou, M. (2018) Social media celebrity and the institutionalization of YouTube. *Convergence: The International Journal of Research into New Media Technologies*: 1–20.

Hyden, L.C. (1997) Illness and narrative. *Sociology of Health & Illness* 19 (1): 48–69.

Hymes, D. (2003) *Now I Know Only So Far: Essays in Ethnopoetics.* Lincoln: University of Nebraska Press.

Iannarino, N.T. (2018) "My insides feel like Keith Richard's face": A narrative analysis of humor and biographical disruption in young adults' cancer blogs. *Health Communication* 33 (10): 1–10.

Jefferson, G. (2004) Glossary of transcript symbols with an introduction. In Lerner, G.H. (Ed.), *Conversation Analysis: Studies from the First Generation.* Amsterdam: John Benjamins, pp. 13–31.

Kleinman, A. (1989) *The Illness Narratives: Suffering, Healing, and the Human Condition.* New York: Basic Books.

Kotyeko, N. and D. Hunt (2018) Special issue: Discourse analysis perspectives on online health communication. *Discourse, Context, and Media* 25: 1–4.

Labov, W. (1972) Languages in the Inner City. Studies in the Black English Vernacular. Philadelphia: University of Pennsylvania Press.

Langellier, K. and E. Peterson (2006) *Storytelling in Daily Life: Performing Narrative*. Philadelphia, PA: Temple University Press.

Liu, S.L., J. Huh, T. Neogi, K. Inkpen, and W. Pratt (2013) Health vlogger-viewer interaction in chronic illness management. *Proceedings of the SIGCHI Conference on Human Factors in Computing Systems*, Paris, France, Apr. 27–May 2, pp. 49–58.

Meese, J., M. Gibbs, M. Carter, M. Arnold, B. Nansen, and T. Kohn (2015) Selfies at funerals: Mourning and presenting on social media platforms. *International Journal of Communication* 9: 1818–1831.

Molyneaux, H., S. O'Donnell, and K.J. Gibson (2008) Singer exploring the gender divide on YouTube: An analysis of the creation and reception of vlogs. *American Communication Journal* 10 (2): 1–14.

Norrick, N. (2005) The dark side of tellability. *Narrative Inquiry* 15 (2): 323–343.

Ochs, E. (1979) Transcription as theory. In Ochs, E. and B.B. Schieffelin (Eds.), *Developmental Pragmatics*. New York: Academic Press, pp. 43–72.

Page, R. (2011) Blogging on the body: Gender and narrative. In Page, R. and T. Bronwen (Eds.), *New Narratives: Stories and Storytelling in the Digital Age*. Lincoln and London: University of Nebraska Press.

Pecchioni, L.L. (2012) Interruptions to cultural life scripts: Cancer diagnoses, contextual age, and life narratives. *Research on Aging* 34 (6): 758–780.

Printsome (Meyer-Delius, H.) (2018) *The 20 types of videos that get the most views on YouTube*. Available at: https://blog.printsome.com/top-20-types-of-videos-with-most-views-on-youtube/. Accessed: 31 Jan. 2019.

Schwalm, H. (2014) *Autobiography*. In Hühn, P. et al. (Eds.), *The Living Handbook of Narratology*. Hamburg: Hamburg University. Available at: http://www.lhn.uni-hamburg.de/.

Senft, T.M. (2008) *Camgirls: Celebrity and Community in the Age of Social Networks*. New York, NY: Peter Lang.

Shapiro, J. (2011) Illness narratives: Reliability, authenticity and the empathic witness. *Medical Humanities* 37 (2): 68–72.

Sharf, B.F., L.M. Harter, J. Yamasaki, and P. Haidet (2011) Narrative turns epic: Continuing developments in health narrative scholarship. In Thompson, T.L., R. Parrott, and J.F. Nussbaum (Eds.), *The Routledge Handbook of Health Communication*. London and New York: Routledge.

Smith, B. and A.C. Sparkes (2004) Becoming disabled through sport: Narrative types, metaphors and the reconstruction of selves. In Twohig, P.L. and V. Kalitzkus (Eds.), *Interdisciplinary perspectives on health, illness and disease*. Amsterdam and New York: Rodopi.

Stage, C. (2017) *Networked Cancer: Affect, Narrative, and Measurement*. London: Palgrave.

Turner, G. (2004) *Understanding Celebrity*. London: SAGE.

Media Sources

BBC (2016) Tributes to teen cancer vlogger Charlotte Eades. *BBC, Newsbeat*, Feb. 26. Available at: www.bbc.co.uk/newsbeat/article/35672481/tributes-to-teen-cancer-vlogger-charlotte-eades. Accessed: 26 Feb.

CLIC Sargent and Charlotte Eades (2015) *I'm Still Here*. Available at: www.youtube.com/watch?v=BnXap21lCzI. Accessed: 11 April 2020.

Marie Claire (Montell, A.) (2018) *What it's like to die online: Chronically ill women are turning to YouTube to share their lives-and deaths*. Mar. 13. Available at: www.marieclaire.com/culture/a19183515/chronically-ill-youtube-stars/. Accessed: 10 Aug. 2019.

Testa, M. (2016) *Vlogumentary*. Available at: https://www.youtube.com/watch?v=1TCN_G-KKHA. Accessed: 11 April 2020.

The Guardian (Heritage, S.) (2017) How to be a vlogger: G guide for wannabe YouTubers. Available at: www.theguardian.com/technology/shortcuts/2017/may/22/how-to-be-a-vlogger-a-guide-for-wannabe-youtubers. Accessed: 12 Aug. 2019.

The Guardian (Petersen, H.E.) (2016) Cancer vlogger Charlotte Eades dies aged 19. *The Guardian, Society*, Feb. 26. Available at: www.theguardian.com/society/2016/feb/26/cancer-vlogger-charlotte-eades-dies-aged-19. Accessed: 31 Jan. 2019.

The Sun (Hanson, K.) (2018) Cancer on camera: What it's like to die online: These chronically ill vloggers are turning to YouTube to share their lives-and their deaths. *The Sun* [Online], Apr. 13. Available at: www.thesun.co.uk/fabulous/6043819/cancer-vloggers-youtube-death-illness/. Accessed: 31 Jan. and 10 Aug. 2019.

The Telegraph (Molloy, M.) (2016) Charlotte Eades: Inspirational vlogger dies from brain cancer aged 19. *The Telegraph, UK News*, Feb. 16. Available at: www.telegraph.co.uk/news/uknews/12174699/Charlotte-Eades-Parents-of-YouTube-vlogger-post-final-message-after-cancer-battle.html. Accessed: 31 Jan. 2019.

VICE (Nolan, J.) (2018) *The YouTuber who created a worldwide community through his cancer*. Oct. 29. Available at: www.vice.com/en_uk/article/gye7ex/the-youtuber-who-created-a-worldwide-community-through-his-cancer. Accessed: 10 Aug. 2019.

YouTube Lesson (2019) *Vlog like a pro*. Lesson 3. YouTube Creators [Website]. Available at: https://creatoracademy.youtube.com/page/lesson/vlogging?hl=en-GB. Accessed: 31 Jan. 2019.

5 Small Stories of Everyday Mourning on Facebook

Introduction

This chapter turns from ante-mortem and peri-mortem activities inadvertently shaping post-mortem activities, discussed in the previous chapter, to cases which illustrate more clearly post-mortem types of death-writing of the moment online from the position of co-telling the story of a loved one's life. Focusing, more specifically, on a case of a Facebook memorial group, I will illustrate how small stories of mourning for the loss of a friend are used for negotiating affective positions of distance or proximity to the death event, the dead, (known and unknown) networked audiences, and the grieving self. This chapter moves on from the consideration of the mobilization of illness, dying, and mourning to the mobilization of death, grieving, and memorialization as resources for different types of identity and affective positioning of members of a bereaved community, which showcase the collectivization of the experience of mourning online.

Social network sites like Facebook facilitate forms of social organization around shared interests, ambient affiliation, in some cases involving the extension of offline groups (Seargeant and Tagg, 2014, p. 13). Research into social network interaction focuses on how these different types of social organization and interactional group norms come about, looking at discourse and communication as situated practices within networked relationships. When Facebook is used for mourning purposes, social network interaction is organized around a specific death event, often as an extension of existing groups of bereaved. To clarify the kinds of connections that sharers develop between them as well as with the dead, it is important to consider not only what they share but also how they share it; in other words, it is important to look for patterns in their situated semiotic and discursive activity.

As a social network, Facebook is organized around sharing as a form of participation, including affordances for broadcasting significant moments of life through updates – and more recently 'Stories' – and for signalling interaction with others via action buttons, such as 'Share', 'Like', and 'Comment'. Facebook participants write themselves into being by entextualizing significant moments with and for network audiences

(Androutsopoulos, 2014), keying their performance both to the context in which a story is told and to the recounted events (Bauman, 1986). Despite recent calls for limiting the use of Facebook or even refraining from it altogether, the platform remains popular – even if among a different age group than before[1] – and continues to be a key point of reference in media and public discussions about social media.

Since 2009, Facebook has offered the option to 'memorialize' the profile page of a deceased user, removing sensitive information and repurposing it as a site for tributes. In addition, users can create closed groups or pages specially dedicated to remembering the dead. These pages are often labelled "R.I.P.", "In Memory of [name of deceased]", or "Remembering [name of deceased]". All these different options for setting up and maintaining tributes on and via the platform offer users multimodal forms of *entextualizing moments of life and death* and *sharing them as small stories of mourning*. These stories are not just vehicles for the representation of denotational content but are also a means for interactionally positioning narrator and audience (Wortham, 2000, p. 166).

The chapter starts with the presentation of the data and details how the analytical framework of sharing small stories of mourning has been adapted for this case study (see Chapter 3). It then moves on to the presentation of the analysis of sharing practices, which unfolds in two parts: the first part discusses the Facebook memorial wall as a whole and the second zooms in on the shared moments of an individual user and her affective trajectory. The discussion provides an empirical investigation of key aspects of the vernacularization and collectivization of grief as participation.

The Case Study

The sampling procedure for this case study included browsing and collecting Facebook memorial sites in English using the "Search" function of Facebook. The criteria applied to the selection of the site in question related to the number of group members, their age, and regularity of posting on the site. The target of the selection process was a group brought together by grief for the loss of a loved one that was set as public. In addition, the selection process targeted a medium-sized group counting at least 500 members, who were also connected offline. The focus on young adults was motivated by their expertise in the use of social media for sharing significant moments of their everyday lives through their increased posting of updates and interaction on the wall (cf. Page, 2010), which would prefigure their increased willingness and readiness to extend the use of those media to sharing significant moments relating to death and mourning.

The group selected for study was created in May 2012 as a tribute to the sudden and tragic loss of a young adult in a U.S. city. The administrators of the group are six of the closest friends of the deceased. The medium-sized group brings together more than 1,000 members including schoolmates and acquaintances of the deceased from the local community (e.g. school, religious community). At the time of writing, the group has accumulated 526 logs of 29,136 words, the first posted one day after the event of death in May 2012 and the most recent on February 16, 2018. Given the sensitivity of the data, pseudonyms will be used throughout for sharers and for the deceased, who will be referred to as *David*. In addition, any references to places that could situate the group or an individual are omitted from any extracts cited (for a fuller discussion of ethics design, see Chapter 3).

To facilitate the handling and analysis of the data, all wall updates were extracted into an Excel spreadsheet. This allowed their coding for themes and content threads and numbers of Likes and Comments attached to each update. Posts making up the most populated content thread were also coded for temporality type (i.e. past, present, future) as a way of bringing to the fore different story types. The linguistic criteria used for the coding of temporality have been devised through an inductive coding process and are summarized in Table 5.1.

The examination of narrative identities connected to practices of mourning on Facebook was based on the analysis of the posts of an individual group member (eight posts shared over a period of six months, from May to October 2012). These will henceforth be referred to as *shared moments* or just *moments*. The user in question was selected on

Table 5.1 Coding scheme for types of temporality in updates

Narrative dimension: Temporality	Linguistic criteria
Past	Use of past tense
	Use of story openings, such as 'I remember', 'I'll never forget'
Recent past	Use of past tense
	Use of temporal adverbials, 'yesterday', 'last night', 'earlier', 'today' (referring to something that has happened), 'just' (followed by past participle)
Present or here and now	Use of present tense, present continuous, present participles
	Use of temporal adverbials 'right now', 'just' (followed by present participle), 'today' (with reference to the present moment)
(Near) future	Use of future tense
	Use of present or present continuous with future reference
	Use of temporal adverbials 'tomorrow', 'this weekend', 'this summer', 'today' (with future reference)

account of her regular contributions to the group in the first couple of days immediately after the creation of the Facebook memorial group. A month after the event of death, the regularity of her posting activity decreased, with bigger intervals between her posts, ranging from one to three months, before altogether ceasing.

The shared moments are examined as *wall events*, relating to multi-authored sequences of contributions displayed on the Facebook wall that consists of a minimum of one contribution (the initiative post, usually a so-called status update) followed by Likes and/or responsive contributions (Comments; Androutsopoulos, 2014). Wall events are visually set off from each other and displayed in reverse chronological order, with posts that were first broadcast appearing at the bottom of the wall and more recent posts on top.

Posts and wall events are analyzed in terms of the projected types of identity positioning as a mourner in a networked community of mourners and modes of affective positioning, which point to the construal of social relations of relative proximity to or distance from the dead (*Level 1*), the networked audience (*Level 2*), and the affective self (*Level 3*; see Chapter 3).

The next section presents the first part of the empirical analysis of sharing practices on the Facebook memorial wall. I will examine in turn practices of selection of shareables, the discourse and narrative styling of posts, and negotiation of identity and affective positions.

The Facebook Memorial Group

Selecting Memorial Content

The Facebook group site under study lacks an explicit 'About' section, but its intended purpose is presented in the first two posts shared by two of the administrators.[2] These posts directly address the group's members with specific requests. The first post invited group members to support the planning of a memorial event on the day of graduation, and the second asked them to share a memorial song written for him. Through these requests, the general motivation for the creation of the group is presented as garnering support and participation for planned memorial activities. In addition, the second post's call for pushing "his name out and let ppl kno he's cared about deeply. Even if he's not here in person" foregrounds the importance of memorial activities for members of this group as a way of contributing to their deceased friend's post-mortem popularity and maintaining a sense of his continued presence.

Out of the 1,265 group members listed on the site, 198 can be considered active participants, having logged at least one post, and 24 members as most active, having shared more than five posts from the day of the site's creation. Comments in the group are posted mainly by people who had known David more or less well and can claim some level of entitlement to the public display of mourning. Distant acquaintances or people who didn't know him tend to make this explicit in their memorial post on the site, where they explain their motivation for posting a tribute. As shown in the examples that follow, common types of such motivations include a sense of the impact the dead has had on others (Example 1) or a need to reaffirm his popularity (Example 2).

Example 1

Davey, I didn't know you very well but you've obviously impacted so many peoples lives. I wish I had the opportunity to meet you . . . Fly high man.

(May 26, 2012)

Example 2

Ayye buddy . . . I didn't really know you, but I heard a lot about you. It sucks that your gone, Its tough down here knowing that a loved one is gone. But while we are all upset down here because of the tragedy, your having a blast with God. It must be really cool to be hanging out with him everyday. I wish you could tell me what things are like up there but that would ruin the whole surprise. Take it easy Bro and see you again someday.

(Oct. 26, 2012)

The Facebook R.I.P. group site is predominantly text centred. Pictures make up just 3.2% of the entire wall; these don't include selfies but a variety of snapshots, contextualized by a short caption in the update box. Snapshots were found to include, more specifically, images of *memorial places*, for instance a tribute on a rock, a tribute on the deceased's parking slot, *memorial items*, such as orange and blue ribbons, orange and blue colours in the sky, and *on-the-spot memorial pictures*, for example a picture of the music score played at the funeral or images taken just before the start of a sports event. Shared images are, thus, used as visual resources for performing acts of remembrance in the here and now anchored in a specific location (the school, a memorial, his parking spot) or connected to items that evoke memories of the deceased. The overall scarcity of images suggests that text-based tributes are the preferred mode for sharing among members of this group.

Tributes and reactions to the news of David's death on the site are organized around specific types of content associated with particular temporal periods or points. These are summarized as follows (also see Figure 5.1):

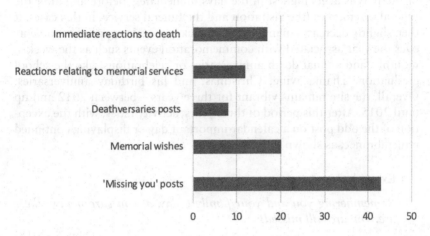

Figure 5.1 Content types in the memorial group

i. immediate reactions to the news of death shared over two days (May 10- May 11 2012; 89 posts)
ii. reactions relating to visitation and funeral services shared during the rest of May (May 12– May 28 2012; 61 posts);
iii. memorial posts on death anniversaries (also known as *deathversaries*) marking the death event from different temporal anchors between 2012 and 2015, that range from days (e.g. 2 days, 20 days) to months (e.g. 2 months, 3 months, 5 months) and years (e.g. 1 year marked in terms of 526,600 minutes, 2 years, and 3 years). As time goes by, the number of these posts declines: for instance, in 2018, only one deathversary post was shared by just one user on the day marking a year after David's death (42 posts);
iv. memorial wishes on calendar important dates, such as the day of the school graduation, birthday anniversaries, Christmas, Thanksgiving, Easter, the 4th of July, and other occasions of culturally marked celebrations between 2012 and 2015 (102 posts);
v. one-off posts that do not fall neatly into any of the above thematic categories. These were coded as a separate category termed *'missing you'* posts, given that their topic focuses on expressions of missing or remembering the dead (220 posts).

The different content types largely shape the texture of mourning in this group. They organize the activity of sharing tributes around a set of key temporal points, which recur across the year, as well as around specific topics, which serve as prompts for reiterative acts of remembrance. Sharing activity is at its highest in the days immediately before and after the funeral ceremonies (the visitation and the funeral service, in this case). It then slightly decreases in intensity and picks up again at specific moments over the year associated with commemoration events such as the weekly, monthly, and annual death anniversaries or celebrations, like the school graduation, Thanksgiving, Christmas, and his birthday anniversaries. Overall, the site remains vibrant for three years – between 2012 and up until 2015. After this period of three years, activity fades, with the exception of the odd post on a calendar-important day or displaying continued remembrance, as shown in Example 3.

Example 3

Remembering you and your family today, as I'm sure many others are. You are still missed!

(May 8, 2018)

This post exemplifies the type of posts described above as '*Missing you*' posts, which emerge as the preferred type of tributes shared in this group. These posts cover a range of affective displays of group members' personal feelings of grief or life moments that invoke or in some way involve their deceased friend in their daily activities. These are going to be considered in more detail later on in this chapter in relation to the types of small story they are found to be associated with. Before that, the next section will examine the practices of styling and interactivity that have been found to characterize sharing on the site.

Styling and Negotiating Posts on the Memorial Wall

The most typical type of posts on the site, the '*missing you*' posts, were found to be shared as contributions that stand apart from posts before or after them: they are addressed directly to the dead rather than to other members of the group. In addition, such tributes do not serve as initiative posts, followed by responsive contributions in the form of comments[3] – this is the case in 93.5% of this type of posts. This apparent lack of interactivity among group members is arguably compensated for by the way individual contributions mirror each other in terms of their discourse style (see also Georgakopoulou, 2016). This mirroring is illustrated in a series of three consecutive posts by different sharers that have been extracted from the first thread of immediate reactions to the news of death (May 10–11) and represented here in the reverse chronological order in which they appear on the wall (see Example 4–6).

Example 4

rip davey! ♥ *love you so much, and miss you like crazyy! i have no doubt in my mind you are doing it big up there! (:*

Example 5

rest in peace davey! i love you & miss you very much ♥

Example 6

rest in peace sweet davey! i love and miss you very much! fly high and watch over us all!

Each post is a personalized tribute, opening with the epitaph "*Rest in Peace*" or "*RIP*" in its short form, expressed in the first-person personal pronoun and directly addressed to the deceased. These so-called R.I.P. posts have by now emerged as conventional forms of online tributes shared across different platforms (Giaxoglou, 2020). Their linguistic style reproduces the informality and register of new media language, as evident in the use of the elongated vowel in the word 'crazyy' (Example 4) or the use of exclamation marks and diminutives as terms of address, e.g. 'davey'. These linguistic choices serve as involvement devices, registering a conventional affective stance to the death event.

Similar examples of mirroring posts are attested in a sequence of fifty-five posts shared on the first birthday anniversary of David. These feature the formulaic expression "*Happy birthday*" with few, if any at all, additions as shown in Examples 7–9:

Example 7

Happy Birthday Davey!

Example 8

Happy birthday! Hope you're having a great day! Came by to see you! Love you see you soon.

Example 9

Happy birthday Davey!! I honestly didn't know you but all I ever hear are good things about you.

Mirroring posts remediate generic forms of remembrance and contribute to the creation of a sense of coherence among this diverse group of networked mourners, made up of friends, acquaintances, and members of the community. Such patterned activity creates sets of expectations for the reception and production of new posts, with users likely to feel compelled to mirror previous posts linguistically and thematically. It also gives rise to a ritualistic form of interaction on the site, which potentially makes it possible for people who were less connected to the dead or the group to post tributes in ways that can be deemed appropriate by other group members.

Not all sharers choose to align to this ritualistic form of interaction and prefer instead to share contributions which are marked off stylistically and thematically from sequentially contiguous posts and which are outside any set temporal point for memorialization. In these posts, which were earlier referred to as '*missing you*' posts and further illustrated in Examples 10 and 11, sharers record sudden and fleeting moments of thinking about their friend. Given their suddenness, they will also be referred to as *memorial outbursts*.

Example 10

the suns setting over the lake right now and it's turning the sky orange and blue. couldn't help but stop and think for a minute about how pretty it must be up where you are

Example 11

MORNING ANGEL! HAVE A GREAT DAY!

These posts are akin to updates on Facebook profile pages breaking news of ordinary, everyday events in slices of mundane life (Georgakopoulou, 2013, p. 20). Sharing memorial outbursts on the site draws attention to an individual's everyday experience of grieving over a friend. It also serves to authenticate their proximity to the dead and hence their claim to mourning.

Selections of the content type and discourse style of posts are associated with different modes of participation in the memorial group. The choice of using conventional tributes, which thematically and discursively mirror sequentially contiguous posts, indexes *ritualistic forms of participation*, which re-affirm emerging norms of collective mourning on the site. Memorial outbursts, on the other hand, stage performances of intimate mourning, indexing *knowing participation* that selects the dead as the main audience or members of the audience who occupy similar positions in the circle of friends. Such mores of participation have been found to be typical in digital interaction around selfies (Georgakopoulou, 2016).

Participation in the memorial is also signalled through the use of interaction with other group members afforded by the platform's social plugins, such as the Like button and the Comments box. These plugins allow users to share content and to co-construct meaning on the site in the absence of face-to-face communication cues. At the time of the creation of the Facebook group, the '*Like*' button was one of the key interactive social plug-ins on Facebook 2.0, visualized via the 'thumbs-up' icon. It was added to Facebook in February 2009 and within less than four years became one of the most pervasive socio-technical objects on the web and a metaphor as well as a method for information sharing spreading to other social media apps (Peyton, 2014, p. 113). Facebook describes the '*Like*' button as a function that lets people share pages and content from their site on friends' Facebook profiles with one click, increasing the visibility of content to friends (Facebook, 2019).

The study of wall events on the memorial site shows users' preference for clicking on '*Like*' rather than '*Share*' or the addition of a comment. This noted avoidance of commenting on others' posts can be seen as a form of *digital silence* comparable to the respectful silence of language surrounding offline bereavement rituals. While on personal Facebook profile pages, the number of *Likes* a post accumulates is generally used as an analogue for the user's social status in the online community, or as action and stance mobilized in capitalist contexts (Peyton, 2014, pp. 124–125), on this memorial group site, it is mainly used as an acknowledge-ment of sharing akin to a nod. It can index a sharer's engagement with other sharers, their support to fellow mourners, and their contribution to the visibility of the group (Marwick and Ellison, 2012, p. 14). Face-book 3.0 now includes a palette of animated emoji reactions to posts, affording the option of displaying digital displays of feeling categories labelled as *love* (beating heart), *haha* (laughing face), *yay* (smiling face – discontinued), *wow* (surprised face), *angry* (red, angry, pouting face) and *sad* (crying face, with a tear; Emojipedia, n.d.). The broken heart and the crying emoji have now become part of the register of mourning online (Seargeant and Giaxoglou, 2018) but were not available at the time of the study of this group.

To sum up so far, selections of moments of mourning on this Face-book group are organized around important memorial or calendar dates, shared as mirroring posts and around posts that stand apart from sequentially contiguous posts. Both types of contributions can be seen as *stopping-by* posts, which allow sharers to update their connection with the dead, however close or distant, in a way that is very similar to putting new flowers on a grave or lighting a candle on a memorial site (Roberts, 2004, p. 63). This type of sharing can be seen as enfranchising the mourn-ing of close friends, acquaintances, and members of the wider commu-nity who may feel affected by the sudden death but not necessarily in a position to claim a central place in official ceremonies where the family has centre stage. The temporal and thematic points of reference, which were found to guide sharing activity on the site, point to the emergence of certain norms and expectations about what and when to post. There is also a shared sense of a duty to keep the group site regularly updated as continued evidence of how much the deceased is cared for and loved (see first post in the group), even if this seems to wane after three years of memorial activity. Affiliative group participation in the group, thus, partly emerges through sharers' adherence to these locally developing norms. Participation in the group also shapes and is shaped by highly individualized performances of grief, affirming individuals' personal grief in the everyday at the same time as highly conventionalized, ritualistic forms, which attest to the collectivization of grief. The next section considers in more detail the modes of storying associated with the latter type of sharing, memorial outbursts.

Storying as Breaking News Stories of Remembrance

Memorial outbursts (or 'missing you') posts were found to be the most popular type of post on the site. These posts are shared as acts of individual participation not connected to a commemorative topic keyed to a calendar-important date – rather, they are found interspersed across the memorial wall. The analysis of temporality in these posts suggests that these moments rarely invoke happenings or memories in the distant past (in only 6 instances) and instead focus on the (immediate) present or the recent past and, to some extent, also the (near) future (see Figure 5.2).

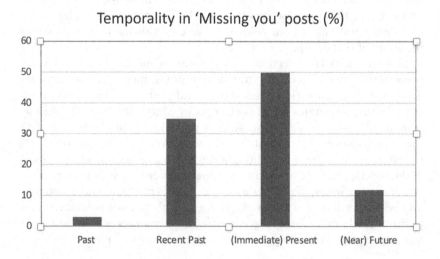

Figure 5.2 Temporality in memorial outbursts (or 'missing you' posts)

The few posts focused in the past are explicitly framed as stories of past memories through the use of the conventional story opening "*I remember . . .* ", as shown in Example 12.

Example 12

Davey I remember u were on the chain gang at the [place name omitted] game and u said u wanted me to run the ball and don't [be] scared and the last kick off of the game the ball was kicked to me on kickoff return and at first I was scared but then [I saw] u stand there and I remembered what u said and ran and wasnt be scared and I ran the ball from the ten yard line to the fifty and I will remember tht game forever man and I just want to u be with me and the team as we play game and [w]ill always remember what u said love you man and miss u

Instead of posting messages anchored in a distant past, sharers opt for accounts in the recent past, reporting, for example, dreaming about their friend (see Examples 13 & 14).

Example 13

Davey, I had a dream about you last night. It was great to see you smile again and be able to talk to you again even if it was a dream.

Example 14

You know . . . Not to be weird or anything but I had a dream last night. Actually more like a memory in my sleep. I watched you walk down the isle for homecoming court again. I watched the homecoming game again. I saw us at the computer Monday morning watching game film. I miss you Jonny . . . I really do.

The majority of memorial outbursts were found to be articulated in the immediate present, often further foregrounded by the use of adverbials denoting the here and now, such as '*right now*' or '*just*'. Through updates on their whereabouts (Examples 15 & 16) or feelings (Examples 17 & 18), sharers offer a slice of their here and now as a public testament to their loss and grief.

Example 15

Well Davey, I'm in [place name] . . .You would have a great time up here . . .Wish you could see it all.

(May 24, 2012)

Example 16

I'm at [name of eatery] right now on lunch break and it's the first time I've been here without you. It's hard man. I couldn't even remember what to get because I always got what you got. I miss you Davey.

Example 17

Just thinking of you

(June 13, 2012)

Example 18

Miss you, but I know you're with me right now! I can feel it. Love you man!

(Oct. 14, 2012)

Other sharers emphasize the continuity (Example 19) or daily recurrence of their grieving experience (Example 20):

Example 19

Not a day goes by that you're not in the back of my mind . . . I miss you Davey . . . . I wish you were still here. Come visit me . . . I could use a really good friend right now . . . . I love you <3.

(emphasis added)

Example 20

I really wish I could hear your voice again man. Miss you everyday, never forgotten.

(emphasis added)

The articulation of posts in the (immediate) present or the recent past is, in fact, typical of Facebook updates (Page, 2010) and stories on social media more generally (Georgakopoulou, 2015). The selection of fleeting moments in the here and now or the just-now allows sharers to display feelings of loss and attest to their experience of 'big' emotions in 'small', seemingly trivial moments of traveling to a new place, sitting at a restaurant, or walking.

Last but not least, a considerable portion of these posts explicitly orients to the (near) future. In these projections, David's friends share a slice of their upcoming life warranting his protection or support, as in Examples 21–22 below:

Example 21

Got a pretty big decision too [sic] make coming up pretty soon Davey boy, please help me make the right one for me . . . love and miss you.

Example 22

Morning Davey, I'm about to head out on my journey to [place] for [purpose], please watch over me as I fly out.

In messages like these, sharers are seen to shy away from explicit displays of sorrowful grief, foregrounding instead their continued connection with their friend in posts styled in vernacular language. For example, it is common for sharers to break through into the point of the message without an explicit opening or feature colloquial, conversational openings, such as direct addresses to David, e.g. (Davey), colloquial terms of greeting "*Hey*", "*Hi*", or discourse markers commonly used in conversation, e.g. '*well*'.

Shared moments on this digital memorial group don't tend to follow plotlines anchored in the (distant) past with a clear beginning, middle, and end (Ochs and Capps, 2001, p. 57) organized around the sharing of past memories, as it has been previously suggested (Brubaker et al., 2013). Happenings and feelings are shared as *breaking news stories of remembrance* in the here and now (or the recent past) or as *projections*, focused on the (near) future of a sharer's life plans offered as updates or calls for support from their 'guardian'-friend. Participation in the site attests to and enhances the deceased's post-mortem popularity as someone who is loved and cared for, allowing group members to negotiate identity and affective positionings at different levels. These are going to be examined in further detail in the next section, which zooms in on the moments shared by a single user, pinpointing key aspects in the selection, styling, and negotiation of sharing grief for the loss of a friend in relation to practices of positioning.

Shared Moments of Mourning

The selected group member, henceforth called Lina, has shared eight posts in the first six months following the death of David, ranging in length from 18 words to 134 words and distributed across the types of content identified earlier. The details of each post, including the date it was shared, its word count, number of Likes, and its position in the unfolding memorial are presented in Figure 5.3.

The first three moments are shared as part of a sequence of the thread aggregating around immediate reactions to the news of the death – in fact, the first two posts are broadcast within a couple of hours from each other on May 10. The next two moments, shared on May 12 and May 13, make part of the thread aggregating around reactions relating to the memorial services. The last three moments do not belong to any thematically focused group thread and are part of what was earlier termed '*missing you*' posts or *memorial outbursts*, shared as individual acts of

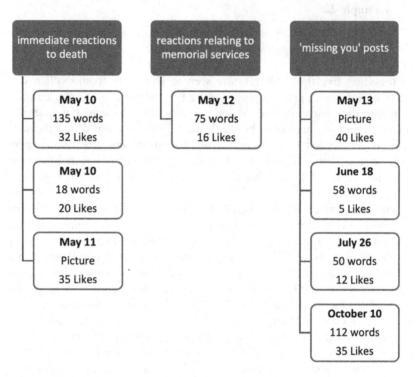

Figure 5.3 Lina's thematic and temporal distribution of posts in the memorial
        group

remembrance over a period of five months, from June to October 2012.
Posts celebrating deathversaries, birthdays, or other calendar-important
events did not feature in this sharer's content. The pattern of the selected
group member's posting activity over a period of six months broadly
reflects levels of posting activity on the wall, which was at its highest
in the immediate period following the death event and then gradually
decreasing.

The eight shared moments are fashioned differently, as the sharer is
crafting her identity positioning as a mourner in the group and negotiating her affective positioning to the dead, to members of the memorial
group, and to aspects of her affective self, as will be discussed in the next
section.

Selecting and Storying Moments of Grief Across Time

In the first three moments shared as part of aggregating reactions to the
news of death, the sharer focuses on the unexpected loss of her friend and
what it means for her. Moment 1 is the longest post of the set, counting

134 words. Its style is less colloquial compared to other examples cited earlier. Instead of an informal greeting or term of address, it opens with the textual adverb "*first of all*", which indicates an attempt to put thoughts in order (see Moment 1). Its closing, "*fly high*", however, echoes the typical structure of R.I.P. posts online (Giaxoglou, 2014).

Moment 1

First of all, I should NOT be writing this about you. You should be here with us, making us laugh & putting huge smiles on our faces. As selfish as that makes me sound, I'm happy you've finally made it home safely & pain free as perfect as we thought you were on earth, you're 1,000 times more perfect now than you ever were. God had you here to show us what love really is & the true meaning of what he is. **Last night at 10:18, we lost the most special angel ever given to us,** *& God gained one. Even though I'm a [US state] girl, I'm gonna be wearin that blue & orange like its goin outa style.[4] I'll be talking to you EVERY night in my prayers. Fly high sweet boy.* [emphasis added]

(No. 18,[5] May 10, 2012, 30 Likes)

In the main body of the message, the sharer praises the dead as a cheery and sociable person who made others laugh and smile. She bids farewell to him through an expression that is often used in eulogies[6] ("we lost the most special angel ever given to us & God gained one"). Her message is oriented to networked mourners through uses of inclusive plural first-person pronoun ("last night, at 10:18, **we** lost . . ."). It's also directed reflexively to herself, as evident in the uses of singular first-person pronoun ("**I** should not be writing . . .), and it's also directly addressed to the dead (". . . about **you**). This first moment, then, can be described as a vernacularized form of eulogy personalizing the expression of intimate loss.

The narrative orientation to the death event emerges out of contrasting external evaluations of the news of death. In particular, the implausibility of this particular death ("*I should NOT be writing this about you*") is contrasted with the deontic modal expression of the desire to retract the irrevocable fact ("*you **should** be here with us, making us laugh & putting huge smiles on our faces*"). The sharer's emotional state ("*I'm happy* ") is also contrasted with the potential negative judgements that the proclamation of a positive emotional state can raise in a mourning context ("*as **selfish** as that makes me sound*"). These evaluations foreground the inconceivability of this death and piece together an overall optimistic approach to the event as a way of coping with it. In the coda of the message, the sharer turns attention to herself in her role and identity as mourner: she commits to honouring her deceased friend by hanging on to memorial items ("*I'm gonna be wearin that blue & orange like* *its goin outa style"*) and by maintaining everyday communication with him mediated by prayers (*"I'll be talking to you EVERY night in my prayers"*). The commitment to remembering David lends authority to her first contribution to the group and authenticates her close relationship with the deceased. It also indexes an optimistic emotional self in line with conventional performatives of mourning enacted within Christian communities in the United States,[7] which is met with the approval of other group members who have 'Liked' the message.

The second moment draws attention to her grieving experience in the here and now, placing the emotional self at centre stage in a way that is markedly different to her first posts or other posts on the site (see Moment 2). The post lacks any explicit opening or closing and it is phrased as a rhetorical question addressed as much to herself as to networked mourners rather than the dead. This post is also the shortest message in the set (18 words).

Moment 2

Can I please just wake up from this nightmare now? there's only so many tears I can handle.

(No. 26, May 10, 2012, 18 Likes)

The moment offers a slice from the sharer's raw and difficult emotional experience of coming to terms with the news of the death of her friend. The use of an interrogative clause leaves the narrative orientation to the death event relatively open as the sharer explores the affective meaning of her friend's death. This moment marks a contrast to the affective stance[8] projected in Moment 1, which settled on optimism and hope. In this small story of grief, the sharer projects an affective stance which foregrounds the personal impact of this intimate loss on her, approaching the death as a *"nightmare"* that's difficult to handle and calling for compassion and support from group members. This post is an act of emotional self-disclosure, which further authenticates the sharer's personal experience of grieving; it allows the sharer to affectively position herself as deeply touched by this loss and in need of support (or attention) from fellow members of the group, and it attests to uses of the memorial as a site for the exchange of support resources (Baym, 2015).

In addition to *"Likes"* that this post attracted, a wall conversation event developed between the sharer and two other group members, with commenters offering verbal recognition of the author's emotional wants, needs, and desires (*"and we all wanna cry"*; *"and im sure you will keep cry"*). They also highlighted the need to manage and restrict overt displays of grief (*"don't cry"*), reorienting the sharer – and, by extension, other group members harbouring similar feelings – back to the emotional optimism typical of the memorial group.

The third moment shows a photograph of the tribute colours for David[9] with a short dedication in the update box as a caption to the photograph (see Moment 3). Sharing a memorial tribute is used here as a form of indirect communication with the dead friend, positioning the sharer to a position of proximity and intimacy with her friend. The sharer projects an affective stance that showcases mourning through 'small', everyday memorial acts, addressing other group members, who are privy to the meaning of colours and other kinds of items turned into everyday emblems of the dead.

Moment 3

Free & [name of sports team] colors for Davey ♥ <3

[image]

(No 50, May 10, 2012, 34 likes)

So far, the examination of shared moments has shown the modal and nar-rative-affective diversification of the moments shared by a single group member as she's navigating the repercussions of the death shortly after the event. The sharer entextualizes her mourning over her friend's death initially by projecting optimism and hope in light of a belief in his tran-sitioning to a "better world" then by self-disclosing her vulnerability in the throes of grieving, and lastly by turning to the possibilities of commu-nication with the dead and other networked mourners through 'small', everyday acts of remembrance. These entextualizations point to the com-plex negotiations involved in the performance of affective positioning at different levels through these memorial posts. The sharer's projected opti-mism allows her to position herself at a relative distance from the death event, while her emotional and memorial 'outbursts' may reveal some level of loss of control over her emotions but also allow her to position herself in proximity to the other members of the group but also the dead.

Similar foci are taken up in the two moments shared as part of the thread relating to the memorial services. On the day of the visitation, Lina shared a public note of excusing herself to her deceased friend but also justifying herself to networked mourners for not attending the ser-vice (Moment 4). She selects this occasion as an opportunity for revisiting her affective experience of loss and reaffirming both the religious opti-mism (*"you're looking 10 times better up there with the big mannn"*) and her commitment to continued interaction with David mediated by God (*"you & God will be hearing me in a few minutes, bc I promised I would talk to y'all every night"*).

Moment 4

I ended up not being able to go tonight & at first I was really upset bc it woulda been my last night seeing you, besides the funeral. But

*then I realized that no matter how you looked tonight, you're look-
ing 10 times better up there with the big mannn I love you & you &
God will be hearing me in a few minutes, bc I promised I would talk
to y'all every night.*

(No 97, May 12, 2012, 16 Likes)

Her optimistic affective stance is reinforced in the visual moment she
shares next (Moment 5). In the image shared in this post, she invokes
the support of God in dealing with difficult situations, while in the caption inserted in the update box, she affirms her belief that her friend is
alongside God, watching over her. This sense of connection is further
underscored by tagging David to the post, making it seem as if they are
indeed together in that moment.

Moment 5

God & davey are watching over me [heart emoji] – with David

[Image of note that reads "God will help you overcome any hardship"]
(No 134, May 13, 2012, 38 Likes)

While so far in her posts the sharer has been reconstructing the relationship between herself and her deceased friend in terms of a one-way communication mediated by prayers and God or memorial items, Moment
5 puts forward a new role accorded to her deceased friend, that of a
guardian of his friends, including her. This is a role which is regularly
invoked by other sharers in this group and is also attested in other memorial practices, where the dead take up the role of an angel caring for the
living (Walter, 2018).

Across these moments, Lina claims visibility for her dead friend, attesting to his pre- and post-mortem popularity. She also claims visibility for
herself as mourner as she navigates the meanings of this unexpected,
intimate loss. Her identity as mourner is created and displayed in and
through personalized, self-reflective performances of mourning that construct her as an *entitled mourner*, that is as someone who knew David,
an *authentic mourner* who has genuinely been grieving over him, and an
involved mourner, who participates in the everyday memorialization and
remembrance of her friend.

The shared moments considered so far were shared during May and
made part of thematically coherent threads on the site, which overlapped
temporally with offline mourning immediately or shortly after the death
event. The last three moments, which will be examined in the next section, were shared across a period of five months, from June to October,
and are indicative of *missing-you* posts (also referred to as *memorial
outbursts*).

Habitual Stories of Mourning as Positioning

The final three moments shared by Lina are not prompted by a key memorial event or a calendar-important date. They are shared as individual acts of remembrance, which, nonetheless, partake to ongoing, collective remembrance as part of a type of small stories oriented to the habitual and the everyday, as will be shown. These moments mark a change in the sharer's posting style and signal a shift in her identity positioning as mourner as well as her affective positioning. The sharer is seen to drop conventional expressions of mourning to project optimistic affective stances lodged in the belief that the deceased is in "God's home". In addition, she adopts a more explicitly vernacularized and personalized style of sharing focused on the everyday experience of grief.

This stylistic and narrative shift is marked by the omission of any explicit references to God or God-mediated communication with her deceased friend. Instead, as shown in Moments 6 through 8, the sharer uses a consistently more informal conversational style, in which David is construed as the sole addressee through the use of colloquial greeting forms and terms of endearment (" *Well Davey*"; "*Hey babyyy!*").

Moment 6

Well Davey, its been a while that I've posted on here. But I still talk to you every night before I go to sleep.
You're still on my mind everyday. I still wear my bracelet & the blue & orange ribbons are still hanging on my purse. So everywhere I go, you're going with me love youu, baby!
(No 248, June 18, 2012, 5 Likes)

Moment 7

Hey babyyy! I was at church tonight, & a song came on & it reminded me of you. Me & XXXXXX couldn't help but smile when we heard it! I miss you so much. you're still & always will be impacting soo many people. I love you sooo much! ♥♥
(No 278, July 26, 2012, 12 Likes)

Moment 8

Hey babyyy. Today, we were on the mats at cheerleading & we were talking about our competition Saturday. When you enter the competition mat, you're not allowed to wear ANY jewelry. So mrs armstrong says "I'm sorry to say it, but the Davey bracelets have to come off while you're competing" all of us got this "oh no, that aint happenin" look on our face. When we wear our davy bracelets, everything goes right. Its safe the say that the [name of high school] cheerleaders have their own guardian angel. So please just keep workin your magic as we take the floor during our competition Saturday! I love & miss you more than ever.

(No. 348, October 10, 2012, 35 Likes)

The 'duty' to remember her friend, which in previous moments was expressed as a promise and commitment, is here presented as enacted in real life. All three moments are organized around the invocation of memorial items, such as the "bracelet" or the "blue & orange ribbons" (in Moments 6 and 8) or prompts, such as a song (in Moment 7) and their use in everyday moments of remembrance. While directly addressing her dead friend, the sharer also aligns herself to the group of mourners by publicly reaffirming her identity positioning as a committed mourner who is thinking about David and interacting with him daily (*"I still talk to you every night"*; *"you're still on my mind everyday"*; *"it reminded me of you"*). The projection of everyday remembrance is achieved through the use of temporal and spatial deixis articulated via combined deictics, "every night", "everyday", "everywhere", "always", which encode repeated action in a futurate present.

The bracelet, referred to in Moment 6 and 8, stands for an important memorial item: it refers to the one hundred handmade bracelets that were passed around at school and the community following David's death. Bereaved friends wrapped the bracelets around their wrists on the day of the funeral and held on to them. People who had never met David also took to wearing them, turning the bracelet into a memorial emblem in the wider community. In Moment 8, the sharer recounts a moment of tension regarding the memorial bracelets, extending their affective value from an index of and prompt for remembrance to a keepsake that brings luck to anyone who's wearing it. The post concludes with a coda section that bridges over to the present moment of writing the post, representing David as a 'magic' agent who can provide support to the cheerleaders when they will be competing.

Moment 8 is linguistically styled as a narrative performance, drawing on audience involvement devices (Bauman, 1986; Tannen, 1984), such as quoted speech (*"Mrs X says 'I'm sorry to say it, but the davy bracelets have to come off while you're competing'"*), imagery (*"All of us got this 'oh no that ain't happening' look on our face"*) and the use of punctuation marks signalling heightened involvement (e.g. exclamation mark, capitalization of 'ANY', emoticon use). In this moment, the sharer moves away from the direct staging of emotional states or moments of remembrance to weaving her affective stance into the story. When referring to how she and other members of the cheerleaders' group reacted to the request to remove the memorial bracelets, she uses performance devices, such as direct speech, as a resource for building in an internal evaluation to her story (*"all of us got this 'oh no, that aint happening' look on our face'"*). She projects feelings of grief to the group of cheerleaders she is a member of, thereby affectively distancing herself from the centre stage of suffering. The weaving of the author's affective stance to the structure of her story and the story characters allows the sharer to place herself among a part of a group of mourners committed to hanging on to the memory of the dead aided by shared symbols of remembrance rather than mourn alone.

Her story affirms the importance of the bracelet as an emblem of mourning and extends its importance as an affective tie among the grieving friends. References to the 'bracelet' are also found in eight additional posts authored by different authors on dates ranging from May 2011 to March 2012, who contribute a little slice of their own experience relating to the bracelet: hand-making it, wearing it, looking at it, talking to others about it, getting attached to it, refusing to remove it, losing it . . . The bracelet is transformed from an emblem of mourning to a keepsake that brings luck to anyone who's wearing it. These stories attest to an additional type of small stories on the site, which focus on the way grief becomes embedded in one's everyday life through small acts of remembrance in the habitual present, which are termed here habitual stories. These stories expand its signification from a memorial bracelet to a bonding icon (see Page, 2018) – a discursive-affective resource which produces interpersonal meaning, bringing mourners together through acts of sharing small moments related to it.

Taken together, the last three 'missing you' posts extend remembrance from the realm of commissive speech acts (cf. Moment 1: *"I'm gonna be wearin that blue & orange like its goin outa style"*) to social fields of mourning activity and habitual events and practices (e.g. church, sports centre), which allow the sharer to affectively position herself in proximity to co-mourners and the dead.

As shown, each shared moment constitutes part of a careful, self-monitored, and highly reflexive writing activity that results in representations of the deceased as loved and worthy to be remembered and contributes to his post-mortem visibility. Sharers participate in the circulation of signs, texts, and discourses on the memorial wall, connecting those who had known the dead in an ambient 'embrace' of intimate publics.

The next section turns to the discussion of the uses of deictic choices as affective positioning resources for projecting affective stances and selves variously aligned to the death and the dead, other members of the memorial group, and the affective self.

Time, Space, and Affective Positioning

In this section, attention is directed more specifically to the role of temporal and spatial deixis in the semiotic and discursive organization of public mourning online that can point to aspects of the dynamic development of affect trajectories on the site.

In the early phase of sharing (see Moments 1–5), the sharer's deictic choices construe the death event in predominantly static terms, encoding time through the use of deictic punctual past or present temporal adverbs (*"last night"*, *"tonight"*). These establish pivot events as the deictic centers to which each moment can be related to. For example, in Moment 1, *"last night at 10:18"* refers back to the exact time of death, while in Moment 4, *"tonight"* refers back to the ceremonial event of the visitation. The use of static temporal points of reference in these moments anchors happenings in time. These static frames are discursively associated with conventional eulogy expressions (Moment 1: *"Last night at 10:18 we lost the most special angel ever given to us, & God gained one"*) or are used to connect back to official mourning events, such as the visitation (Moment 4: *"I ended up not being able to go tonight"*).

In addition to static construals of time, the use of combined temporal deictics (*"every night"*, *"everyday"*; *"always"*) was also attested across shared moments; for example, in the coda sections of Moment 1 (*"I'll be talking to you EVERY night in my prayers"*) and Moment 4 (*"bc I promised I would talk to y'all every night"*), the main body of Moment 6 (*"But I still talk to you every night before I go to sleep"*, *"You're still on my mind everyday"*), or the coda section of Moment 7 (*"you're still & alwayswill be impacting soo many people"*). Combined temporal deictics propose a dynamic construal of mourning as communication, focused on repeated (inter)action with the dead in a futurate present, as shown in the examples. Such construals were also found to co-occur with ordinary greetings of separation, for example *"love you baby"* (Moment 5, 6). As affective positioning resources, dynamic construals of time allow the sharer to situate herself among a group of mourners committed to continued, everyday remembrance rather than to official ceremonies fixed in time.

In terms of spatial deixis, the first moment featured binary distinctions of space that separate 'here' from 'not-here' (or *"up there"*). Uses of such contrastive deictics of space in this early phase of sharing construct the sharer as (physically) separate from the dead (I–you) and as proximal to the living (us; see Moment 1). The physical separation between the sharer and the dead locates the sharer in the social role of mourner bidding farewell through ritual expressions and greetings of farewell (e.g. Moment 1: *"You should be here with us"*, *"Fly high"*). Gradually, these deictics give way to spatial construals that blend taleworld sites and sites of remembrance (e.g. 'church', Moment 7; 'sports centre', Moment 8). In other cases, they give way to combined deictics of space co-occurring with combined deictics of time (Moment 6: *"So everywhere I go, you're going with me"*).

These shifts in the use of deictic choices point to the sharer's affective positioning to the event of death in static frames that anchor death as fact (e.g. Moment 1, l. 8: "*last night at 10:18 we lost the most special angel ever given to us*") versus more dynamic and fluid frames that construe death in terms of everyday life (e.g. Moment 5: "*So everywhere I go, you're going with me*"). Along the same lines, the dead is constructed as distal, via the spatial differentiation of the sharer's location of the sharer compared to the location of the deceased, or as proximal and 'high focus', in other words as an absent present.

The spatiotemporal frames identified in the memorial group under focus are related to two key orientations to socially recognizable forms of mourning that shape individual mourner identities: the first one is sharers' orientation to Christian Baptist master discourses and the seeking of a spiritual relationship to the dead mediated by God. The second type of orientation involves a concern with peer-group norms for continued interaction mediated by the mourner's self-presentations and increased visibility online. Each sharer negotiates the two types of orientations in different ways, adapting them to their projected place in the religious community and the peer group and participates in the production of routinized forms of mourning mediated by digital performances of self.

Based on the observations, the following general pattern about trajectories of the discursive representation of public mourning online is suggested:

- proximity to the time of the event of death is associated with spatiotemporal frames of distancing from death and the dead through which the boundaries between the living and the dead are discursively articulated.
- distance from the time of the event of death is associated with spatiotemporal frames of proximity to the dead through which continued bonds with the dead are discursively constructed.

(Giaxoglou, 2015)

These insights point to the changing identity of the mourner and shifts in her affective positioning in the context of digital public mourning, signalled by the use of deixis. Members of the memorial group construct, negotiate, and re-affirm their membership to the group of grieving in and through narrative activity and take up positions of the 'good' mourner, in affective proximity to each other and to their absent friend, and commit themselves to continued remembrance in line with the developing norms of the group.

Summary

The chapter examined how significant moments are shared on a Facebook memorial group site and discussed key aspects of patterned semiotic, discursive, and narrative activity shaping and shaped by the entextualization of death and mourning online. I showed how this Facebook memorial group site emerges as a semi-public diary of grief and sadness, whereby grief becomes socially intelligible and shareable through its weaving into everyday life, which affords members of the group to enact and inhabit different identity and affective positions that place them in proximity to the dead and with networked mourners at a relative and 'safe' distance from the death event and the grieving self.

Sharing mourning on Facebook over the loss of a friend is found to be organized around themes and topics relating to calendar-important dates – especially at the early phase of the site – which invite acts of ritual appreciation in mirroring posts. A large part of the memorial is also textured around one-off *missing-you* posts or memorial outbursts, which index forms of knowing participation, whereby sharers select the dead and members of the closed circle of his friends as addressees. Memorial outbursts were found to fall into three different types of small stories: (i) *breaking news stories of mourning* – acts of remembrance in the here and now or the recent past; (ii) *projections* – stories about the sharer's plans in the (near) future inviting the dead's participation or support as a 'magic' guardian; and (iii) *habitual* stories of grief – small acts of remembrance in the everyday, which establish the dead as an absent present with a lasting impact on the living. Uses of Facebook for mourning in the case of the loss of a friend encourage, thus, the weaving of death and grief into everyday life. These practices challenge pervasive conceptions of death, dying, and mourning as a site of 'big', extraordinary crisis and disruption fraught with emotional challenges (see Foster, 2007) and bring to the fore young adults' ways of connecting the experience of mourning with a sense of the mundane (Ellis, 2013). This analysis provides an empirical account of practices of forming *continuing bonds* with the dead (Klass et al., 1996; Kasket, 2012) as *small stories*, whereby sharers rework and continuously negotiate their affective positioning to the dead.

Furthermore, the analysis of shared moments foregrounded the highly reflexive style of writing activity on the memorial wall. In addition to projections of post-mortem mediated sociality, shared moments of mourning online are also acts of identity positionings vis-à-vis members of the group as the 'good' mourner, someone who has (or can claim) entitlement to taking part in mourning for a particular death and who does so in the context of a performance of emotional sincerity. In addition, a 'good' mourner for this group is someone who views death as a transition to a better life and who commits themselves to the 'duty' of remembering the dead, showing that commitment by sharing moments of engagement in group memorial activities or in personal, everyday acts of remembrance. These ideas of 'good' mourning are also found to be pervasive in conventionalized tributes shared online more generally. They are connected to ideas of a 'good' death,[10] where the emphasis is on the avoidance of suffering and the use of communication to ensure a sense of support in the experience of dying and also bereavement. These ideas are, however, socio-culturally situated and should not be seen as universalizing models of dying and grieving; it is expected that group mourning on Facebook will vary across groups or cultures whose norms and beliefs about death differ from the ones discussed here.

In the analysis of shared moments, time and space deixis were found to play a key role as affective positioning resources that help to organize discursively the personal and social experience of mourning across time. The uses of deixis pointed to the way that the identity and affective positioning of sharers is not static and fixed but rather changes over time. Articulating space and time deixis in shared moments of mourning was shown to involve different images of death (i.e. as contrasted to life or as embedded in the everyday) and the dead (i.e. as separate from the living or as integrated in everyday activities as a 'guardian angel' or 'magic agent'). Sharers were seen to modulate their affective positioning to the death event, the dead, the bereaved community, and their own grieving self with the passing of time, showing a tendency to increase their proximity and intimacy to the dead, reconstructed as their 'guardian angel', as they gain some distance from the death event and their own experience of grieving.

Conclusion

In online memorials, the dead become an empty vessel to whom mourners pour their preoccupations, whatever they may be, producing routinized forms of mourning mediated by sharers' self-presentations. Mourners gain centre stage in continued mediated projections of affect and post-mortem sociality that point to the complexity of the individual and social experience of mourning.

This type of death-writing of the moment illustrates a type of mourning focused on memorialization that can be termed *participatory*, in that it creates increased opportunities for individuals – known or unknown to the dead – to participate in the weaving of the story of his life as a life worth grieving. This case study shows how mourning is mobilized for (re)creating (existing) communities of the bereaved and increasing the visibility of individuals within them, as well as claiming visibility for the dead as a micro-celebrity.

This chapter and the previous one focused on small-scale death events, drawing attention to story sharing and curation towards the (hyper-) personalization and collectivization of experiences of death and mourning. The next two chapters turn to the consideration of big-scale death events, where mourning is mobilized for emblematic purposes, capitalizing on its potential for connective action.

Notes

1. According to a Newsweek article, the use of Facebook by young users is in decline (see Newsweek. 2018. *Facebook is officially for old people*, Dec.

2. Available at: www.newsweek.com/facebook-officially-old-people-803196. Accessed: 11 Aug. 2019.

2. Note that these posts were recovered at the first stage of the analysis in 2014. At the time of writing, these posts have been removed as part of the administrators' maintenance of the Facebook group.

3. The largest number of comments accumulated in response to the posting of a tribute song, which was created by friends of David. These comments were mainly addressed to the creators of the song, thanking them for sharing it and showing appreciation to its creators for making and sharing it.

4. The sharer refers here to the tribute colours, which are colours associated with a U.S. state different to the state she – and most members of the group – are from.

5. The number indicates the sequential position of this post on the memorial wall.

6. A funeral oration in praise of a person. Conventionally, it includes nice words and praise of the dead and ends with the expression of some kind of hope and optimism. Eulogies serve as a formal act of farewell in funerals.

7. Notably, Julian Barnes (2014) p. 107) remarks that "in the US emotional optimism is a constitutional duty".

8. Affective stance refers to the expression of personal feelings, attitudes, or judgements towards a stance object (Barton and Lee, 2013)

9. The tribute colours are the colours of David's favourite sports team and were used in various acts of memorialization, offline and online.

10. A 'decent' or 'good' death is defined by the Institute of Medicine as "death that is free from avoidable distress and suffering for patients, families, and caregivers; in general accord with patients' and families' wishes and reasonably consistent with clinical, cultural, and ethical standards" (Emannuel and Emannuel, 1998, p. 21).

References

Androutsopoulos, J. (2014) Moments of sharing: Entextualization and linguistic repertoires in social networking. *Journal of Pragmatics* 73: 4–18.

Barnes, J. (2014) *Levels of Life*. London: Vintage.

Barton, D. and C. Lee (2013) *Language Online: Investigating Digital Texts and Practices*. Oxon: Routledge.

Bauman, R. (1986) *Story, Performance, and Event: Contextual Studies of Oral Narrative*. Cambridge: Cambridge University Press.

Baym, N.K. (2015) *Personal Connections in the Digital Age*. 2nd ed. Cambridge, UK, and Malden, MA: Polity Press.

Brubaker, J., G. Hayes, and P. Dourish (2013) Beyond the Grave: Facebook as a site for the expansion of death and mourning. *The Information Society* 29 (3): 152–163.

Ellis, J. (2013) Thinking beyond rupture: Continuity and relationality in everyday illness and dying experience. *Mortality* 18 (3): 251–269.

Emannuel, E.J. and L.L. Emannuel (1998) The promise of a good death. *Lancet* 351: 21–29.

Emojipedia (n.d.) *Facebook*. Available at: https://emojipedia.org/facebook/. Accessed: 20 Jan. 2019.

Facebook (2019) *Social plugins: Like, share, send & quote*. Available at: https://developers.facebook.com/docs/plugins/#like-share-send. Accessed: 20 Jan. 2019.

Foster, E. (2007) *Communicating at the End of Life: Finding Magic in the Mundane*. London: Lawrence Erlbaum Associates.

Georgakopoulou, A. (2015) Small stories research: Methods-analysis-outreach. In De Fina, A. and A. Georgakopoulou (Eds.), *The Handbook of Narrative Analysis*. Malden, MA: Wiley Blackwell, pp. 178–193.

Giaxoglou, K. (2014) 'R.I.P. man... u are missed and loved by many': entextualising moments of mourning on a Facebook Rest in Peace group site. *Thanatos*, 3 (1): 10–28.

Giaxoglou, K. (2015) 'Everywhere I go, you're going with me': Time and space deixis as affective positioning resources in shared moments of digital mourning. *Discourse, Context and Media* 9: 55–63.

Giaxoglou, K. (2020) From Rest in Peace to #R.I.P.: Tracing shifts in the language of mourning. In Tagg, C. and M. Evans (Eds.), *Message and Medium: Historicizing English Language Practices*. Berlin, NY, and London: Mouton de Gruyter.

Kasket, E. (2012) Continuing bonds in the age of social networking: Facebook as a modern-day medium. *Bereavement Care* 31 (2): 62–69.

Klass, D., P.R. Silverman, and S.L. Nickman (Eds.) (1996) *Continuing Bonds: New Understandings of Grief*. London: Taylor & Francis.

Marwick, A. and N.B. Ellison (2012) "There isn't wifi in heaven!" Negotiating visibility on Facebook memorial pages. *Journal of Broadcasting & Electronic Media* 56 (3): 378–400.

Ochs, E. and L. Capps (2001) *Living Narratives: Creating Lives in Everyday Storytelling*. Cambridge: Harvard University Press.

Page, R. (2018) *Narratives Online: Shared Stories in Social Media*. Cambridge: Cambridge University Press.

Peyton, T. (2014) Emotion to action? Deconstructing the ontological politics of the "Like" button. In Benski, T. and E. Fisher (Eds.), *Internet and Emotions*. London and New York: Routledge.

Roberts, P. (2004) The living and the dead: Community in the virtual cemetery. *Omega: The Journal of Death and Dying* 49 (1): 57–76.

Sànchez-Querubín, N. H. and W. M. van Laarhoven (2019) Vlogging at the end-of-life. *The Lancet* 20 (7): 911–912.

Seargeant, P. and K. Giaxoglou (2018) What effect is social media having on the way we mourn global tragedies? *Open Learn*, Mar. 28. Available at: www.open.edu/openlearn/languages/what-effect-social-media-having-on-the-way-we-mourn-global-tragedies.

Seargeant, P. and C. Tagg (2014) *The Language of Social Media: Identity and Community on the Internet*. London: Palgrave Macmillan.

Tannen, D. (1984) *Conversational Style: Analyzing Talk Among Friends*. Norwood, NJ: Ablex.

Walter, J. (2018) The pervasive dead. *Mortality*. DOI: 10.1080/13576275.2017.1415317.

Wortham, S. (2000) Interactional positioning and narrative self-construction. *Narrative Inquiry* 10 (1): 157–184.

6 Small Stories of Ecstatic Mourning on Twitter

Introduction

This chapter turns to the consideration of digital mourning in reaction to big-scale death events. In these types of practices, death-writing of the moment is related to the mobilization of mourning for emblematic purposes, capitalizing on its potential for connecting affective publics (Papacharissi, 2014). This and the next chapter draw attention to shared mourning as a form of affective engagement with the news, which contributes to the social-mediatization of mourning as a mode of witnessing global events in the here and now. The analysis considers the key event of the *Charlie Hebdo* attacks and the reactions to it as a case of the *ecstatic sharing* mode.

The storm of reactions on social media and in the streets across European cities after the attack at the offices of the *Charlie Hebdo* magazine in January 2015 arguably heralded a particular mode of media and public affective mobilization in the wake of similar attacks that followed it. In that sense, it is considered a key event almost on a par with the live footage on TV covering the 9/11 attacks in New York in 2001, which signalled a new form of news, which Chouliaraki (2006) termed *ecstatic news*. In this type of news, television spectators are called into positions of reflexive identification with others' suffering through discursive practice. Ecstatic news demands some form of public speech – even if this is just the spectator's whisper to themselves – and seeks to universalize the spectacle of suffering in terms of moral values and ethical norms, constituting a broader 'public' of judgement and action (Chouliaraki, 2006, p. 46). This demand for public speech has stirred polarized debates about the potential of television – and media more broadly – as an ethical and moral agent.

In these debates, the optimistic view sees the exposure of spectators to suffering as something that can awaken them to a new sensibility and sense of responsibility. The pessimistic view, on the other hand, sees the focus on tragedies and death as an instance of over-exposure to human suffering with numbing effects on their willingness or ability to act. Chouliaraki points out that these two extremes are grounded in different models of public life. The optimistic view is grounded in an ideal of public life as *dissemination* and capitalizes on the promise of technology to cultivate new collective sensibilities among media publics. The pessimistic view is grounded in a model of public life as a *dialogue* grounded in the condition of co-presence and reflecting the ethics of proximity as its public norm, which involves "acting on those who are close to us, or at best, translating distant events into our own lifeworld, as its public norm" (ibid, p. 35–36). To move away from either of these two positions, Chouliaraki suggests instead a turn to the study of particular practices of mediation as "a politics of pity" (see also Boltanski, 1999).

In an age of social media, the spectator's whisper turns into loud echoes as spectators turn to social media platforms to publicly share and amplify reactions to spectacles of disaster and tragedy, often through practices of social tagging. Such new, amplified forms of public speech and public formation has stirred debates about the role and ethical responsibility of social media, similar to the debates about television publics discussed earlier. In a similar vein, these debates recycle polarized ideals of public life as dissemination or dialogue reflected in public norms of *proximity* or *distance*.

This chapter presents an empirical study of small stories and participation in the case of sharing reactions to the *Charlie Hebdo* attacks. Looking at how these 'loud echoes' emerge in practices of live news making online and social tagging, I clarify the types of narrative positions afforded to participants as part of a *politics of pity* but also as part of a *politics of mourning*, whereby social media users are affectively positioned as proximal or distant witnesses to media-spectacular death.

After a brief introduction to Twitter as a platform for sharing news, the chapter moves on to the examination of how social tagging emerges as a form of discourse and shared storying and how hashtags serve as resources for narrative and affective positioning. Finally, it turns to the use of these resources as cues for the poly-storying of the event and its assessment across and outside social media platforms.

Twitter as a Hub of Sharing

The microblogging platform Twitter allowed users to post messages capped at 140 characters until 2017 and at 280 characters thereafter. In 2009 Twitter was categorized as a social network company, then in 2016 switched to a news company aspiring to "connect everyone to what's happening in the world right now [. . .] as it unfolds" (Twitter, 2016). The platform currently brands itself on the Apple Store as follows: "Twitter is what's happening in the world and what people are talking about right now".[1] Its users are invited to "see what's happening, follow your interest, join the conversation, stay in the know". The tagline on its welcome page is: "Connect with your friends – and other fascinating people.

Get in-the-moment updates on the things that interest you. And watch events unfold, in real time, from every angle" (Twitter, 2018). Twitter is a dynamic platform constantly adapting to trends and user needs, as evident in the way its taglines change from time to time (Spilioti, 2015). It is promoted as a platform in between a news and social network platform, which allows users to find out breaking news in the world but also to connect in the moment with others.

Twitter often turns into a hub of communication in the wake of national elections, world sports events, or natural disasters and helps spread messages quickly and widely. It allows users to remain tuned in to latest developments and updates from both professional journalists and witnesses on the ground. At the same time, and in parallel to live updates on events as they happen, Twitter feeds also serve as a form of a backchannel to live events through the sharing of direct-experience reports, thoughts, and feelings, often accompanied by pictures or videos. For instance, according to the New York University's Social Media and Political Participation data report (2013, p. 1), during the 2013 protests in Turkey, more than 22 million tweets featuring the hashtags #direngezipark and #occupygezi associated to the demonstrators were mentioned more than 4 million times and 1.9 million times, respectively. It is not surprising, then, that Twitter is often viewed as a barometer of public opinion or political participation, even if its skewed demographics are not always taken into account (Mislove et al., 2011).

Similarly to views of mediation polarized around optimistic and pessimistic models of communication, claims about Twitter as a democratizing force are pitted against claims about Twitter as mobilizing 'mobs' and prompting violence and riots. Both these views are expressions of technological determinism. As Fuchs observes, "social media in a contradictory society (made of class conflicts and other conflicts between dominant and dominated groups) are likely to have a contradictory character: they do not necessarily and automatically support/amplify or dampen/limit rebellions, but rather pose contradictory potentials that stand in contradictions with influences by the state, ideology and capitalism" (Fuchs, 2014, p. 206).

Twitter constitutes a rich site for exploring the surfacing and receding of such contradictions, avoiding alignment to either of the two forms of technological determinism (Spilioti, 2015). Twitter practices are to be studied empirically in practices of sharing (or not sharing) as a form of social and discourse practice intersecting with other online and offline domains of discourse. While there has been a focus on the rhetorics underlying the emergence of sharing as a concept and practice in Web 2.0 environments (John, 2013, 2017), its relationship to linguistic repertoires on Facebook profile pages (Androutsopoulos, 2014), to affective trajectories on Facebook memorials (Giaxoglou, 2015), and to practices of rescripting on YouTube (Georgakopoulou, 2015), more recent approaches have pointed to the need to extend the focus from local to global contexts of sharing. Page (2018), for example, has highlighted the importance of studying shared stories beyond the small-scale level of analysis, combining qualitative with quantitative approaches, and especially corpus methods. This chapter shows how the study of small stories and 'small' data can be extended to the analysis of supra-local sharing, using a qualitative and small-scale lens. The analysis attends to the incipiency of shared stories via hashtags and their associated modes of participation through an emphasis on emblematic social media events and moments in phases of circulation (see Chapter 3).

Hashtags: Forms and Functions

The hash or pound symbol #, technically known as 'octothorpe', is used together with a word or phrase (preferably with no spaces between the words, e.g. #openuniversity) as a clickable link used to categorize and search content. It has been used by some computer users since the late 1980s until the symbol was adopted by Twitter, with other social media platforms, like Google, Facebook, Pinterest, and Instagram, following suit. On Twitter a hashtag is a symbol used to index keywords or topics on Twitter created to allow people to easily follow topics they are interested in. In order for a hashtag to work properly, no spaces or punctuation should be added, and it's advisable to avoid using more than two hashtags per tweet, even though it is possible to use more than that (Twitter, n.d.).

Product designer Chris Messina is credited with inventing the hashtag in an attempt to enhance Twitter's relevance and discovery function and enhance online relationships via the platform back in 2007. Despite Twitter's initial scepticism, the hashtag made its break when one of Messina's friends and San Diego resident Nate Ritter started posting tweet-bit sized messages about the unfolding wildfires in San Diego, using Twitter as an *ad hoc* news aggregator from local radio and police reports, TV news, but also from text messages and emails from friends in the affected areas. This turned into one of the first exercises in citizen journalism (The Wired, 2017, May 19). Messina asked Ritter to apply a hashtag in his live reporting as a first live attempt to show how hashtags can bring people together around a common term (Messina, 2007, Oct. 22).

In a recent TEDx talk, Messina describes the hashtag as a "rhizomatic structure" whereby every part of it has enough information to replicate itself (Messina, 2019). This rhizomatic structure has led to some unexpected outcomes, such as the hashtag becoming a driver of 'citizen conversations' about breaking news, personal journeys (e.g. of fitness), controversial topics, small and large protests, or crises. It has also turned into a driver of offline 'conversations' about brands, advertising, and fashion featured in print, billboards, placards, or on walls in the form of graffiti and tagging. It is telling that the Oxford Dictionary decided to include "hashtag" in its list of entries in 2014.

The hashtag is not just "a particular form of social metadata" (Zappavigna, 2015) used for annotating posts; it's also a form of linguistic innovation (Cunha et al., 2011). A tweet published on a public account and using a hashtag may be retrieved by anyone who performs a search for that hashtag, using Twitter's search bar or other specialized apps. The enhanced visibility for tweets afforded by hashtags has led to their repurposing as "the cachet of internet fame" and as a commercial trademark (MacFarlane and Stobbe, 2018; Shulga, 2013). Trademarks confer intellectual property rights that typically protect a name or logo and thus serve to create brand identity. In addition to brand hashtags, attempts to obtain trademark protection have included applications for words which are widely used in and beyond a particular industry. Attempts in the U.S. for trademarking the word 'hashtag' in connection with TV advertising and entertainment services in 2014 as well as an application to the Intellectual Property Office in France in 2015 to trademark the hashtag #JeSuisCharlie (Champeau, 2016) have not been successful. They attest, though, to the increasing commodification of popular hashtags in anticipation of their commercial uses.

Hashtags have been connected to activism also termed "hashtag activism" (Yang, 2016), which is often enhanced by the use of storytelling and the prompting of second stories that serve to amplify the message, as in the case of the #MeToo campaign. From a linguistic perspective, hashtags can be described as technomorphemes (Saki, 2015), which are syntactically very flexible and can either occur as an adjunct to the lexis, clause, or clause complex constituting the main content of a post or, alternatively, can integrate themselves seamlessly into that content (Zappavigna, 2015) in the position of *infix, prefix, or suffix* (Tsur and Rappoport, 2012). The variable functions of hashtags can be broadly classified as *annotation*, recording the author's feelings or comments on the content of a tweet (e.g. #happy #joking) or *community*, a topical entity that links the tweet with an external community (e.g. #music #BecauseItIsTheCup; Yang et al., 2012). Previous literature has drawn attention to hashtags as searchable talk (Zappavigna, 2012), an aid to the formation of ad hoc publics (Bruns and Burgess, 2011), supporting visibility and participation (Page, 2012). More recently, hashtags have been described as pragmatic markers of relevance guiding the reader's inferential processes (Scott, 2015) but also as metadiscursive markers (Zappavigna, 2015) and storytelling devices (Papacharissi, 2015; Giaxoglou, 2018). Hashtagging is also viewed as a social and discourse practice (see special issue Lee, 2018), which can contribute to investigations of discourse and sharing online (Varis and Blommaert, 2014).

In this chapter, I examine hashtagging as a discourse and narrative practice, which can shed light on the narrative and participation modes of sharing death as a social-mediatized event via hashtags, a form of digital mourning activity that will be referred to as *hashtag mourning*.

The Case Study

The findings reported in this study are based on the examination of the hashtag #JeSuisCharlie, which became viral in response to the attacks against the French satirical magazine *Charlie Hebdo* in Paris on January 7, 2015 around 11:30 local time. The attack left twelve people dead, among whom were eight employees, including five well-known cartoonists-journalists, a guest at the offices, a maintenance worker, and two police officers. From January 7 to January 9 seventeen people were killed in the offices of the magazine *Charlie Hebdo*, a kosher grocery store, and the Paris suburb of Montrouge (CNN, 2018, Dec. 24).

Journalists immediately started covering the events in live reports appearing on television, radio, news blogs, and Twitter. At 12:52 p.m. (local time), French designer Joachim Roncin posted via his Twitter account a logo using the masthead of the magazine featuring the words 'Je Suis Charlie'. Seven minutes later, the logo was retweeted by Twitter user Thierry Puget, who further added the hashtag '#JeSuisCharlie'. The hashtag was used 1.5 million times that day and about 6 million times over the week after on Twitter, Instagram, and Facebook (BBC, 2016, Jan. 3).

Tracking the emergence and circulation of hashtags qualitatively using a 'small' data angle can be a challenging task, given the range of ways in which keywords are selected, appended to messages as hashtags, and shared among large numbers of users across social media platforms. Live-coverage blogs offer rich sites for studying hashtag selection practices in the context of breaking news stories that report on the events 'as they happen' and archive news 'as it happened'. In the next section, I will provide a situated snapshot of the hashtags' emergence focusing on critical moments in the unfolding coverage of the events in *The Guardian* live coverage of the events. The analysis will tap into the linguistic forms and functions of hashtags in tweets as they become embedded in public writing practices. I'll be looking more specifically at (i) how hashtags emerge and circulate at a global scale, (ii) how the circulation of hashtags relates to modes of sharing as small stories, both online and offline, and (iii) in what respect such sharing practices can be considered to be part of mourning activity.

Drawing on small stories methods (see Chapter 3), I selected for analysis the live blog on the *Charlie Hebdo* attacks by *The Guardian* updated by Claire Phipps and Alexandra Topping (in London) and Tom McCarthy (in New York), which started on January 7, 2015, 11:20, and ended on January 8, 2015, 00:04. The live report covers eleven e-pages, in which thirty-three posts picked up from Twitter were embedded. One of these tweets, posted by Salman Rushdie and attracting thirty-five replies, was selected for further analysis as a tweet event, including, that is, the replies and conversations in response to it. Social media metrics, using social media tool Hashtagify, were also used to track the popularity of the hashtag and its association with other hashtags. Finally, a corpus of posts returned from hashtag searches for the keyword 'Je Suis Charlie' on Twitter was collected as supplementary data (January 7, 2016, circa 10,000 tweets) and "I am Charlie" (circa 302 tweets; January 7, 2016–March 3, 2016).

The analysis combines a metafunctional optic for the study of hashtags with a discourse trajectories lens informed by small story heuristics (Georgakopoulou, 2013, 2017). The metafunctional optic on hashtags (Zappavigna, 2015) draws attention to the linguistic functions of hashtags that work together to realize a social function of enacting ambient community at the following different though interrelated levels: (i) the *experiential* level, where tags are used as type, i.e. as 'same kind' post aggregators, (ii) the *interpersonal* level, where hashtags are used as evaluative meta-comments construing relationships and evaluative stances, and (iii) the *textual* level that relates to the organization of the post (e.g. hashtags functioning as a form of punctuation). This approach is used as a starting point to tap into hashtag functions in context, recognizing the integration of hashtags into the linguistic system as a linguistic unit with full grammar functions. Given that this approach proves less useful when considering the trajectories of hashtags and the dynamics of their circulation, a small stories research perspective is employed in the analysis to address questions of incipient narrativization and audience considerations. This approach emphasizes the incipience, transportability, and circulatability of events, the alignment/disalignment potential of digital sharing for negotiating participation frameworks, and the potential of small stories sharing for different kinds of identity and affective positioning (see Chapter 2).

The discussion is organized into three sections. The first section focuses on the level of selecting practices, looking at how the phrases 'Charlie Hebdo' and 'Je Suis Charlie' emerged as keywords in the context of the live news coverage of the events. The second section deals with the level of storying, considering how the hashtag #JeSuisCharlie is shaped as a reference shared story. It also deals with practices of positioning, examining the uses of the hashtag for encoding moral stances and positions of distance from or proximity to the events and those involved in them, both online and offline. The third section will discuss the place of hashtag mourning in mourning practices in the urban landscape.

Hashtag Storying

#CharlieHebdo as a Microstory Resource

Live-coverage blogs offer a rich site for studying hashtag selection practices in the context of breaking news stories that report on the events 'as they happen' and archive news 'as it happened'. *The Guardian* live coverage, in particular, often features tweets, filtered to fit the profile of its readers, at various points of the reporting timeline in a bid to enrich the report with local witness reports and reactions representing an array of public voices.

The Guardian's live coverage of the *Charlie Hebdo* events starts on January 7, 2015, 11:20, with a brief report on the attacks and ends on January 7, 2015, 00:04. It spans eleven e-pages and features thirty-three tweets in total. The majority of those tweets (7) are drawn from *The Guardian* correspondent in Paris, Kim Willsher and journalists from a range of agencies and organizations (13) as well as politicians (2), institutions (e.g. Elysée, U.S. embassy) news organizations (4), or Twitter users from around the world (2).

The majority of tweets (66.6%) included reference to *Charlie Hebdo* (or, in its short form, Charlie; in two tweets), while there fewer instances (21.2%) that included the hashtag #JeSuisCharlie. In particular, tweets at the start of the blog feature references to *Charlie Hebdo*, lacking any form of hashtag annotation altogether. The noun phrase 'Charlie Hebdo', referring to the magazine, recurs across these updates, which were posted within thirty-eight minutes from the start of the live blog (see Examples 1, 2, 3; emphasis added).

Example 1

*11:24 @MartinBoudot: Attaque en cours de deux hommes en cagoule dans les locaux **de Charlie Hebdo***. *On est refugié sur le toit [link to pic]*

[Translation: Attack by two men in balaclavas in the offices of *Charlie Hebdo*. People find refuge on the rooftop]

Example 2

*11:54 @kimwillhser1: Police say it was carnage 'a butchery' **inside Charlie Hebdo**.Can see police car riddled with bullets.*

Example 3

*11:58 @kimwillsher1: Police say there had been specific threats **against** Charlie Hebdo and other media recently.*

In the examples, the noun phrase *Charlie Hebdo* is selected as the topic of this breaking news story; it points to the satirical magazine and its staff, the offices where the *Charlie Hebdo* magazine is situated, as well as the place of the attack.

In other tweets embedded in the blog, a hashtag is appended to references to *Charlie Hebdo* (or its abbreviated form, 'Charlie'). With the exception of the first occurrence of the hashtag in a tweet posted within less than an hour of the events (Example 4), hashtagged uses of the noun phrase *Charlie Hebdo* appear in the form of a concatenated phrase (Examples 4–10). In the majority of these posts (Examples 4–6), hashtags are embedded in the grammatical structure of the post in the syntactic role of an adjunct, similarly to non-hashtagged uses of the keyword (Examples 1–4). They occupy either infix position (Examples 4 and 5) or suffix position (Example 6 and 7).

Example 4

11:45 a.m. @EliseBarthet: Les tireurs de #CharlieHebdo face a une voiture de police. Ils ont fait feu, les policiers ont replique puis recule [picture of the two shooters]
   [Translation: The shooters of #CharlieHebdo in front of a police vehicle. They fired, the police officers fired back then retreated]

Example 5

6:34 p.m. @BenQuinn75: Images from #charliehebdovigil in Trafalgar Sq. Cartoons & people holding pens [picture]

Example 6

1.22 p.m. @EliseBarthet: Des familles des victimes son accueillies dans l'immeuble qui fait face a #Charlie. [Picture of sign Accueil Familles]
   [Translation: Families of the victims are accommodated in the building opposite #Charlie]

Example 7

7:03 p.m. @LexyTopping: Camille Rousseau, a French student in London holds up the drawing she made to honour #charliehebdo. [picture of JeSuisCharlie].

Uses of the keyword in suffix position in some cases serve textual functions, explicitly adding a metacomment to the update, as in Examples 8–10:

Example 8

20:04 p.m. @Elysée: Le president @BarackObama a exprime au president @fhollande la solidarite des Etats-Unis #CharlieHebdo [picture of President Hollande on the phone]
   [Translation: President @BarackObama expressed the U.S.'s solidarity to President @fhollande]

Example 9

20:14 p.m. @fquairel: La une de @libe demain #CharlieHebdo
[image of Liberation's cover 'Nous sommes tous Charlie']
   [Translation: The cover of @libe tommorrow #CharlieHebdo]

Example 10

10:30 p.m. @sullduggery "An assault on democracy": Thursday @
guardian front page with former Le Monde editor Natalie Nou-
gayrede #charliehebdo [picture of Guardian cover]

In all the examples considered so far, the noun phrase *Charlie Hebdo*
is selected as the keyword for hashtagging, highlighting the key focus
of interest and rendering it into searchable and viewable content. Uses
of the hashtag #CharlieHebdo or #Charlie mark content as part of a
hyper-linked chain of updates relating to the attacks against *Charlie*
Hebdo, serving the experiential function of hashtags as same-kind post
aggregators.

The final set of examples (Examples 11–14[2]) illustrates less frequent
uses of the hashtag #CharlieHebdo in prefix position, all of which are
linked to *The Guardian*'s correspondent in Paris, Kim Willsher – with
the exception of one micropost broadcast by AFP (Agence France-Press).

Example 11

12:50 p.m. @kimwillsher1: #CharlieHebdo. It was press day at the
magazine so all important staff were there. Now 10 assassinated
along with 2 police officers.

Example 12

1:39 p.m. @kimwillsher1: #CharlieHebdoFrench Islamic leaders at
scene to condemn the attack. "They have hit us all. We are all victims.
These people are a minority".

Example 13

1:45 p.m. @afp: #CharlieHebdo: Charb, Wolinski, Cabu et Tignous
sont morts u.afp.com/Rse #AFP.
   [Translation: @afp: #CharlieHebdo: Charb, Wolinksi, Cabu and
Tignous are dead]

Example 14

3:59 p.m. @kimwillsher1 #CharlieHebdo funeral services vans have
just arrived at scene.

In these examples, posted within the first five hours from the launch of the blog, the hashtag #CharlieHebdo appears in non-concatenated form. It is used as an opening frame to each individual micropost, which adds to the accumulating breaking news story. Placing the keyword at the start of the tweet also foregrounds the story as a shared story that journalists are already reporting on. In functional terms, the use of the hashtag, here, is related to the organization of the micropost text, opening the post and marking its content as part of a chain of related posts on the same topic.

The type of hashtag practice noted earlier, which moves from the non-hashtagged use of a keyword that captures the main topic of the breaking news reporting to its hashtagged fronting, echoes Nate Ritter's live citizen reporting of the San Diego wildfires back in 2007, which prefigured the uptake of hashtags on Twitter for connecting breaking news to those concerned. In the initial posts, Ritter referred to the 'San Diego fire' and offered related updates (see Example 15). Then his friend Chris Messina, who was, at the time, looking to show the world the potential of hashtags, suggested to him to use the hashtag #sandiegofire (even though that wasn't the most popular hashtag related to the wildfires used on Flickr or the ideal form of a hashtag). However, given that it was the keyword Ritter was using across his live reporting from the ground, it was selected as the tag that had the best chance to be widely adopted and be recognizable in a stream of updates (Messina, 2007). Ritter adopted the hashtag, appending it to the fronted topic of his updates (see Example 16). Even though the hashtag didn't become as popular as other hashtags since, it is now part of the history of the hashtag and the growth of Twitter hashtag communication in emergency coordination and disaster relief (Messina, 2007). About ten years after the use of hashtags by citizen journalists, similar practices of hashtag selection based on their potential for wide adoption as well as for their recognizability in a stream of updates are an integral part of professional journalists reporting live via Twitter.

Example 15

3:03 a.m. @nateritter: San Diego fire: Current highway closures include: N-bound l-15 (between 56–78). 76 to 79, S-bound l-15 from scales to Mercy Road [Oct. 23, 2007]

Example 16

3:29 a.m. @nateritter: #sandiegofire Mandatory evacuation for Harbison Canyon and Crest [Oct. 23, 2007]

This snapshot of a phase of the emergence of the hashtag 'Charlie Hebdo' showcases key aspects of its selection as a keyword in breaking news updates. First of all, its recurrent use in early updates highlights the focus of updates and creates coherence across posts; its use as a coherence device makes it more likely to be recognized and thus searched for, viewed, and shared. By making part of a cumulative chain of tweet-bite size updates, updates from a single user or multiple users become part of a shared story in the making.

This section will turn to the emergence of the #JeSuisCharlie hashtag in *The Guardian*'s live blog and beyond.

Sharing #JeSuisCharlie as a Reference Small Story

In *The Guardian*'s live blog on the *Charlie Hebdo* attacks, the hashtag #JeSuisCharlie appears far less frequently compared to the instances of the hashtag #CharlieHebdo (in 21.2% of the tweets embedded in the blog, as mentioned).

The hashtag originated in a tweet by Joachim Roncin,[3] a designer working in an office situated very near to the offices of the *Charlie Hebdo* magazine, posted shortly after the news of the attack broke, at 11:52 a.m. In the live news blog, the first update in which the hashtag #JeSuisCharlie features is broadcast just seven minutes after the tweet was shared on Joachim Roncin's account (see Example 17).

Example 17

11:59 a.m. @titi1960 **#JESUISCHARLIE** [pic of logo]

Embedding this tweet so quickly after it was first posted attests to the immediate and fast-paced sharing of the hashtag on Twitter, including mainstream reporting outlets, such as *The Guardian*. The tweet is one of the few posts on the live blog posted by a Twitter user with no formal link to professional networks of journalists. Its embedding in the live feed suggests an attempt to include voices that encode a wider public reaction to the events that is developing in parallel to the journalistic coverage of the events.

In other cases, the hashtag #JeSuisCharlie was found to co-occur with hashtagged uses of #CharlieHebdo (Examples 18–20). These tweets attest to the emergence of additional symbolic meanings relating to the attack against *Charlie Hebdo*. One tweet, for example, cites the proverb 'the pen is mightier than the sword',[4] pointing to the power of the pencil and writing to defeat any gunman and violence more generally (Example 18).

Example 18

1:19 p.m. @shumylaj: ***The pen is mightier than the sword, and the cowards were afraid of it. So don't stop writing.*** *#JeSuisCharlie #CharlieHebdo.*

The trope of the pencil as a weapon turned into one of the main symbols of defiance against terrorist acts and was featured in tribute cartoons to the journalists at *Charlie Hebdo* (BBC, 2015, Jan. 9). The symbol was also taken to the streets, with demonstrators holding small or large pencils aloft, sometimes alongside the phrase 'Je Suis Charlie'.

Twittering voices from the ground in *The Guardian*'s blog were found to blend with voices from select public figures, such as that of novelist Sir Salman Rushdie. His concise tweet (see Example 19) includes the hashtag #JeSuisCharlie as an accompaniment to a short statement he shared via Twitter on behalf of PEN, in which he condemns the attacks and defends the art of satire (EnglishPEN, 2015). The tweet event created around this post will be discussed in more detail later in this chapter.

Example 19

3:08 p.m. @*SalmanRushdie*: *#JeSuisCharlie* [link to PEN statement]

Finally, the live blog picks up a tweet from Twitter data reporting on the huge impact of the hashtag #JeSuisCharlie on Twitter, quickly rising to 2.1 million shared tweets and retweets on the day of the attacks (see Example 20) and to 5 million tweets the next day (source: Twitter Data 2015).[5] The impressive and fast-paced sharing of the hashtag led to claims that this was one of the most popular tweets in the history of Twitter (MailOnline, 2015).

Example 20

23:29 p.m. @*Twitter Data: By 7.15 p.m., Paris time, there had been 2.1m Tweets for #JeSuisCharlie* (via @**TwitterFrance**).

In all the examples considered in this section, hashtagged uses of the phrase Je Suis Charlie feature the phrase in the standard hashtag format, as a concatenated string of words with capital letters marking word boundaries (#JeSuisCharlie). According to the search results from Hashtagify, this is the most popular spelling variant in which the hashtag has been used, indicating a preference for the digitally most readable version (see Figure 6.1).

Uses of the hashtag in suffix position further indicate that the hashtag can also fulfil a textual function, serving as a form of punctuation to the tweet. Unlike uses of the hashtag #CharlieHebdo, however, uses of #JeSuisCharlie in the blog did not make part of the unfolding breaking news story, given that the tweets they were embedded in did not provide additional information or further details about the attacks. This suggests that uses of the hashtag were not associated, here, with experiential functions but mainly served interpersonal functions, orienting to an *ad hoc*

Spelling Variants Used

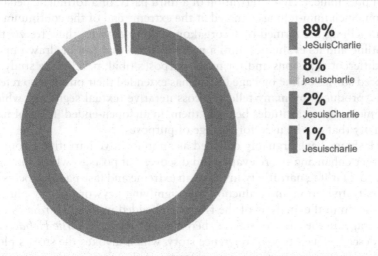

89%
JeSuisCharlie

8%
jesuischarlie

2%
JesuisCharlie

1%
Jesuischarlie

Figure 6.1 Hashtagify results for spelling variants of hashtag 'Je Suis Charlie'
Source: Search results retrieved on Jan. 22, 2019.

community banding and bonding around sentiment of solidarity (Yang et al., 2012).

The hashtag 'Je Suis Charlie', expressed in the concise form of a stand-alone utterance that intertextually invokes Stanley Kubrick's 'I am Spartacus,' Robert Kennedy's 'Ich bin ein Berliner', and 'We are all Americans' following the September 11, 2001, attacks, encodes a personalized and at the same time portable stance to the attack, which is shared as an evaluative metacomment to the story. Its short and memorable format expressed in a declarative statement, which asserts an (empty) subject's position in the affirmative has proved apt as a recognizable slogan, facilitating its reiteration as a sloganized, portable hashtag tribute through which networked users have connected.

Looking beyond the metafunctional dimensions into its narrative dimensions, the hashtag #JeSuisCharlie can also be viewed as a special type of *shared story*. Shared stories refer to mini-tellings in face-to-face interactions among peers, which feature a narrative skeleton, i.e. a brief reference to or reminder about the main events and their resolution, and mainly capitalizing on the point or evaluation of those events (Georgakopoulou, 2007, pp. 50–56). Shared stories are often used to highlight the point of the tale in the moment of telling and to draw up analogies to what is currently happening or what may happen in the future (ibid, p. 51). Some of these mini-tellings, especially of less recent events, gain emblematic status after a series of retellings, which result in the gradual de-narrativization or reduction of the stories to a bare minimum of a reference that is typically brief, frequently one line long, and takes the form of a punchline, a characterization of a third party, or a formulaic personation. Such mini-tellings situated at the extreme end of the continuum of mini-tellings are termed by Georgakopoulou *references*; they 'freeze' the plotline and its evaluation into a portable form that can be drawn upon in different occasions and for many purposes (ibid, p. 53). The study of shared stories online by Page (2018) has extended their purview to retellings, produced by many tellers, across iterative textual segments, which promote shared attitudes between them, in an 'open-ended' form of narrativity that can be used for a range of purposes.

Hashtags have arguably emerged as an innovative narrative resource, further enhancing the relevance and discovery of posts to which they are added. Hashtag narrativity involves an extreme and fast-paced process of de-narrativization and reduction to a signifying keyword or key phrase, as shown in the analysis of the tweets embedded in *The Guardian*'s live coverage. In the case considered, here, the key phrase *Charlie Hebdo* can be described as a type of reference story, which invokes the story's plotline in an extremely reduced summation of the name of the magazine, the target, and place of the attack as well as the cartoonists-victims of the attacks selected as the main focus. The slogan 'Je Suis Charlie' is a different type of reference story, in that it does not feature a plotline but rather sums up and 'freezes' the point of the story in the form of a portable evaluation, which is recontextualizable and can be drawn upon as an emblem of solidarity to band and bond users around a shared sense of solidarity.

The narrative function of hashtags is further highlighted in cases when more than one hashtag are appended to a tweet in a line clearly separated from the main body of the message (even though this practice goes against Twitter's recommendation to avoid using more than two hashtags, Twitter, n.d.). The sequential ordering of hashtagged key words can result (more or less consciously) in a mini-narrative, which is searchable and retrievable as part of a bigger shared story online. An example of this type of hashtag narrativity is offered in Example 21, posted in January 7, 2019, four years after the attacks, the fronting of key phrase '*Charlie Hebdo*' invokes the bare skeleton of the story alluding to the events at the *Charlie Hebdo* offices, while the key phrases 'Paris attacks', 'January 7' that follow it provide additional orientation information about the place and time of the events. Finally, the hashtagged slogan 'Je Suis Charlie' emphasizes the main point of the story. It is used as an evaluative device and an affective positioning resource, allowing sharers to claim their personal involvement in the story as the condition of public participation in the story.

Example 21

@CtrlSec, Jan 7: *Always in our mind and in our heart. We don't forget* [French flag emoji]
   #CharlieHebdo #ParisAttack #January7 #JeSuisCharlie

The continued appeal of the hashtags #CharlieHebdo and #JeSuisCharlie with related hashtags that contextualize the shared story and the portable stance they invoke in each case is evident in social metrics data from 2016, one year after the attack, and comparable data from 2019, four years after the attack. In 2016, #JeSuisCharlie was found to be in close association with hashtags relating to the main event and its victims, e.g. *Charlie Hebdo*, Paris Shooting, or additional orientational information, e.g. Paris, France. It was also associated with hashtags about related street rallies, e.g. Marche Republicaine or media sources, e.g. AFP (Associated French Press), and evaluative stances either generalizing the personalized stance into 'Nous Sommes Charlie' (trans. 'We are Charlie') or directed to expressions of solidarity with the dead police officer (see Figure 6.2).

In 2019, the association of the hashtag with *Charlie Hebdo* remains popular (see Figure 4.3), even though at a lower level compared to 2016 (see Figure 4.2). Additional associations which have developed over time include associations to the date of the attacks, e.g. 7 janvier 2015, reorienting the focus from references to place to reference to the time of the events, marking a date for commemoration. The emphasis of these associations to commemoration is further attested in the hashtags '4ansdeja' (4 years already), '4ans' (4 years) and 'ToujoursCharlie' (Always Charlie). Other terror attacks, such as the van attack on April 24, 2018, in Toronto that resulted in the death of ten pedestrians, also come to be associated with the hashtag #JeSuisCharlie, extending the symbolic value of the hashtag to similar attacks across the world.

Uses of hashtags #jesuistoronto and #jesuistorontois in Example 22 attest to the widening of the scope of the expression 'je suis' in the subsequent months after the attacks and until the present moment, to an extent that it has now acquired a more general meaning associated with mourning, solidarity, or alignment.

Example 22

@KenVanhoecke: *#jesuischarlie #jesuistoronto #jesuistorontois #jesuisalek #jesuismotherfucker* @Toronto. Ontario [link to Instagram] (April 24)

The hashtag was used, for example, in the wake of other terror attacks, as in the case of 'Je Suis Ankara' referring to the bomb attacks in Ankara in October 2015, or the case of 'Je suis Orlando' in 2016, expressing

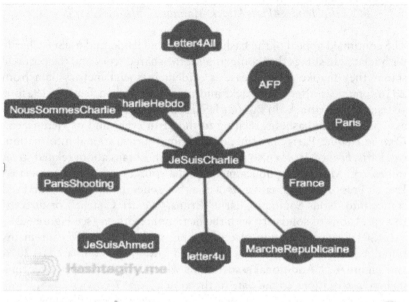

#JeSuisCharlie: Top 10 Related Hashtags

#JeSuisCharlie
Popularity: 69.1 W -3.7 M -3.7

Figure 6.2 Top 10 related hashtags to #JeSuisCharlie, 2016
Source: Hashtagify, 2019.

solidarity with the victims of the terrorist attack in the gay nightclub Pulse in Orlando, Florida. In Example 10, the fronting of the portable hashtag stance #JeSuisCharlie in a sequence of Je Suis-ims sets the tone for this message of solidarity with the victims and the sarcastic use of "Je Suis Alec' referring to the attacker Alek Minassian built up cumulatively through the sequencing of hashtags.

The discussion has so far foregrounded the close links between the type of hashtag keyword or key phrase, the type of content shared, the metafunction, and small story type that can be arguably gleaned from a focus on different key phases of the hashtag's circulation. The examination of the occurrences of the hashtags #CharlieHebdo and #JeSuisCharlie in the tweets featured in the live blog of *The Guardian* showed their different metafunctions and narrative functions. The hashtag #CharlieHebdo was found to serve experiential functions in the context of

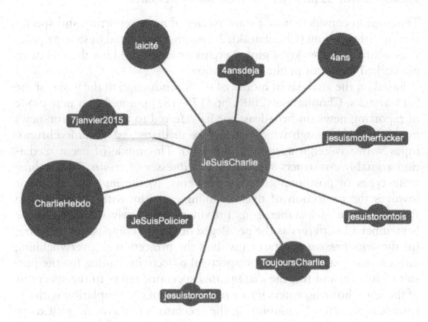

Figure 6.3 Top 10 related hashtags to #JeSuisCharlie, 2019
Source: Hashtagify, 2019.

breaking news updates aggregating content relating to the events' news coverage, while the hashtag #JeSuisCharlie was found to serve interpersonal functions, encoding and (re)sharing a personalized evaluative stance to the events. Both hashtags were described as a special type of shared small story, a reference story, which in the case of #CharlieHebdo invoked the plotline reduced in its bare essentials. The hashtag #JeSuisCharlie invoked the main point or evaluation of the story, 'frozen' as a portable stance, allowing its meaning to widen both semantically and narratively. It was also suggested that the sequencing of hashtags emerges as an important dimension of narrative meaning making in microposts, which form an integral part of the hashtags' extension of semiotic and narrative scope.

The next section turns to the close analysis of three tweet events – two taken from *The Guardian*'s blog and an additional one taken from Twitter – attending to the specific participation positions afforded by the sharing of the hashtag #JeSuisCharlie. It shows how the hashtag, in addition to a portable stance 'frozen' into a reference story, is also an affective positioning resource, which prompts displays of alignment or disalignment, extending 'spectatorships of suffering' into *ad hoc* mourning publics.

#JeSuisCharlie as an Affective Positioning Resource

This section considers how extant modes of news reporting and spectatorships of suffering (Chouliaraki, 2006) are remediated in sharing practices online in the wake of global events or crises and how they relate to networked modes of public participation.

Based on the analysis of modes of news production in the wake of the 9/11 attacks, Chouliaraki (2006, pp. 179–181) pointed to a new mode of reporting news on broadcast media referred to as the 'ecstatic news mode' in and through which events are mediated as "ecstatic chronotopes with sovereign agency" (ibid: 159). This mode of event mediation arguably constructs spectators as *witnesses of events* cast in three main types of positionings to those events: (i) the *involved* spectator involves the projection of overwhelming empathy with the victims in the space-time of instantaneous proximity, selectively singling out the September 11 sufferers as the privileged objects of compassion and care; (ii) the *omnipresent* spectator involves the projection of overwhelming anger in the space-time of a-perspectival objectivity, calling for the pursuit of justice; and (iii) the *distantiated* spectator refers to the spectator of the long shot who enters into a relationship of contemplation with the spectacle of suffering, mobilizing the spectator's fantasy and reflexivity in the space-time of the sublime and promoting a reflective stance on the events.

The wide circulation of the hashtag #JeSuisCharlie attests to the social mediatization of the ecstatic news mode described earlier, indicating a shift from spectatorships of suffering to affective publics of mediatized suffering and ad hoc mourning publics. This ecstatic sharing is further facilitated by poly-languaging in the hashtag spaces in 'big' languages, such as English, Spanish, and Arabic, accentuating sameness in difference and attesting to the worldwide reach of the message (see Giaxoglou, 2018). To clarify the nature of this mode of mediatized experiencing of global events, I will draw on the concept of narrative stancetaking, which implies a choice of the affective position of a 'teller' with a specific point of view to the events and characters of the referred events. This discourse identity has implications for networked audience participation roles: the teller proposes a specific understanding of the events and characters rendering certain audience responses (e.g. retweeting, replying, or recontextualizing) more relevant than others (Georgakopoulou, 2015). Applied to the case of the hashtag #JeSuisCharlie, it is suggested that its broad circulation is a case of *ecstatic sharing*, which is indexical of the user's narrative stance as *a mediated witness of suffering* orienting to certain audiences more than others and projecting specific types of the affective self.

Three examples of #JeSuisCharlie used as evaluative devices in a reference small story will serve as key illustrations of the different narrative stances and their associated type of affective positioning as a mediated witness of suffering, which emerge in the context of its global circulation.

The first example is the tweet of Joachim Roncin. The tweet involves the resemiotization of the media slogan 'Nous sommes tous Americains' ('We are all Americans'), which had appeared on the cover of the French journal *Le Monde* in the wake of the 9/11 attacks. In this case, the resemiotization is adapted to the affordances of Twitter as a personal broadcasting tool through the shift from first person plural 'nous' to first person singular 'Je'. The narrative stance encoded in the hashtag is co-articulated with its intertextual resonances of national solidarity in Western contexts, where an attack 'at home' challenges Western citizens' feelings of safety from war and armed conflict. At the same time, this use of the hashtag encodes proximity to the victims and the place of the attacks and hence contributes to the evocation of ecstatic feelings. The foregrounding of the magazine in both the slogan and the choice of typeface projects an overwhelming empathy with the victims in a space and time of instantaneous proximity and selectively (even if not intentionally) singles out the cartoonists-journalists sufferers as the privileged objects of compassion and care. Based on this, it is suggested that the slogan encodes an *involved narrative stance* and invites agreement with the shared values it encodes through reiterative sharing (e.g. through retweeting or posting on other platforms) without any further critical reflection or elaboration. This involved position is re-enacted in tweets that contribute pictures from rallies, vigils, and protests around the world that create a kind of experiential backchannel to events and marches across France and other European countries. This type of sharing is typical of what is termed here an *ecstatic mode of sharing* in the here and now, which contributes to the reproduction of evaluative stances to the events and amplifies the flow of high levels of emotion.

The second example is the tweet of Salman Rushdie's appropriation of the hashtag used as a caption and pointer to his tribute written in PEN in response to the events. In this case, there's a notable shift from the involved narrative stance to a stance that involves elaboration of the key, shared assumptions. In the tweet in question, Salman Rushdie 'speaks out' his reaction to the events and foregrounds his own stance to what's happening revolving around the denunciation of religion and the defence of free speech. In this respect, Rushdie's message cross-linking to his statement can be said to encode an *omnipresent stance*, characterized by overwhelming indignation and anger expressed in the time of a-perspectival objectivity that requires the denunciation of religious totalitarianism and calls for "fearless disrespect of religion" (EnglishPEN, 2015). It also abstracts from the here and now of the attacks and moves attention to its broader, symbolic importance, contributing to the emblematization of the hashtag as a symbol of the defence of free speech.

Example 23

7 Jan, 03:05 p.m. @Salman Rushdie #JeSuisCharlie [link to PEN statement]

> PEN Statement: "Religion, a mediaeval form of unreason, when combined with modern weaponry becomes a real threat to our freedoms. This religious totalitarianism has caused a deadly mutation in the heart of Islam and we see the tragic consequences in Paris today. I stand with Charlie Hebdo, as we all must, to defend the art of satire, which has always been a force for liberty and against tyranny, dishonesty and stupidity. 'Respect for religion' has become a code phrase meaning 'fear of religion'. Religions, like all other ideas, deserve criticism, satire, and, yes, our fearless disrespect".

The post received 1,382 retweets, 612 Favorite clicks, and 19 replies from January 7 to January 10 (excluding retweets that included the addressivity marker @Salman Rushdie). By appending an extended statement voicing concerns over religion and free speech, the tweet also prompted individual replies and comments (see Examples 24–26) and invited the opening up of a public conversation.

Example 24

Thank you Mr Rushdie. It is a great pity Christopher Hitchens is not physically with us to add his polemical anger to your gentler, but still effective, statement. We are all Charlie now.

Example 25

We are all Charlie. Condemn stupid religion.

Example 26

We are all Charlie. Hey world, no more try to deny brutality of Muhammed soldiers. No more compromising with the islamists for economy reasons.

As the examples show, the omnipresent stance prompts affiliative replies in which users affirm their belongingness to the networked affiliative public united in solidarity with the victims of the attack ('We are all Charlie'). In their replies, users are also seen to rework and selectively amplify key aspects of the author's interpretation of the events, calling forth and legitimating a specific course of action (e.g. 'condemn stupid religion', 'no more compromising with the islamists').

Finally, the third narrative stance, that of the distantiated or reflexive spectator, emerged at the same time as the hashtag #JeSuisCharlie was trending, with the appearance of hashtags such as #JeSuisAhmed, articulating the position of the Muslim dead police officer (the twelfth person killed at the attack) and #JeNeSuisPasCharlie, giving voice to diverse positions on free speech, Western attitudes to Islam, Islamophobia, and so on. Such stances arguably reflect attempts to move beyond the instantaneously expressed overwhelming empathy or the emotionally charged pursuit of justice and to draw attention, instead, to the paradoxes inherent in the construction and solidification of Western identity. By asserting 'Je ne suis pas Charlie' and 'I am not Charlie', users reflectively point to the exclusionary nature of the identification performed in the sharing of the hashtag #JeSuisCharlie and call attention to the need to assess and re-evaluate the underlying premises of ecstatic identification with Charlie from one's own narrative-affective position. This type of reflective narrative stance invites further and diversified (re)appropriations of the slogan across different contexts.

Reactions to the attacks at the offices of the *Charlie Hebdo* magazine arguably illustrate a new mode of collectively and emotionally historicizing and experiencing tragic events at a global scale through hashtag mourning, a particular mode of sharing on social media. This mode involves acts of narrative stance taking in the space-time of instantaneous proximity. The positions afforded through such acts fall largely within three different types:

i. reflexive identification with sufferers
ii. omnipresent stances encoding demands for the pursuit of justice
iii. reflexive stances challenging presumably shared assumptions and beliefs

Similarly to the 9/11 attacks, which marked a shift to ecstatic modes of news reporting that gave rise to universal moral stances and legitimized certain courses of political action (e.g. the war against terror), hashtag mourning in the wake of the *Charlie Hebdo* attacks marked a shift to ecstatic modes of sharing, creating dividing lines of identification and giving rise to both legitimizing and critical moral stances. This ecstatic mode of sharing global news and reactions attests to the emergence of social tagging as a contemporary and emerging form of discourse (Lee, 2018) and of public modes of participation as a mode of mediatized witnessing of global events and crises through practices of hashtag mourning.

Ecstatic Sharing in Affective Landscapes

The ecstatic sharing of reactions to the breaking news story of the attack at *Charlie Hebdo* shows the inter-connections between traditional media, social media, and semiotic landscapes (see Seargeant and Giaxoglou, forthcoming). Tweets broadcast live from Paris were recontextualized in mainstream media coverage of the events. The hashtag #JeSuisCharlie was reshared on Twitter but also on Facebook and Instagram; it gave rise to cartoon tributes shared online and adorning walls on the streets of Paris. The very phenomenon of this ecstatic sharing became the topic of media articles and discussions on TV and broadcasting media. On the day of the attack, an image was circulated on Instagram and shared by more than 100,000 people under a fake Bansky account, even though the original creator-illustrator was the next day revealed to be Lucille Clerc (The Independent, 2015).

During the day of the attack, both the logo and hashtag migrated from Twitter onto the streets of cities in France in personalized placards held up by demonstrators. Images of people holding these placards were then remediated on social media, accompanied by messages re-using the hashtag as a metadiscursive marker and tagging the message as part of a developing backchannel to people's rallies on the ground which remediated the experience of 'being there'. The slogan also became part of the physical landscape, featuring as a sticker and graffiti on the monument of the Place de la République, as well as on walls, trains, and beaches across France: a mural of *Charlie Hebdo* cartoonist Cabu in Haute-Savoie signed by tagger 463; the slogan 'Je Suis Charlie' in a street wall in Nice, Bois-Colombe, and other cities; the phrase 'Vive Charlie Hebdo' tagged on an SNFC train or simply 'Charlie' written in red and followed by a heart in La Reunion; the tag 'JeSuisCharlie' next to a pencil dripping blood by graffiti artist DZIA at the Belgian gare d'Anvers-Luchtbal, and tags 'Charlie' and 'JeSuisCharlie' around Shoreditch quickly emerged as testimonies to the event (Le Figaro, 2015, Jan. 9). The logo 'JeSuisCharlie' written in white letters against a black background, seemed to have invaded the screens, the streets, the restaurant menus – even schoolchildren had the letter C written on their hands. Global stars like George Clooney also took part in the spectacle, closing his Globe Awards speech with the slogan and wearing a 'JeSuisCharlie' badge on his tuxedo, while his wife Amal Alamuddin had hers pinned on her Christian Dior clutch bag (The Guardian, 2015).

These different creative acts point to the transmedia poly-storying possibilities this media event offers for bringing together different plots and for users' multiple modes of participation in them (Georgakopoulou and Giaxoglou, 2018). They can also be seen on a par with the vigils, memorials, and rallies held in the aftermath of the attacks as spontaneous vernacular shrines, which take an ever-diversifying range of forms. Their function is similar to the function of (semi)-public sites for public mourning, whereby collectivized grief is performed, calling for unity in the face of safety threats 'at home'. They create affective spaces which demand public attention and invite members of the public to take up participant positions as spectators or witnesses to what becomes a shared, public history of the event (Seargeant and Giaxoglou, forthcoming).

The articulation of the slogan in these different modalities extended further the semiotic scope of the slogan so that it very rapidly turned into a meme, i.e. a shared cultural reference and public sign of solidarity and alignment shaped as much as shaping affective publics within and beyond Paris. This pragmatic and semiotic extension of the expression attests to moments of heightened interconnectivity between traditional media, social media, and landscapes through which local events are 'up-scaled' to global events, creating super-spectacles that spread across modalities, platforms, contexts, and people. This phenomenon attests to the way social media overlaps and interconnects with traditional broadcast and print media, as well as physical spaces of gathering (see also Kavada, 2018), in a "close choreography between traditional and new forms of communications technology" (Seargeant and Monaghan, 2017, n.p.).

Despite their seemingly ephemeral nature, transmedial discourse assemblages are organized as moments of stancetaking in the here and now or *narrative stancetaking* (Georgakopoulou, 2013, 2017), which invite audiences to take up affective positions of more or less distant witnesses to key events and align or disalign themselves to already-circulating stances. Importantly, they also contribute to shaping the direction of discourses about particular events and issues by sedimenting particular types of affective positionings to the events and to select victims, hence increasing the visibility of certain privileged voices in physical and (social) media landscapes.

For some, this mode of ecstatic and transmedia sharing was an instance of mass hysteria. As Todd (2015, pp. 15–16) noted, in these early days of January 2015, a critical analysis of the events, their reception, and their fast-paced up-scaling into a global spectacle of media, social media but also national and supranational communion, was beyond bounds. This excluded, for example, a number of important points that such a critical analysis would raise, including among others the unnecessary conflation of condemning the terrorist act and deifying *Charlie Hebdo*, the distraction of the public debate from an analysis of the global jamming of Islam into the contemporary West or the risk of government-backed mass demonstrations at glorifying brothers Kouachi. Importantly and for what concerns us here, the ecstatic experiencing of the events led to a 'demand mode' for everyone to pronounce the ritual formulation 'JeSuisCharlie' as a synonym with 'JeSuisFrancais' (I am French; ibid, pp. 11–12). Todd's critical angle on the events and their reception in his country are important to bear in mind in order to avoid an over-celebratory tone when considering the role of social media and mass mobilizations. His call for a sharper critical perspective echoes other scholars' acknowledgement that the repetition of frozen concepts falls short in a world of flux and violence (Sreberny, 2016).

Since the attacks at the *Charlie Hebdo* offices in 2015, the expression 'je suis' has turned into an emblem of social identity (De Cock and

Pizarro Pedraza, 2018, p. 209) which selects and privileges particular types of positionings of alignment to shared values. At the same time, this homophiliac mobilization prompts counter-pronouncements of disalignment to such identities. Statements like 'Je ne suis pas Charlie' or 'I am not Charlie' or 'Not in my name' reject the proposed social identities in reaction to what many viewed as an empty expression reducing really complex issues or in an attempt to mark distance from *Charlie Hebdo*'s satirical humour, which is seen by some as offensive.

Summary

This chapter has considered mass death events in attacks 'at home' which mobilize performances of mourning at a national and global scale and result in their emblematization as symbols of national identity and global solidarity. The examination of the case study of reactions to *Charlie Hebdo* showed how the attack turned into an emblematic event, whereby ecstatic news modes that emerged in the live broadcasting of the 9/11 attacks were reconfigured into modes of ecstatic sharing of affective reactions, described here under the umbrella term *hashtag mourning*.

This form of mourning is an activity of poly-storying death events, whereby hashtags emerge as shared reference stories, i.e. reduced, de-narrativized plotlines keyed to place names or the key event's date and 'frozen', portable assessments of the events. Hashtag mourning encompasses tributes on social media walls but also on street walls and the broader semiotic landscape, attesting to the interconnected ways in which the semiotic scope of signs and affective indexes is extended and up-scaled. Hashtags, as well as public spaces and semiotic artefacts, are used to demarcate *places of affect*, bringing into relief specific types of narratives along with participant positions of alignment or disalignment to discourses already in circulation about key events (see also Seargeant and Giaxoglou, forthcoming).

The focus on key phases of the circulation of the hashtags #CharlieHebdo and #JeSuisCharlie attending to practices of selection shed light into their different metafunctions. Attention to the styling of these hashtags in tweets pointed to their association with other hashtags in narratively oriented sequences and recognized them as the key ingredients of the social-mediatized emplotment and poly-storying of the attacks as moments of narrative stancetaking. This means that hashtags were not just used to mark content as searchable and viewable aggregating content; they were mainly used as affective positioning resources affording sharers the 'right' to participate in the unfolding story in positions of the involved, reflexive, or omnipresent witness. The consideration of positioning practices suggests that this form of mediated experiencing of mass death marks a shift from the rather passive witnessing roles afforded to television's 'spectators of suffering' to roles and positions of mediated witnesses of events who take the position of a more or less distant witness to spectacular death. This shift needs to be seen as part of a broader normalization of memorialization acts and the instrumentalization of mourning for rallying (social) media attention around public narratives about an event or issue while leaving others in the shadow.

Conclusion

The type of digital mourning examined in this chapter attests to phenomena of *connective mourning* (see van Dijk, 2013), whereby witnessing death and mourning is becoming subject to media and social media logics.

This chapter extends attention to practices of mourning as a form of affective engagement with the news and adds to our empirical understanding of public participation online afforded by different types of affective positioning as a form of proximal or distant witnessing to spectacular death.

The next chapter will turn to the death of the Other and consider the way positions of intimacy, proximity, or distance to death are negotiated through particular kinds of social media- and narratively afforded resources in image-based stories.

Notes

1. On the app store the description of Twitter is the following: "From breaking news and entertainment to sports, politics, and everyday interests, when it happens in the world, it happens on Twitter first. See all sides of the story. Join the conversation. Watch live streaming events. Twitter is what's happening in the world and what people are talking about right now".
2. Examples are cited in the actual chronological order in which they were posted.
3. In an interview, Joachim Roncin said he didn't intend the post to get viral, and he felt that the message doesn't belong to him but rather to the whole world (Huffington Post, 2016).
4. The proverb is attributed to novelist and playwright Edward Bulwer-Lytton. In his historical play *Cardinal Richelieu*, written in 1839, Cardinal Richelieu upon finding out a plot to kill him says *"The pen is mightier than the sword . . . Take away the sword; States can be saved without it!"*. The expression had gained currency among English speakers by the 1840s (BBC, 2015, Jan. 9).
5. The quoted numbers do not include the tweets that featured the slogan without making use of the hashtag.

References

Androutsopoulos, J. (2014) Moments of sharing: Entextualization and linguistic repertoires in social networking. *Journal of Pragmatics* (Special Issue on Pragmatics of Participation in the New Media) 73: 4–18.

BBC (Gee, A.) (2015) Who first said 'The pen is mightier than the sword'? BBC News, 9 January 2015. Available at: https://www.bbc.co.uk/news/magazine-30729480. Accessed: 11 April 2020.

BBC (Devichand, M.) (2016) How the world was changed by the slogan "Je Suis Charlie". *BBC Trending*, Jan. 3. Available at: www.bbc.co.uk/news/blogs-trending-35108339. Accessed: 20 Jan. 2019.

Boltanski, L. (1999) *Distant Suffering: Morality, Media and Politics.* Cambridge: Cambridge University Press.

Bruns, A. and J. Burgess (2011) #ausvotes: How Twitter *covered the 2010 Australian Federal Election. Communication, Politics & Culture* 44 (2): 37–56.

Champeau, G. (2016) Les hashtags de plus en plus déposés comme marque commerciale. *NUMERAMA* [online magazine]. Available at: www.numerama.com/business/154174-hashtags-de-plus-plus-deposes-marque-commerciale.html. Accessed: 10 July 2016.

Chouliaraki, L. (2006) *The Spectatorship of Suffering.* London: Sage Publications.

CNN (2018) 2015 Charlie Hebdo attacks fast facts. *CNN Library*, Dec. 24. Available at: https://edition.cnn.com/2015/01/21/europe/2015-paris-terror-attacks-fast-facts/index.html. Accessed: 20 Jan. 2019.

Cunha, E., G. Magno, G. Comarela, V. Almeida, M.A. Goncalves, and F. Benevento (2011) Analyzing the dynamic evolution of hashtags on Twitter: A language-based approach. *Proceedings of the Workshop on Language in Social Media* (LSM 2011), Portland, Oregon, June 23, pp. 58–65.

De Cock, B. and A. Pizarro Pedraza (2018) From expressing solidarity to mocking on Twitter: Pragmatic functions of hashtags starting with #jesuis across languages. *Language in Society* 47 (2): 197–217.

EnglishPEN (2015) PEN condemns savage attack on French satirical magazine, Charlie Hebdo. *EnglishPEN*, 7 January 2015. Available at: https://www.englishpen.org/campaigns/pen-condemns-savage-attack-on-french-satirical-magazine-charlie-hebdo/. Accessed: 11 April 2020.

EnglishPEN (2015) Salman Rushdie condemns attack on Charlie Hebdo. *EnglishPen*, 7 January 2015. Available at: https://www.englishpen.org/campaigns/salman-rushdie-condemns-attack-on-charlie-hebdo/. Accessed: 11 April 2020.

Fuchs, C. (2014) *Social Media: A Critical Introduction.* London: Sage Publications.

Georgakopoulou, A. (2007) *Small Stories, Interaction and Identities.* Amsterdam and Philadelphia: John Benjamins Publishing Company.

Georgakopoulou, A. (2013) Small stories research & social media: The role of narrative stance-taking in the circulation of a Greek news story. *Working Papers in Urban Language & Literacies* 100: 1–18, King's College London.

Georgakopoulou, A. (2015) Sharing as rescripting: Place manipulations on YouTube between narrative and social media affordances, *Discourse, Context & Media* (Special Issue on Communicating Time and Place on Digital Media, edited by A. Georgakopoulou) 9: 64–72.

Georgakopoulou, A. (2017) Narrative/life of the moment: From telling a story to taking a narrative stance. In Schiff, B., E. McKim, and S. Patron (Eds.), *Life and Narrative: The Risks and Responsibilities of Storying Experience.* Oxford: Oxford University Press, pp. 29–52.

Georgakopoulou, A. and K. Giaxoglou (2018) Emplotment in the social mediatization of the economy: The poly-storying of economist Yanis Varoufakis. *Language@Internet* 16, Article 6: 1–15.

Giaxoglou, K. (2015) "Everywhere I go, you're going with me": Time and space deixis as affective positioning resources in shared moments of digital mourning. *Discourse, Context, and Media* (Special Issue on Communicating Time and Place on Digital Media, edited by A. Georgakopoulou) 9: 55–63.

Giaxoglou, K. (2018) #JeSuisCharlie? Hashtags as narrative resources in contexts of ecstatic sharing. *Discourse, Context and Media* 22: 13–20.

Hashtagify (2019) Top 10 related hashtags to #JeSuisCharlie. Hashtagify [online hashtag tracking tool]. Available at: https://hashtagify.me/hashtag/StaySafe.

The Independent (Selby, J.) (2015) Banksy's illustrated response to the Charlie Hebdo attack isn't by Banksy: But it is striking. *The Independent*, Jan. 8. Available at: www.independent.co.uk/news/people/banksys-striking-illustrated-response-to-the-charlie-hebdo-attack-9964198.html. Accessed: 11 Aug. 2019.

John, N.A. (2013) The social logics of sharing. *The Communication Review* 16 (3): 113–131.

John, N.A. (2017) *The Age of Sharing*. Malden, MA: Polity Press.

Kavada, A. (2018) Editorial: Media and the "populist moment". *Media, Culture & Society*: 1–3.

Lee, C. (2018) Introduction: Discourse of social tagging. *Discourse, Context, and Media* (Special Issue: Discourse of Social Tagging) 22: 1–3.

Le Figaro (Paulet, A.) (2015) Le street art rend homage à Charlie Hebdo. *Le Figaro Culture*, Jan. 1. Available at: www.lefigaro.fr/culture/2015/01/09/03004-20150109ARTFIG00231-le-street-art-rend-hommage-a-charlie-hebdo.php. Accessed: 10 Jan. 2019.

MacFarlane, L. and R. Stobbe (2018) #Hashmarks: Can a hashtag be a trademark? *The Medium: Intellectual Property Technology Law Newsletter*. Available at: www.fieldlaw.com/portalresource/can-a-Hashtag-be-a-Trademark. Accessed: 20 Jan. 2019.

MailOnline (2015) #JeSuisCharlie becomes one of the most popular hashtags in Twitter's history. *MailOnline*, Jan. 10. Available at: www.dailymail.co.uk/news/article-2904689/JeSuisCharlie-one-popular-hashtags-Twitter-s-history.html. Accessed: 11 Aug. 2019.

Messina, C. (2007) Twitter hashtags for emergency coordination and disaster relief. *Factory Joe (Blog)*, Oct. 22. Available at: https://factoryjoe.com/2007/10/22/twitter-hashtags-for-emergency-coordination-and-disaster-relief/. Accessed: 20 Dec. 2018.

Messina, C. (2019) The unlikely lesson from inventing the hashtag. *TEDx Talks*, Jan. 15. Available at: www.youtube.com/watch?v=sL8i-dIFOY0. Accessed: 25 Jan. 2019.

Mislove, A., S. Lehmann, Y.-Y. Ahn, J.-P. Onnela, and J.N. Rosenquist (2011) Understanding the demographics of Twitter users. *Proceedings of the Fifth International AAAI Conference on Weblogs and Social Media*, July 17–21, Association for the Advancement of Artificial Intelligence, Barcelona, Spain.

Page, R. (2012) The linguistics of self-branding and micro-celebrity in Twitter: The role of hashtags. *Discourse and Communication* 6 (2): 181–201.

Page, R. (2018) *Narratives Online: Shared Stories in Social Media*. Cambridge: Cambridge University Press.

Papacharissi, Z. (2014) *Affective Publics: Sentiment, Technology, and Politics*. Oxford, USA: Oxford University Press.

Papacharissi, Z. (2015) Affective publics and structures of storytelling: Sentiment, events and mediality. *Information, Communication & Society.* DOI: 10.1080/1369118X.2015.1109697.

Saki, M. (2015) Notinmyname comme heterotopie: Twitter comme un espace sans lieu. *Presentation in Colloque Internationale Les Nouvelles Journees de l' ERLA 15,* Universite Bretagne Occidentale, mai 28–29.

Scott, K. (2015) The pragmatics of hashtags: Inference and conversational style on Twitter. *Journal of Pragmatics* 81: 8–20.

Seargeant, P. and K. Giaxoglou (forthcoming) Discourse and the linguistic landscape. In De Fina, A. and A. Georgakopoulou (Eds.), *The Handbook of Discourse Studies.* Cambridge: Cambridge University Press.

Seargeant, P. and F. Monaghan (2017) Street protests and the creative spectacle. *Diggit Magazine,* Mar. 20. Available at: www.diggitmagazine.com/articles/ street-protests and-creative-spectacle. Accessed: 3 June 2018.

Shulga, A. (2013) Who owns # hasthags: Lexis Nexis Lega newsroom intellectual property. *Lexis Nexis.* Available at: www.lexisnexis.com/legalnewsroom/ intellectual-property/b/copyright-trademark-law-blog/archive/2013/05/13/ who-owns-hashtags.aspx?Redirected=true. Accessed: 15 July 2016.

SMAPP Data Report (2013) A breakout role for Twitter? The role of social media in the Turkish protests. In *Social Media and Political Participation Lab.* New York: New York University Press. Available at: https://smappnyu.org/ wpcontent/uploads/2018/11/turkey_data_report.pdf. Accessed: 10 Jan. 2018.

Spilioti, T. (2015) Digital discourses: A critical perspective. In Georgakopoulou, A. and T. Spilioti (Eds.), *The Routledge Handbook of Language and Digital Communication.* London: Routledge.

Sreberny, A. (2016) The 2015 Charlie Hebdo killings, media event chains, and global political responses. *International Journal of Communication* 10: 3485–3502.

The Guardian (2015) Golden Globes: Hollywood stars pay tribute to Charlie Hebdo victims. *The Guardian/Agence France-Presse,* 12 Jan. 2015. Available at: https://www.theguardian.com/film/2015/jan/12/golden-globes-hollywood-stars-pay-tribute-to-charlie-hebdo-victims. Accessed: 11 April 2020.

Todd, E. (2015) *Qui est Charlie? Sociologie d'une crise religieuse.* Paris: Editions du Seuil.

Tsur, O. and A. Rappoport (2012) What's in a hashtag? Content based prediction of the spread of ideas in microblogging communities, *WSDM 12,* Seattle, Washington, Feb. 8–12. Available at: http://people.seas.harvard.edu/~orentsur/ papers/wsdm12.pdf.

Twitter (n.d.) How to use hashtags. Twitter Help Pages. Available at: https://help. twitter.com/en/using-twitter/how-to-use-hashtags. Accessed: 11 April 2020.

Twitter. 2016. About: Brand. *Twitter.* Available at: https://brand.twitter.com/ en.html. Accessed: 26 July 2016.

Twitter. 2018. *Sign up for Twitter.* Available at: https://twitter.com/account/ new?lang=en. Accessed: 20 Jan. 2019.

van Dijk, J. (2013) *The Culture of Connectivity: A Critical History of Social Media.* Oxford: Oxford University Press.

Varis, P. and J. Blommaert (2014) Conviviality and collectives on social media: Virality, memes and new social structures. *Tilburg Papers in Culture Studies* 108: 1–21.

The Wired (Wiseman, B.) (2017) An oral history of the #hashtag. *The Wired*, May 19. Available at: www.wired.com/2017/05/oral-history-hashtag/. Accessed: 20 Dec. 2018.

Yang, G. (2016) Narrative agency in hashtag activism: The case of #BlackLives Matter. *Media and Communication* 4 (4): 13–17.

Yang, L., T. Sun, M. Zhang, and Q. Mei (2012) We know what @you #tag: Does the dual role affect hashtag adoption? *WWW '12: Proceedings of the 21st International Conference on World Wide Web*, pp. 261–270. http://dx.doi. org/10.1145/2187836.2187872. Accessed: 11 Aug. 2019.

Zappavigna, M. (2012) *Discourse of Twitter and Social Media: How We Use Language to Create Affiliation on the Web*. London: Bloomsbury.

Zappavigna, M. (2015) Searchable talk: The linguistic functions of hashtags. *Social Semiotics* 25 (3): 274–291.

7 Visual Small Stories of Mourning on Twitter

Introduction

The previous chapter presented an analysis of the emergence and circulation of the hashtag #JeSuisCharlie, showing how affect can be scaled up into small stories of global mourning through the ecstatic sharing of hashtags on Twitter. This chapter extends the narrative approach to mourning in social media developed in this book with the examination of the circulation of image-driven stories and metastories of death, i.e. reworkings of stories.

The focus, here, is on the death event of a three-year old child, which became iconic of the refugee crisis in 2015. The boy was Alan Kurdi,[1] although he became internationally known as Aylan, after his name was misspelled in initial reports of his death. He was found drowned on a Turkish shore in the morning of September 2, 2015, after the inflatable boat he was in with his family – in an attempt to cross the Mediterranean – capsized. His death was added to the drowning of his mother Rihanna, brother Ghalib, and nine others on board of the boat and to the toll of 3,770 people who lost their lives during migration to Europe in 2015 (IOM, 2015).

This death event obtained high media and social media visibility through the public circulation of the photographs of Turkish journalist Nilüfer Demir for the Dogan New Agency (CNN, 2015, Sept. 3). Three images from this series of stills have become widely known. The first image shows the lifeless body of the boy lying facedown half in the sand, half in the water of a beach in Bodrum. The second one shows the boy's body and a Turkish officer standing by and taking notes. The third image shows a Turkish officer carrying the child away. In a video from the scene, the series of these stills is shown as it unfolded, starting with the frame of the body from behind, then cutting to a view from the front, while the waves continue their relentless movement. Then the camera cuts to another scene from the beach, where two men are dragging the body of an adult to the shore. It then returns to the scene where Alan's body is lying, where a police guard is seen standing near him taking notes, before the next cut, in which the guard is shown carrying the body away (*Daily Mirror*, 2015, Sept. 4).

The photos won the photographer the Press Photo of the Year award in the 2016 Turkey Photojournalist Association Press's Photos of the Year contest (*Hürriyet Daily News*, 2016, Mar. 28), the Sedat Simavi award for Journalism for 2015, and the gold medal of the 2016 Elizabeth Neuffer Memorial Prize awarded by the United Nations Correspondents' Association. Its emblematicity was highlighted in collections of pictures summing up the years 2015 and 2016 in English-speaking media, including the BBC, *The Guardian* World Press Photo 2016 Winners, and *The New York Times*. It was also selected by *TIME* as one of the top 100 photos of 2015 (*TIME*, 2015). According to Vis (2015), this deeply personal tragedy became one of the most iconic image-led news stories of our time, engaging a global audience within less than twelve hours and ultimately changing the way social media users talked about the issue of immigration.

The ecstatic sharing of the image online before it even hit the headlines opened this story up to public evaluations and reworkings. These invite empirical investigation as small stories of mourning associated with specific forms of online participation and affective positioning. A critical angle on meaning-making practices in the process of this image's circulation is also warranted, given the widespread claim about the change that this image brought about in the global reception of the refugee crisis (see Vis and Goriunova, 2015).

In the previous chapter, the focus was on hashtag reactions as one emerging mode of the mediatized experiencing of global events along dividing lines of identification and affective positioning. In this chapter, the analysis draws attention to the increasingly important role of the visual mode in sharing as a mode of affective positioning, broadening our understanding of different types of digital mourning phenomena. The exploration of multimodal modes of meaning making in different phases and moments of circulation of the story of Alan Kurdi in social and print media will clarify the different types of stances and positions for approaching the death of the distant 'Other' through specific visual, textual, and story frames.

The chapter starts by considering the conditions that allowed the circulation of the distressing image of a dead child in the first place, showing the close connection between media and social media, and raising important questions for an empirically based approach to the sharing and uptake of this image-based story. Then I present the data and the analytical framework for sharing as affective positioning as adapted to this case study before discussing how the identified story frames drive the sharing and reception of the story of a child's drowning, turning it into an emblem of mourning for refugee death at a distance.

Sharing the Image of a Dead Child

The images from the scene of the drowning in Bodrum became available via press release distribution at 11:30 a.m. on September 2. At 12:20 a.m., the image zooming in on the toddler's body was shared by Peter Bouckaert from Human Rights Watch on Twitter.[2] Sharing the image online gradually became associated with a series of hashtags either unique to the specifics of this event, such as #kiyiyavuraninsanlik (trans. *humanity washed ashore*), #JeSuisAylan, or existing hashtags relating to the refugee crisis, such as #RefugeesWelcome.

Given that the visual portrayal of death is considered to be a taboo, in particular the death of a child (see also Chapter 3), the availability of the images of Alan Kurdi inevitably raised debates among news editors, journalists, and members of the public about the ethics of publishing a highly graphic image of a child's death. *The Guardian* Media Group's editorial code guide, for example, calls for special care when dealing with images of children (under the age of sixteen; see PCC[3] code, section 6) and sensitive treatment of people during periods of grief and trauma (see PCC code, section 5). In a footnote, however, possible exceptions to the publication of images of children are acknowledged, in cases where their publication can be demonstrated to be in the public interest,[4] such as the detection or exposure of crime or serious impropriety or when material is already in the public domain or is likely to become so. In such exceptional cases, editors are committed to demonstrate how the public interest is served.

This need for editors to demonstrate how the public interest is served explains why many of the newspapers that opted for publishing the images took care to devote space in explaining the decision-making process and motivation for publishing a photograph of a toddler without parental consent and for intruding into the grief of his surviving family. *The Guardian*'s editors, for example, waited for the photographs as well as the details of the full story to be verified before proceeding with publication. They eventually went ahead to run the image of the Turkish policeman carrying Alan's body on their front page, adding the more distressing image of his lifeless body in an inside page and in a smaller size, with a warning to readers. Their motivation had to do with the potential of this image to stir the conscience of the public but also the political establishment's regarding the 'saga' of refugees. As the newspaper's deputy editor Paul Johnson explains:

> The enormous poignancy and potential power of the photographs was evident from the start. Could they be the images that provided a tipping point? Would public sympathy, and perhaps anger at Britain's role as an apparent bystander in this saga, be moved by them? We decided that both of these were highly likely. Those

factors had to be balanced against the real shock that some readers would feel.

(*The Guardian*, 2015, September 7)

Warnings about the sensitive content of the image were also displayed on Twitter. In the tweet of human rights activist Peter Bouckaert, which included the image of the lifeless body (and which is analyzed later in this chapter), a warning about the media potentially containing sensitive content is displayed instead of the image.[5]

Transgressing editorial codes for publishing images of children (not to mention a dead child) and for safeguarding the privacy of the bereaved was, thus, inflected by the consideration of this image as being a transgressive story in its own right, which would be in the public interest of revealing a crime against some groups of people. In addition, the availability of the image on Twitter within a few hours after it was made available through news wires offered to editors part of the justification they needed, given that the images were already in circulation in the public domain, tagged as sensitive content.

In this case, the inter-connection between media and social media in terms of shifting publishing and shareability norms at the boundaries of the transgressive becomes evident. This connection was pointed at explicitly by Hugh Pinney, at the time vice president of news image distributor Getty, who said that despite the rules around never publishing a picture of a dead child, in the case of Alan Kurdi, this "golden rule" was bypassed because "individuals have had the balls to publish the pictures themselves on social media [. . .] [giving] the mainstream media the courage and the conviction to publish this picture" (*TIME*, 2015, Sept. 4).

Those directly involved in the circulation of the images, namely the photographer and the human rights activist who was among the first ones to publish it on Twitter, pre-empt criticisms of the photograph as potentially offensive and present it instead as an act of hope and a 'message in the bottle' for European leaders and the public. As the photographer Nilüfer Demir explained to CNN Turk:

> When I realized there was nothing to do to bring that boy back to life I thought I had to take this picture . . . to show the tragedy. I hope the impact this photo has created will help bring a solution.
>
> (*Daily Mirror*, 2015)

Peter Bouckaert, the human rights activist who shared the graphic image of the lifeless body of the boy on Twitter, also offered a detailed explanation of his decision to share the image:

> Some say the picture is too offensive to share online or print in our newspapers. But what I find offensive is that drowned children are

washing up on our shorelines, when more could have been done to prevent their deaths. It was not an easy decision to share a brutal image of a drowned child. But I care about these children as much as my own. Maybe if Europe's leaders did too, they would try to stem this ghastly spectacle.

(Bouckaert, 2015)

Both the photographer and the human rights activist projected personalized moral and affective stances to the ethical issues raised by the sharing of the images. In these journalistic or editorial post-publication reflections, there is rarely an explicit reference to the need to safeguard the bereaved family of the boy. Articles and interviews with the father and the aunt were featured in most of the newspapers that covered the events, in which none of the two expressed an explicit objection to its public circulation. Their acceptance of this intrusion to their grief is reportedly motivated by their expressed hope that this terrible image would touch people and help change the world. Tima Kurdi, the sister of the father of the boys, Abdullah, was reported saying, "I only saw that image once, when the rest of the world, saw that image. And I cannot look at it anymore". Since then, Tima Kurdi has appeared in various interviews, is tweeting about refugee matters, and also recently published a memoir entitled *The Boy on the Beach* (2018), telling her story of her childhood in Syria, her emigration to Canada and her thrusting onto the world stage after what happened in Bodrum. While for many viewers around the world, the image of little Alan turned a political issue into a personal moment of sympathy, for Tima Kurdi, this death turned her personal tragedy into an opportunity for her political envoicing on behalf of Syrian refugees. As for the father of Alan Kurdi, Abdullah Kurdi, the motivation for allowing this picture to circulate was stated in a clear and stark tone in the early days after his family's death, where he was reported saying that: "We want the whole world to see this".

Regarding the Death of the Other

Despite the division provoked by the publication of this image, its sharing has arguably contributed to a shift in the framing of the debate about *migrants* to a debate about *refugees* (Vis and Goriunova, 2015, p. 10) and a concomitant shift in framing the so-called *refugee crisis* as a *political crisis*. These shifts have drawn attention to the inadequacy of institutions and systems to cope with the increased numbers of people entering the European Union. For Blommaert (2015, n.p.), for example, this image became emblematic not just as an image of the crisis "but also as [a pointer] to the moral positions people can assume in relation to it [. . .] fuelling a new type of formal-informal voluntarist politics organised around moral causes". This process of emblematization and turn to this new form of political engagement are associated with an emerging visual regime of meaning-making, which is intricately associated with social media publishing forms. They are, however, also linked with humanitarian discourses and media representations (Pantti and Tikka, 2014, p. 190).

As this analysis will show, however, it is important to avoid adopting an over-celebratory tone when considering the implications of such public mobilization in favour of an empirically based critical perspective, especially given that the sharing of this image has also important ramifications for publication norms of images of the death of the Other and the shaping of approaches to it. The focus on practices of public mourning for Alan Kurdi provides insights into social-mediatized mourning for a distant 'Other'. As Boltanski (1999) has argued, the mediatization of suffering enacts 'politics of pity'. It also constitutes 'spectators of distant suffering' (Chouliaraki, 2004, p. 194), which in this case also encompasses networked publics of distant suffering and distant death.

From a discourse-narrative perspective, it is important to ask how events like Alan's death become a media fixture and fixation and how they get to accrue meanings over time through their iteration in the context of different forms of story sharing and participation. It is also important to look for any continuities or shifts in the topics of suffering to those described in the wake of the 9/11 attacks by Chouliaraki (2006, p. 195) or of more recent attacks, e.g. the attacks at the offices of *Charlie Hebdo* (see Chapter 6), seeking to point to how stances and positions to the Other's life and death get reconfigured in the context of new events and crises, (trans)forming the available moral positions available and the conditions of their becoming visible.

Chouliaraki's work on spectatorships of suffering has shown the importance of looking at chronotopic configurations to show the relations of proximity and distance created in and through televisualized events. Given that chronotopic configurations are at the heart of emplotment, it makes sense to use a narrative lens when pursuing such analyses (see Chapter 3). The next section presents the data and the analytical framework of narrative and affective positioning as it has been adapted for addressing research questions relating to this case study.

The Case Study

The focus on photographs and their use in story sharing practices relies on the acknowledgment that in photographs, types of people emerge as the key characters in the storying of moments, which become part of emblematic events or spectacles shaping perceptions of history (Giaxoglou and Spilioti, 2017). In the case of 9/11, for instance, the mass-mediated circulation of spectacular images of the event shaped its experiencing as an "iconographic event", which was represented in live audio-visual-textual images broadcast for global audiences (Topinka, 2016, p. 3). This focus also calls for analytical vocabulary for the examination of visual modes and meanings to address the following questions:

1. How are the boy's life and death emplotted visually, verbally, and/ or multimodally? In other words, how are characters, time, place, or space encoded, and what meanings arise out of different configurations of key narrative elements?
2. How are these visual stories recontextualized in the media and social media? What types of positions and stances do such mediatized emplotments make available to (networked) publics?
3. What types of emotion are articulated in these acts of story participation, and how are these negotiated in different contexts?

The different sources drawn upon to address these questions cover different phases of the circulation of the image and its evaluations:

1. The images of the photographer Nilüfer Demir that became popular through their publication in the media and social media (see Appendix 1).
2. The front pages (headlines and images) of UK print newspapers on Thursday, September 3, and Friday, September 4, 2015 (*The Independent, The Guardian, The Daily Telegraph, London Evening Standard, Daily Mirror, Daily Express*). These were recovered using the online tool Paperboy's UK Newspaper Front Pages archive (see Appendix 2).
3. Key Twitter events, i.e. the tweet event created when human rights activist Peter Bouckaert posted the image on this timeline on September 2, attracting 207 replies. Replies were coded for content, alignment or disalignment, and story frames.
4. A corpus of Twitter reactions aggregated around the hashtag #JeSuis-Aylan via the Twitter's API on September 3, 2015 (205 tweets in total).
5. Creative reworkings of the images drawing on compilations of artists' responses to the image (97 images and comments to images published on the Bored Panda blog, 2018).[6]

Shared images and their accompanying verbal posts are analyzed here as *visual small stories* (see also Georgakopoulou, 2016). Images put forward particular kinds of meanings that create visual frames for the interpretation of the events and figures portrayed. These can be described using the analytic vocabulary of visual semiotics. The meanings of these images are reworked and negotiated further in print headlines, where they get embedded and coupled with headlines. In addition, their meanings are further extended, negotiated, or sedimented depending on how users respond to these visual small stories through different types of sharing, namely sharing as storying and restorying and sharing as rescripting (see Georgakopoulou, 2015). Sharing as storying and restorying is analyzed through a focus on the patterns of participation in the story. Drawing on De Fina's (2016) framework used in her study of participation in a You-Tube story, these are examined in an analysis of patterns of alignment or disalignment and story frames.

De Fina starts from the widely established distinction in narrative analysis (Young, 1987) between the *taleworld*, that is the world in which characters move and live, and the *storyrealm*, that is the storytelling event at the center of which the taleworld lies and which is embedded in conversation or in another communicative activity. These categories bracket a discourse activity as a story (Taleworld) or reveal attitudes toward the story or the storytelling event (Storyrealm; De Fina, 2016, p. 479). Story frames can offer insights into participation patterns, given their association with participants' taking up of positions of alignment or disalignment to a situation and those involved in it. Story frames are, thus, sites where participants' displays of alignment or disalignment are articulated. In the present case, the aim of the analysis of story frames is twofold. It seeks to point to the different types of participation positions taken up in reactions to the story of Alan Kurdi and to show the connections of these frames with the semiotic meanings of the images and visual and textual news frames within which these images were shared. The coding scheme used for the analysis of the tweet event and tweets shared via the hashtag #JeSuisAylan is presented in Table 7.1.

Creative reworkings are examined as *rescriptings*, which involve specific types of plot manipulations to be empirically identified (Georgakopoulou, 2015). The analysis presented in what follows takes the images of Alan Kurdi as a single, emblematic moment of the crisis. This echoes Chouliaraki's discourse-analytic approach that focuses on selected moments, aligning with Foucault's "analytics of truth" or "the quest to define the conditions under which knowledge is possible, acceptable and legitimate" in the present (Chouliaraki, 2004, p. 189) and with more recent advances in small story research that draw attention to key events and moments in the circulation of stories online (Georgakopoulou, 2015; see also Georgakopoulou and Giaxoglou, 2018). In this case, this focus allows an insight into modes of story participation that contribute to the circulation, reiteration, and sedimentation of storylines and story positions (see also small story methods, Chapter 3). Addressing these research questions will shed light into the uptake and negotiation of broader discourses on the refugee crisis and enhance our understanding of the narrative practices associated with mourning in social media.

Table 7.1 The coding scheme used to identify story frames in tweet events and tweets shared via the use of #JeSuisAylan

STORYREALM	Posts focusing on:
	(i) Comment on the sharer as sharer: comments on Peter Bouckaert as the sharer of the boy's picture and story
	(ii) Comment on participants: comment about fellow commenters, including viewers of the image outside Twitter
	(iii) Comment on the tellability, shareability, or viewability of the story: comment on how worthy the story is for telling or why it is worth sharing. featuring the hashtag "#JeSuisAylan" or a series of hashtags, e.g. "#basta #helptherefugees #fightforpeaceintheworld #facethereality #refugeeswelcome #jesuisaylan".
	(iv) General attitudes to the story, e.g. "We are not going to just sit back and watch this happen. Hope this will be of some help ❤ #vigörvadvikan #jesuisaylan".
TALEWORLD	Posts focusing on:
	(i) the character(s) of the visual story, e.g. "Il n'avait que trois ans . . . #jesuisaylan ☹".
	(ii) comments on the main event of the story as story evaluation or R.I.P. posts, e.g. "R.I.P petit ange, un ange partit trop tôt . . . ☹😭❤ #JeSuisAylan#RIP#AllahYRahmo ☹😭❤☹☁".

Images as (Re)sources of Semiotic Meaning

Social semiotics provides an analytic vocabulary for the study of visual communication at three interrelated, though analytically separable, levels of meaning: (i) the *ideational* level, which refers to the way participants are represented as figures as well as to the processes that link these together (visually portrayed as vectors), (ii) the *textual* level, which refers to the organization of the image and the salience assigned to different elements through tonal contrast or framing of the different elements for example, and (iii) the *interpersonal* level, which refers to the relationships between figures in the image and viewers via devices, such as perspective, gaze, close-up, or distance. These levels will be considered in turn as they apply to the image of Alan Kurdi as a first step into its semiotic meanings.

In terms of the ideational level, Nilüfer Demir's images deal with the most difficult topic to represent, namely the death of a child. The portrayal of this death is summed up in the still portrayal of the lifeless body of little Alan Kurdi. His pose, lying on the shore, evokes a passive state of stillness, which can be considered the visual equivalent of silence (Jaworski et al., 2005), inviting a mournful contemplation of the event. The event of death is captured as the tragic culmination of the boy's life story, presenting the viewer with a powerful visual narrative whose evaluation is opened up for reflection and commentary.

At the textual level in the case of the close-up frame of the image that features the figure of the child lying on his front, facing down to the sand with eyes shut, it is notable that other figures associated with the child character, for example parents, guardians, other adults, or children, are notably absent from the frame. The child figure dominates the image space. The place portrayed is the open space of a sandy beach, with limited visual cues signalling where that beach is actually situated. The lack of spatiotemporal indicators or additional details to the frame offers space for moves between the specific and the general or the more abstract.

In long-shot frames, an additional figure is included, that of a police officer whose vest signals that the scene unfolded on a Turkish shore. Later news reports identified him as paramilitary officer Sgt Mehmet Ciplak (*The Independent*, 2015, Sept. 6). In the first image, the police officer is standing at a slight distance from the child's body, with his back turned towards the camera, and taking notes, presumably recording the death. In terms of the visually depicted relations between the figures of the police officer and the child, no direct connection between them is signalled. Although the police officer's body is turned towards the direction of the child, his position – standing, his back turned towards the camera – makes it impossible for the viewer to discern gaze or movement that could have been revealing of a particular relation between the two figures. The officer's position in the frame signals an indirect relationship of relative distance. In this image, the officer is portrayed as a distant witness to the scene.

In the second image, the same officer is figured in physical proximity to the child, carrying his body. Under different conditions, this image could stand for the police officer's heroic gesture of saving the child. This possibility is, however, ruled out by the knowledge that the child is already dead. This is further underscored in the visual depiction of the officer cradling the boy's body in his arms yet directing his gaze sideways, away from the boy, or straight ahead. The officer is portrayed, in this case, as an involved witness to the event yet powerless.

Images as particular semiotic configurations position viewers as recipients of the events, creating particular kinds of interpersonal relations with them through the ideational and textual functions described, as well as through the use of specific devices, such as gaze, close-up, or distance. In the images of death considered here, there is a notable absence of gaze that could be termed a *non-gaze*. This lies in sharp contrast with the gaze of smiling, full-of-life children common in pictures of children (Blommaert, 2015) or the direct, 'demand' gaze of children in shock advertising invoking empathy (Jones, 2012). The lack of gaze places the viewer in a contemplative and reflective mode about the life and death of this child. In the case of images which include the figure of the officer either at a distance from the body or at physical proximity, the viewer is placed in a position of witness, more or less distant and powerless.

The powerful visual narrative emerging from the three images anticipates possible displays of mourning as ways of engaging with the story. These include, more specifically, displays of emotional identification with the bereaved family of the child (i.e. grieving as if for one's own child), the felt duty for tribute-like gestures, and the need to ask why and how this happened and who should be held responsible for it, i.e. the assignment of blame. Associated with such modes of engagement, the selection of particular moments and their visual depiction projects particular stances on the reported events. In the case of Alan's story and the 2015 events, Blommaert has summarized the stance projected to the viewer as follows: "children like Aylan and Ghalib should not be dying like this" (Blommaert, 2015).

This reading of the semiotic meanings of the most popular images of Alan Kurdi's death points to a visual emplotment of the event, which foregrounds the vulnerability and helplessness of a specific child, presented though in an abstract mode (e.g. no clear image of the boy's face, no clear indication of place, no clear indication of other characters and figures). This double-edged visual articulation of the story along the specific and the generalizable makes it possible for the image to become a carrier of other meanings and ultimately be emblematized as a symbol of the plight of refugees.

The semiotic ideational, textual, and interpersonal meanings of the images identified afford different types of identity positions to the death event for viewers. These can be summed up as including positions of (i) the mournful, contemplative witness, (ii) the distant witness, and (iii) the involved though powerless witness. These positions put forward particular visual frames focused on the taleworld for approaching its main figure as an innocent child who shouldn't have died like this and his death as an emblem of the human suffering of refugees. Their viewing calls forth a reaction, opening up its evaluation, i.e. assessments of its importance and tellability to the viewers.

The association of the three images with these different types of positions and frames arguably explains why it was these which were picked up among many other images (earlier or concurrent) from the scene as newsworthy images and as objects of sharing, quickly becoming part of a metaculture of refugee death and mourning.

Multimodal Frames in Print Headlines

The images selected for covering the front pages of print newspapers combined with headlines of varying fonts and sizes create or 'fix' frames for the interpretation of reportable events. Even though the term *news frames* has been used to uncover and study these types of journalistic stances and positions suggested to readers, more recently, the term *multimodal frames* has also been used, given the increasing importance of images in the public understanding of media(tized) events. Jungblut and Zakareviciute (2019), for example, compare visual and textual frames in the case of the 2014 Israel–Gaza conflict in terms of their thematic convergence or divergence. They found that despite their initial thematic correspondence, in later coverage, visual and textual frames begin to diverge: textual frames uphold the original, middle-ground and solution-seeking stances, while visual frames shift to increasingly graphic portrayals of the conflict, foregrounding the escalation of the conflict and its implications.

In the case under focus here, seven UK print headlines from September 3, 2015, have been examined (see Appendix for full listing and details; see also Giaxoglou and Spilioti, 2018). On September 3, four newspapers' front covers featured the image of the Turkish officer carrying the boy's body away from the scene[7] (*Daily Mirror, The Guardian, Daily Mail, The Independent*), accompanied by headlines which thematically converged with the visual (emplotment) frames identified earlier.

The visual frames of alignment to the plight of the boy and refugees created by the dramatic portrayal of the officer in a position of an involved yet powerless witness to the event (see earlier) thematically concur with the headlines' textual frames. These verbally reiterate the sense of shock at this death, with a focus on the human-interest aspect of this drama, either avoiding its politicization (Examples 1 and 2) or underlining the relevant political dimensions, assigning blame for the lack of adequate interventions that could have saved the boy's life.

Example 1 (*Daily Mail*)

Tiny victim of **a human catastrophe.**

Example 2 (*Daily Mirror*)

A three year-old boy washed up on a holiday beach in Turkey . . . **the heartbreaking human face of a tragedy** *the world can no longer ignore.* **UNBEARABLE.**

Specifically, Europe is portrayed as an inefficient and failed agent in resolving the crisis (Example 3) or 'deadlocked' (Example 4), while the Prime Minister at the time, David Cameron, is called out for being 'in denial' (Example 4).

Example 3 (*The Guardian*)

The **shocking, cruel reality of Europe's refugee crisis** – Picture raises questions over EU's response

Example 4 (*The Independent*)

SOMEBODY'S CHILD

The tide of desperate humanity seeking safety in Europe is rising. Yesterday's victims include this Syrian boy, drowned in his family's attempt to reach Greece from Turkey. The EU is deadlocked: our Prime Minister is in denial. A **vast human catastrophe** is unfolding. *Do we really believe that this is not our problem?*

In all of the examples, the headlines approach the so-called refugee crisis using various affect-laden descriptions, such as 'the unbearable' and 'heartbreaking human face of a tragedy' (Example 1), a 'human catastrophe' (Example 2), 'a vast human catastrophe' (Example 3), or rephrasing it as 'the tide of desperate humanity seeking safety in Europe' (Example 4). *The Guardian*'s headline, more specifically, draws a direct connection between the image of the dead boy and 'the shocking, cruel reality of Europe's refugee crisis' (Example 3). The headlines' emphasis, thus, foregrounds its implications for human suffering not unlike that of large-scale natural disasters and calls for comparable sympathy and support. Concurrent visual and textual frames are reinforced by the use of evaluative adjectives, such as 'heartbreaking', or adjectives of scale, such as 'vast', proposing stances of alignment to the child – and refugees more broadly – as innocent, non-threatening, tragic victims.

Not all newspapers, however, displayed alignment to the plight of Alan Kurdi or refugees more broadly. For *Daily Express* and the *London Evening Standard*, Alan's story was not selected as the most relevant piece of breaking news. Instead, another piece of news relating to the Eurostar's train line cancellations of trips as migrants were walking on the tracks in their attempt to cross the border made the headlines. In the case of the *Daily Mail*, the headline was not accompanied by any image, while the *London Evening Standard*'s cover page featured the image of a group of migrants walking en masse.

Example 5 (*Daily Express*)

EU blamed for migrant chaos. Europe's border crisis is totally out of control

Example 6 (*London Evening Standard*)

MIGRANT CRISIS: 13-HOUR EUROSTAR ORDEAL

The headline and image, where available, counters other newspapers' focus on the refugee crisis as a human-interest story, indirectly expressing a stance of disalignment to border crossers as suffering humans. The textual frames foreground the 'chaos' and 'crisis' brought about by this crisis, referred to as 'migrant crisis' and focus, instead, on its implications for Eurostar travellers (Example 6), using it as an opportunity to hit back at the European Union (Example 5). The image chosen by the *London Evening Standard* for its cover page suggests border crossers as coming over in large numbers, feeding into dominant portrayals of them as 'threatening invaders' (see earlier).

The *Daily Telegraph* stands somewhere in the middle, not explicitly aligning or disaligning to the plight of Alan Kurdi and other refugees. Instead, it combines the two pieces of breaking news, displaying an ambivalent position. The front cover image features a soldier carrying a toddler – who is not Alan Kurdi – while people are standing in a queue in the background; the headline draws attention to a more general issue of children embroiled in these difficult conditions as attracting Europe's attention.

Example 7 (*The Daily Telegraph*)

Plight of migrant children stirs Europe's conscience.

As this examination of headlines from September 3 has shown, visual and textual frames tend to concur thematically in the first day of reporting the breaking news in four out of seven newspaper covers under study. The close-up image of Alan's body does not feature in any of the print cover pages of these newspapers. While there is a congruence of visual and textual frames in the newspapers that expressed an alignment stance to the boy, his family, and refugees, the *Daily Express* opted for news stories and images that consistently countered the angle of empathetic support with an emphasis on migrants as a threat to the UK.

The avoidance of humanitarian-focused coverage of the refugee situation has been found to be typical of the UK press, where a high proportion of articles consistently emphasizing the threat that refugees and migrants pose to Britain's welfare and benefits system has been found (*Daily Telegraph* 15.8%, *Daily Mail* 41.9%, *Sun* 26.2%, EU average 8.9%) against articles featuring humanitarian themes (*Daily Mail* 20.9%, *Sun* 7.1%, EU average 38.3%; Berry et al., 2016).

The multimodal frames identified in the select newspapers foreground the positions of the involved though powerless witness afforded by the image of the officer cradling the child in his arms that was reiterated across cover pages. The description of the semiotic meanings of the images and the way these are embedded in print headlines of September 3, 2014, sheds light into one phase of the circulation of Alan Kurdi's story and uptake. In the next section, I will consider how these meanings and positions are taken up in visual rescriptings of the images before turning to the examination of the use of the images in reactions on Twitter.

Rescripting the Plot of Alan Kurdi's Visual Story

Reactions to these images also included creative visual reworkings, mostly by artists. These were shared on social media and (some of them) also appeared in compilations online or in print media. This analysis draws on such a compilation in the blog Bored Panda (n.d.), where ninety-seven[8] of these reworkings are gathered from various sources, e.g. Facebook and Twitter, and cite the name of the creator where known. The collection is introduced with the reiteration of the position that this image is as an emblem of the unacceptable death of refugee children (see Blommaert, 2015):

> These touching responses range from grief to rage, and regardless of where you stand on the Syrian refugee crisis and Europe's response, one thing is certain – children like Aylan and Ghalib should not be dying like this.

Among the fifty most popular reworkings analyzed here, most of them involve reworkings of the close-up image of Alan Kurdi lying on the beach of Bodrum. There were also four reworkings of the long shot of the body featuring the officer in the background recording the death. These reworkings are instances of rescripting, i.e. social media enabled practices of sharing which involve manipulations of the taleworld of already circulated stories, often leading to the presentation of new stories as comments on the breaking news story (see Georgakopoulou, 2015).

Considering these rescriptings in terms of their emplotment features, i.e. the way events, agents, and objects are configured as part of a larger whole and their relation to types of identity and affective positioning, two main types have been identified.

The first type of reworking of the close-up image involves the re-emplotment of the figure of the boy maintaining it in its pose of stillness in new scenarios, either by manipulating the place or by adding further figures to the frame. An example of rescriptings involving place manipulation is the image where the boy's figure is re-emplaced in the same motionless, face down pose in the UN council or other similar high-status decision-making places. Other examples of place manipulation are drawings that emplace Alan's body in an imagined setting which projects an alternative life for the boy, as in the case of the image with the boy lying on a bed as if sleeping in his bedroom. The addition of figures includes, for example, leaders from the Middle East looking down at the body and holding shovels or various types of figures (e.g. sea creatures, fairies, his mother, and brother or the Virgin Mary) embracing, holding, or mourning over Alan.

A further distinction in this type of emplotment, based on the change of place or the addition of figures, has to do with the type of modality in which the images are articulated. Two main modalities have been identified as key in the way these rescriptings make meaning. The declarative modality of the 'here, now' foregrounds the urgency of the need for action. This modality can be also reflected in the image's headline, e.g. 'Do you see it now?'. In these rescriptings, the boy's figure is repositioned as a key character in the political arena and a resource for political action: the lifeless body becomes an accusing body asking for justice change. The second type is the subjunctive modality of the 'what if', imagining a different ending to Alan's story. These rescriptings project alternative scenarios, proposing an alternative ending to Alan's story and imagining he is still alive or is in a better place. They, thus, appeal to the viewer's need to restore order in the face of the most marked of deaths and accommodate in more familiar terms this 'unbearable' death. These reworkings form visual expressions of distant mourning, where viewers occupy positions of mediated witnesses to the death of the 'Other'.

The prevalence of the use of the subjunctive mode in sharing of the story helps us to better understand how this image has turned into a viral icon of Syrian migrants' suffering. As Zelizer notes in her analysis of the 'about-to-die' images, such images provoke strong emotional reactions on account of their articulation in the subjunctive voice of the visual – the 'as if', which forms a visual prelude to an invisible unfolding of events (Zelizer, 2010, pp. 66–67). Rescripted images of Alan's death invite viewers to imagine alternative possibilities that could have prevented that outcome or alternative realities that deny its irrevocability.

Similar meanings are produced in the case of reworkings of the image of the boy's body which includes the officer in the background. Examples of these rescriptings involve the addition of figures, as in the case of the image where sea creatures cry over the boy's body, while the officer stands at a distance, keeping notes, juxtaposing the cold humanity to the spontaneous mourning of the sea creatures. In other cases, Alan is shown lifted by an angel. Through such rescriptings, the boy's body is re-invested with dignity, and his life is deemed worthy to be mourned and remembered. This type of rescripting invites an emotional response through positionings of distant witnessing and parasocial mourning to the other's death and suffering.

The second type of rescriptings of Alan's visual story involves the re-emplotment of the main figure of the close-up image in the same place. For example, in one reworking, the body of Alan is replaced by an EU representative. In another, the artist Ai Wei Wei stands in his place, posing upon the request of a photographer as Alan on the shore of Lesbos. A similar re-enactment was performed by a group of Moroccans in a beach in Rabat.[9] This type of rescriptings foregrounds the plight of refugees and transforms the personal tragedy of Alan Kurdi into an emblematic story revelatory of the refugee crisis.

The reproduction and slight reworking of plots is found to mobilize, amplify, and diversify the story, projecting particular kinds of narrative stances in a blending of mass and social media frames and logics. Through reiteration with slight changes, such rescriptings create participation positions for viewers and sharers who are prompted to view, share, or like the image. Rescriptings also project specific types of story frames. While the images of Nilüfer Demir focus on the taleworld, prompting affective identification with the victim and tributes, rescriptings focus on the storyrealm, given that their reworking redraws the story and contributes an evaluation of the story.

Rescriptings like the ones identified contributed to the visual emblematization of the two images by using character and place as key resources for reworking the plot of the migrants' suffering and encoding particular stances to it. The series of rescriptings and artistic recreations of the emblematic image on social media arguably amplifies their power and also their impact.

Their sharing provokes strong emotional responses from viewers in the form of what Beck (2006, p. 7) calls *cosmopolitan empathy*, i.e. an extended capacity to imagine and empathize with the suffering of others beyond one's immediate existence, and they also instil an individualized sense of moral responsibility. In an age of sharing (John, 2017), the mobilization of *cosmopolitan emotions* (Nussbaum, 2007) through images is increasingly realized through social media users' sharing and commenting on certain media images, often in various reworked forms, attesting, thus, to vernacular creativities in participatory cultures (Burgess, 2006). Such practices bring about 'new' forms and practices of visual emblematization, which enter the telling and showing of stories and their extension as metastories, i.e. stories about stories. More specifically, these frames echo stances to refugees identified in previous research and include, for example, compassionate stances, tenderhearted, blame-filled, shame-filled, powerlessness-filled (Hoijer, 2004), or generally emotional sympathetic reactions (Smith Dahmen et al., 2017), which are often combined with the expression of strong political emotional reactions, directing blame to national targets, governments, and 'humanity' (Mortensen, 2017; Olesen, 2017). The next section turns to the consideration of the story frames within which reactions to the image on Twitter were couched in the context of a specific Twitter event and across Twitter more generally.

Sharing Viewable Stories

The close-up image of Alan Kurdi was shared on Twitter by human rights activist Peter Bouckaert a few hours after it became available, on September 2 at 12:29 p.m., as already mentioned at the start of this chapter. It preceded the images of the little boy that hit the headlines the next day, which are examined in the next section. The post turned into a tweet event, which attracted 208 replies, 2,134 retweets, and 769 likes and which was also cited in the media. This tweet event, thus, forms a key phase in the circulation and reception of the image by social media users but also by media as it helped push further and challenge the norms of shareability of this graphic image, as discussed earlier.

Bouckaert's multimodal post is made up of the close-up image of the boy (not reproduced here) and a message that contextualizes it: "Just pause 4 moment & imagine this was your child, drowned trying 2 flee #Syria 4 safety of #EU. #solidarity. The tweet caption is prefaced by a direct address to Twitter readers and punctuated by the hashtag #solidarity, explicitly marking it as a message of global solidarity. By sharing this image, Bouckaert puts the story of the boy's death up for viewing and explicitly calls his readers to contemplate the image ("just pause 4 a moment") from a personalized, empathic perspective ("imagine this was your child"). Details about the name of the child or the place and circumstances of the death are not included in the tweet, presuming that these are already known or that they can be recovered from other sources. The breaking news of this death is shared as a multimodal small story focused on the here and now of viewers' feelings and reactions, putting forward a stance of affective solidarity as the position that readers are also invited to take up.

The coding of the replies for content, alignment, or disalignment and story frames (see Appendix) allows us to consider whether and how readers respond to this call. The thread of replies is found to be predominantly made up of individual, one-off contributions posted as part of accumulating messages under Bouckaert's tweet and including the @ bouckap to explicitly mark their tweet as a reply to him. This type of comments points to the nature of Twitter communication exchanges: even though the terms used on the platform draw on terms from face-to-face interaction, e.g. 'Reply', 'Comment', and 'Conversation', to designate communication affordances on the site, these practices in fact rely on what in previous work has been termed *inter-reaction*, i.e. a form of public communication which involves the sharing of individual contributions as part of accumulating comments on and across threads and sites, in which the act of sharing is an act of story participation (Giaxoglou and Spilioti, 2020). Additional @usernames can be inserted in the post space to publicly invite other users to view or participate in the unfolding activity.

The majority of inter-reactions involved verbal displays of alignment either to the sharer, to the boy and his family, or to refugees more generally (in some cases, to all of these), replying to the sharer's call for displays of solidarity. Online participation in the story proves to be largely ritualistic in that posts tend to reproduce a set of related stances of alignment, which either reflect or complement one another. Convergence in content and style contributes to the creation of a sense of online affinity among people who don't necessarily know each other outside the platform. The production of this echoing, a convivial style, is evident in the use of the evaluative adjective ('heartbreaking') in ten inter-reactions for describing users' affective reaction to the image (see later in this section) or the use of the term of address 'mate' in Examples 8 and 9:

Example 8

@Backs[10] @bouckap it's sickening **mate**

Example 9

@FelixGee @bouckap Yeah **mate**, hope we find some humanity pretty fucking soon.

Comments displaying disalignment were limited, counting up to twenty-five posts. In these posts, users either criticized the sharer for posting the graphic image of the boy's death (e.g. "@bouckap @medusanet if it were my child I would die a little bit more each time I saw someone else posting this picture"). Others expressed negative views about the parents for not safeguarding their child in the first place ("@bouckap SORRY . . . But who left the child? Where are his parents There should be a safe zone in Syria so All can go and then go home") or about refugees more generally.

Expressions of disalignment disrupted the flow of the accumulating thread of inter-reactions as users felt the urge to engage directly with specific users and counter their view. This prompted the creation of unanticipated pairs of posts displaying alignment to the boy's family and to the sharer (Examples 10–11) or to Syrians (Examples 12–13), countered by displays of disalignment.

Example 10

@bouckaert Sad for Aylan's family; glad you went public. Transparent reality is key to elevating the "civilized" world.

Example 11

@bouckaert @bear heres some transparent reality 4 ya. you'll just probaly dismiss it but wth? [link to youtube video entitled: 'Syrian boy drowning because his Father wanted new teeth'].

Example 12

@bouckap I hope this image haunts all of those who refused to help Syria in the last five years. No forgiveness ever.

Example 13

@bouckap @james45 Um, won't happen. Normal parents don't kill own kids for dental care. They were not fleeing Syria you fool. Plus, screw them anyway.

These patterns of participation point out the extent to which reactions to the images are shaped by the affordances of Twitter, given that the norm for inter-reactions in a solidarity thread is to reflect or echo each other's style and stance. This trend for convergence is what seemingly makes these posts a target for disagreeing readers, who strike back with direct replies to users disrupting the flow and the emerging ambient affiliation, in some cases even verging on trolling. These observations on the form of the unfolding Twitter discussion are a prerequisite step for the examination of the content of these comments, given that form (the 'how') and content (the 'what') in discourse are inextricably linked as constituents of meaning.

In terms of their content, inter-reactions were found to fall into two main types: (1) emotional reactions to the image (e.g. "awful. This is painful") and (2) contributions to the evaluation of the breaking news story (e.g. "this is Assad's doing"). In some cases, comments covered both types (e.g. "absolutely dreadful. So sad. Politicians need to grow some. Deal with it guys"). There were also comments that were not directly relevant to the post (e.g. "@user1 How are you [first name]? We met a few months ago. Do yo know where?") or attempts to push away trolls (e.g. "@userX move on please. Troll some one who gives a damn. One more tweet and you're blocked"). These were excluded from the analysis.

Examining the story frames created in these comments, it was found that users predominantly oriented to the storyrealm (in 182 posts) rather than the taleworld (in 10 posts). The majority of posts draw attention to storytelling as the sharing activity at hand, to the tellability of the story, or both. In these comments, users make an explicit reference to the act of sharing the image-story, thanking the sharer as in Example 14 and offering an evaluation of the image in terms of its possible implications ("a shocking image that can get European politicians to act"), thus signaling the tellability of the story it portrays.

Example 14

@bouckap Thanks! It takes a shocking image such as this to get European politicians to act.

Other posts focused on the storyrealm provided the user's explanation of their own motivation for retweeting the image as in Example 15, acknowledging its ambivalent nature whose viewing is impossible and at the same time necessary, while others were seen to reflect critically on the act of sharing it, as shown in Example 16.

Example 15

I'm going to RT a truly heartbreaking photo posted by @bouckap – impossible to look at but impossible to turn away from. #refugeecrisis.

Example 16

@bouckap @maryonthenet I do appreciate what you are doing but remember, his father who did survive this tragedy (1/2)

@bouckap @maryonthenet I posted it too not thinking abt the father but It would kill me to see it over and over again. #respectfamily (2/2)

Other types of comments focused on the storyrealm offered assessments of the story in the form of additional angles and reports from other related media and social media sources, as in the case of the user in Example 17, who points to reports about the father being a trafficker.[11]

Example 17

@MillionZ and now Reuters reports that there are hints the father might be a trafficker

Fewer posts focused on the taleworld, i.e. on the child as the main figure of the story. An example of such a comment is given next, where the user picks out the shoes of the boy as a symbol of maternal love (see Example 18).

Example 18

JSSR Retweeted Peter N. Bouckaert His mum must have bought those little shoes for him with so much love :(@bouckap @Beemzx @EyeofTheTiger.

Other examples of taleworld-focused comments concerned tributes, through which users projected their affective identification with the suffering of the boy (see Examples 19 and 20).

Example 19

@bouckap the shoes-that was worn by the kid with a dream of a new journey for 'freedom' from barbarians to 'free world' drowned #AylanKurdi

Example 20

Jesus have mercy : (RIP, kid.

Lastly, there were posts which combined a focus on the storyrealm and a focus on the taleworld, as shown in the following example, where the emboldened part of the sentence signals the focus on the taleworld (affective identification with the boy) and the rest of the message focuses on the storyrealm, referring to the importance and tellability of his story.

Example 21

93 @bouckap **This sweet little boy is my child as well. As a mother I mourn his death.** I demand justice for these innocent victims. #solidarity.

This examination of comments as inter-reactions enacting particular types of story frames clarifies the different forms of uptake of the image-story in this thread of solidarity. It highlights that users' messages tend to converge stylistically and narratively, in their shared concern with different aspects of the storyrealm, such as the activity of story sharing, the viewability of the image, and the tellability of the story it portrays. Their contribution of comments in support of the act of sharing or their offering of evaluations of the visual story constitute moments of affective positioning, in which sharers take up positions signaling alignment or disalignment to other sharers, the father of the child, and (Syrian) refugees more generally, and the sharer's own self in the here and now.

Comments focused on the main figure of the visual story, even though fewer, which show an orientation to the taleworld, constitute moments of affective positioning in the here and now, which resonate directly with Bouckaert's call for solidary identification with Alan Kurdi. Such displays of solidarity point to users' taking up identity positions to the story as mourning, contemplative witnesses to the death event.

These different types of witness positions and stances suggest that through similar threads or messages of solidarity, a metastory of Alan Kurdi's death gradually emerges, as a story that is less about his short life and more about his tragic ending, his family, the plight of Syrian refugees, or the boundaries of acceptability in visual representations of death. The emergence of the metastory of Alan Kurdi's drowning on Twitter in this early phase of the image's circulation mainly relied on verbal forms of positioning rather than hashtag use (cf. Chapter 6). In fact, across this thread of immediate reactions to the just-shared image of Alan Kurdi, hashtags were sparsely used, and when they were, they were not necessarily mirroring other sharers' hashtags. Hashtags that instantiated in the corpus included place names referring to countries implicated in the refugee crisis, e.g. #Syria, #SaudiArabia, #UAE, #Egypt, #Kuwait, or institutions, e.g. #EU and explicit references to the crisis, e.g. #refugeecrisis, #SyrianCrisis. There was one instance of a hashtag which mentioned the name of the boy #Aylan Kurdi and various references to hashtags as metacomments to posts, highlighting invoked emotions, e.g. #solidarity, #respectfamily, #prayers, #nowords, or suggestions for general actions of solidarity, e.g. #savethechildren, #nomore war. There were no instances of the hashtag #JeSuisAylan or #HumanityWashedAshore, which became associated with this story at a later phase. The next section will consider in some more detail the emergence and uses of stances of solidarity in the hashtag #JeSuisAylan on social media on Twitter.

The Hashtag #JeSuisAylan as an Affective Positioning Resource

As the following diagram shows, over time, the hashtag #JeSuisAylan has been associated with hashtags in different languages (English, French, and Spanish), mainly with names of countries 'Turkey' and 'Syria', the first or full name of the boy, 'Aylan' and 'AylanKurdi', references to refugees rather than migrants ('refugies') and solidarity stances to them, e.g. 'refugeeswelcome', 'yosoyrefugiado'. It also became associated with feelings of nausea, 'nausee', and dividing lines of alignment to the boy versus to *Charlie Hebdo*, 'JeNeSuisPasCharlie'.

The hashtag #JeNeSuisPasCharlie started circulating as a reaction to a series of cartoons by *Charlie Hebdo* using drawings of the death of Aylan in September 2015 and satirizing his death under the headline "Welcome to migrants!" and a caption on his body reading "So near his goal . . . promotional offer: kids menu 2 for the price of 1". Another cartoon by *Charlie Hebdo* shows what appears to be Jesus next to the drowned boy with the caption: "Proof that Europe is Christian. Christians walk on water – Muslim children sink" (The Independent, 2015, Sept. 14). Then, after an incident in January 2016 about immigrants allegedly involved in an assault case, *Charlie Hebdo* republished a drawing of the image

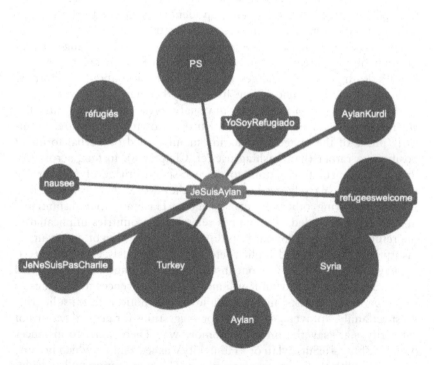

Figure 7.1 Hashtagify analysis of popularity of hashtag #JeSuisAylan
Source: Hashtagify, 2018.

of Alan Kurdi's body, asking, "What would little Aylan have grown up to be?" and offering the following answer at the bottom: "Ass groper in Germany". *Charlie Hebdo*'s satirical uses of the image on these different occasions sparked a huge wave of outrage against the newspaper, with many torn over whether its cartoons were racist or satirical of dominant perception of Muslims and immigrants in the West (*The Guardian*, 2016, Jan. 14). This explains its prevalent association with the hashtag #JeSuisAylan noted in the Hashtagify analysis.

A search for tweets including the hashtag #JeSuisAylan on Twitter retrieved few posts from September 2 (six posts) and 205 tweets from September 3 (182 after cleanup). The emergence of the hashtag as a popular choice among commenters on the event on September 3 seems to confirm the finding from the analysis of the #JeSuisCharlie hashtag (see Chapter 4), which suggested that the emergence of a story-specific hashtag was part of a different phase of the circulation of the story.

The hashtag #JeSuisAylan arguably emerges as an instance of solidified involved narrative positions of empathic solidarity shortly after the breaking news of the death has been anchored to related locations, institutions, persons, emotions, and acts of solidarity in Tweet events picked up by mainstream media. Its uses affirm as well as prompt further the public visibility of the story and the constitution of loosely bonding affective publics around it. The story frames identified in this corpus of tweets are discussed in more detail in what follows.

Similarly to the story frame orientation of the tweets in the thread under Bouckaert's post, tweet inter-reactions hashtagged as #JeSuisAylan were also predominantly oriented to the storyrealm (117 instances). The majority of commenters focused on the shareability of the story and contributed to its further circulation and hence visibility online by resharing one of the images already in circulation in print media or Twitter, a visual meme of the hashtag or a reworking of the image (in 79 instances), accompanied by a series of hashtags (e.g. *#IamAylan #AylanKurdi #refugee #crisis #humanitarian #innocence #Syria #RIPlittleone. #JESUISAYLAN; #JeSuisAylan #AylanKurdi*).

The majority of the images in the corpus focused on the storyrealm, i.e. images involving some form of visual rescripting (in 33 instances). These were predominantly rescriptings of the image of the boy's dead body on the shore, projecting positive afterlife scenarios (in 20 instances). Shared images concerning the taleworld, i.e. the visual representation of the boy's death as portrayed in Demir's widely shared images, were found in fewer instances (15).

Posts directed to the storyrealm mainly shared comments on the broader issues the story raised about Europe, the world and humanity, attributing blame and responsibility to different social and institutional actors (38 instances; Example 22). They were also found to call networked publics to action (18 instances; see Example 23) or offer an explicit comment about the tellability of the story (12 instances; see Example 24).

Example 22

Jusqu'à quand? L'Europe doit prendre ses responsabilités et les Euro-péens montrer leur solidarité #UE #Réfugiés #Syrie #JeSuisAylan
(Trans.: 'Until when? Europe has to assume its responsibilities and the Europeans show their solidarity #UE #Refugees #Syria #IAmAylan').

Example 23

Time for action #JeSuisAylan; Hug your children.

Example 24

#jesuisaylan Cette photo qui fait la une de tous les journaux remue toutes les consciences
(trans.: 'This photo which has hit the headlines moves all consciences').

Lastly, a limited number of posts categorized as 'storyrealm' called attention to the use of the hashtag, either negotiating the metamessage expressed by the hashtag (Example 25) or ironically nodding to the quick succession of hashtags in reactions to very different kinds of events, turning 'JeSuis . . . ' statements into a cliché, i.e. an empty expression (Example 26).

Example 25

On est à deux doigts du #JeSuisAylan ou #JeSuisUnMigrant
(trans.: 'We are within a hair's breadth from #IAmAylan to #IAmaMigrant')

Example 26

#jesuischarlie #jesuisaylan et dans 15 jours #jesuiséquipedefrancederugby
(trans.: '#iamcharlie #iamaylan and in 15 days #iamteamfrancerugby')

Posts categorized as invoking the taleworld included posts which explicitly referred to A(y)lan as the main character of the story (Example 27) or invoked some of the details of the life of the boy and his brother, Ghalib, who also died when the boat they were on capsized (Example 28).

Example 27

#JeSuisAylan cet enfant est le mien
(trans.: '#IamAylan this child is mine')

Example 28

Aylan et Ghalib fuyaient la guerre pour un avenir meilleur
(trans.: 'Aylan and Ghalib escaped the war for a better future')

To sum up, the hashtag #JeSuisAylan was found to be associated with comments pertaining to the storyrealm, pushing further the visibility of the story by reiterating its wider importance and relevance in a mimetic way. The identification of considerably fewer comments pertaining to the taleworld in the corpus seems to suggest that users' affective engagement with the main characters of the story is limited. Instead, affective engagement online appears to be driven by associations of the boy's story to other stories and reactions to them, such as the *Charlie Hebdo* attacks or the outside world, for example the broader refugee crisis. Users' participation in the story was found to be centred around the shareability of the story in the recognizable and portable format of the hashtag story #JeSuisAylan, extending the mediatization of the story online and reproducing existing affective positions to the event and those involved in it.

This mode of sharing creates affective positions of ambient solidarity as a form of phatic and evaluative communion of networked publics around the refugee crisis at a distance from the main protagonists of the event. The emotional response that such images promote seems to prompt urgent action that takes the form of a political spectacle intermeshed with audience engagement modes of 'politainment' (Schultz, 2012) rather than a critical and in-depth engagement with the root causes of the refugee crisis or the deep-rooted views about migrants more broadly. As Jaworski et al. (2005, p. 10) point out, the 9/11 live news coverage was characterized by a reporting of feeling and emotions, organized around the "politics of pity" (Chouliaraki, 2006). In this type of news reporting, viewers engaged with the news, focusing on its affective and moral dimensions on the basis of a politics of mourning.

After the Outpouring of Grief

The story of Alan Kurdi remains emblematic not only of the plight of refugees but also of fading memory and compassion fatigue. September 2 of every year that's passed since 2015 has turned into a memorial day, when articles or artistic interventions remembering Alan re-appear. The more recent example at the time of writing is the publication of a UN report on those seeking refuge in Europe prefaced by Khaled Hosseini, the novelist and Goodwill Ambassador for UNHCR, the UN Refugee Agency, who also wrote an illustrated (and virtual reality) story as a tribute to families forced from their homes by conflict and persecution. Some commentators in the media have drawn parallels of the image to earlier emotionally evocative paintings, such as Nicolas Poussin's 1627 painting *Massacre des Innocents* (Renard, 2018). More recent rescriptings of the visual story of Alan Kurdi tend to involve fewer plot manipulations or comments: for example, an image drawn by Eduardo Sales, entitled *La Memoria Colective Siempre es de corto plazo* (trans. Collective Memory is always short-term) shows the same image of the boy's lifeless body in nine frames, moving from a full representation of the boy's to a blank frame, as a way of making a poignant comment on the quickness with which the effervescence of collective memory tends to fade away.

Summary

The circulation of visual small stories on Twitter in reaction to the images of Alan Kurdi's death illustrates how media spectacles extend to social media spectacles of affect, which prompt mediated participation in the death and suffering of the Other. In cases of reporting instances of sensational and tragic death, like the boy's death, which are inherently reportable, the tellability of the story is extended on social media to shareability via the reiteration of emblematic images, their rescripting, and the affirmation of equally emblematic stances and positions in print headlines, threads of solidarity on Twitter, and hashtagged posts on Twitter. The circulation drive of the story and metastory of Alan Kurdi does not rely so much on the detail about the story or the clarification or further exploration of related events, causes of the events, or second stories. Rather, the circulation drive of these stories lies in the opportunities they create for social media users to participate in the telling of the moment, constructing and sharing affective stances on characters and events, which draw on familiar tropes and frames and allow them to affectively position themselves as witnesses to events of global resonance. The resharing and reworking of the image shifting from taleworld to storyrealm frames partly explains how this shared story continues to accumulate affective value over the time of its circulation as an index of cosmopolitan emotions.

Similarly to the YouTube videos of disaster appeals studied by Pantti and Tikka (2014, p. 190), visual stories of #JeSuisAylan shared online "create objects and subjects of feelings as well as communities of feeling [that relate] to other humanitarian discourses and media technologies". As Chouliaraki (2010) has argued, humanitarian appeals have been moving away towards a post-humanitarian style of appeal, avoiding the use of 'shock images' and the elicitation of 'traditional' emotions of guilt and empathy in favour of short-term and low-intensity forms of engagement.

The identified story frames and modes of story participation in this chapter arguably emerge as forms of *vernacular post-humanitarianism* online, promoting a cosmopolitan sense of moral responsibility and an obligation to show and share emotions of sadness but also shame and disgust at contemporary humanity. In these types of sharing, acts of stancetaking and displays of emotion arguably contain the individualized reception of these stories of suffering into moments of emotional upheaval that make people feel better about their own moral universe.

Even though the images shared can be said to rehumanize refugees, the sentimental portrayal of refugee stories as tragedies can be harmful in different ways. Instead of mobilizing public and political agency, they end up creating spectacles of human suffering, turning reporting into acts of voyeurism and raising "vague awareness" of largely apathetic spectators (Rae et al., 2017; Chouliaraki and Stolic, 2017).

In the era of news (social) mediatization, such affective and moral engagements with unfolding global events are not only circulated through professional news discourse, but they are spread further and rescaled through modes of ecstatic sharing in which viewers and networked publics recycle or remix emblematic images to feel united in their 'shock' and 'outrage' and restore their sense of 'safety at home'. Rather than giving, though, a particular directionality (e.g. attributing responsibility to key actors, decision makers, etc. or radically challenging the deeply rooted suspicion, fear, or pity stances to refugees), it is argued that this process of news spreading through mimetic restorying of the Other's suffering primarily achieves some form of phatic communion among networked audiences as witnesses of the reported events, exhausting criticality and the possibility of change to mediating mourning engagement. Networked users are increasingly urged to affirm already circulating stances and positions instead of investigating widely shared stories in relation to the 'bigger' stories of war and power and the 'small' stories of suffering and death these are enmeshed in.

Conclusion

Participation in stories of migrant suffering and death online needs to be understood as part of cosmopolitan forms of reflection and engagement in contexts of digital late modernity characterized by reflexive individualization (Svensson, 2014, p. 20), where users manage and control the display of their emotions in order to connect with peers and gain or increase their own visibility online. As Zelizer notes (2010, p. 336), the impact and reception of images of death is very much an open debate – it is yet unclear whether images of the dead nurture or kill compassion (see also Sontag, 2004) and whether – or when – they can actually impact policy and change.

Despite the rapid dissemination of such images and their contribution to the upscaling of global outrage and empathy, their scope tends to be limited to the digital realm, positioning sharers as empathetic witnesses to the death of the 'Other' and connecting sharers with each other through the expression of cosmopolitan empathy.

While in this type of large-scale mourning in social media, the emphasis is on creating a moment instead of a movement based on bonds that extend beyond the media spectacle of a death. If mourning in social media is to claim political significance, it needs to explicitly connect to and emerge from offline movements fostering positions of active witnessing of deaths caused and silenced by rampant inequalities. Rebellious forms of mourning encompass mourning for the tragedies of the Palestinian struggle, AIDS, border crossings, police shootings; they are organized beyond the insularity of the personal, around a collective sense of grief and feelings as words or action that "can open up cracks in the wall of the system, [. . .] pry open spaces of contestation and reconstruction, intervulnerability and strength, empathy and solidarity" (Milstein, 2017, pp. 8–9).

The final chapter brings together the key insights drawn from the examination of these four case studies and sets out further direction in the study of dying, death, and mourning, narrative, affect in social media.

Notes

1. I will be referring to the boy as Alan unless quoting directly from users' posts or popular hashtags.
2. Some other sources, however, including Wikipedia, cite a Dutch news source for the initial posting of the image instead.
3. PCC refers to the Press Complaints Commission www.pcc.org.uk/. The PCC is charged with enforcing the newspaper's Code of Practice, which it ratified on August 7, 2006.
4. "1.   The public interest includes, but is not confined to:

    i.   Detecting or exposing crime or serious impropriety;
    ii. Protecting public health and safety;
    iii. Preventing the public from being misled by an action or statement of an individual or organisation.

    2.   There is a public interest in freedom of expression itself.
    3.   Whenever the public interest is invoked, the PCC will require editors to demonstrate fully how the public interest was served.
    4.   The PCC will consider the extent to which material is already in the public domain, or will become so.
    5.   In cases involving children under 16, editors must demonstrate an exceptional public interest to over-ride the normally paramount interest of the child."

    (*The Guardian*'s Editorial Code, 2007, p. 10)

5. Note that this might vary across users, depending on the user's media settings.
6. The use of visual online material abides by the current *UK Copyright, Designs and Patents Act 1988* Sections 29 and 30 which state respectively that:

    "Fair dealing with a work for the purposes of research for a non-commercial purpose does not infringe any copyright in the work provided that it is accompanied by a sufficient acknowledgement" (www.legislation.gov.uk/ukpga/1988/48/section/29) and

    "Fair dealing with a work for the purpose of criticism or review, of that or another work or of a performance of a work, does not infringe any copyright in the work provided that it is accompanied by a sufficient acknowledgement (unless this would be impossible for reasons of practicality or otherwise) and provided that the work has been made available to the public". For this reason, we acknowledge the creators of visual material (where known) and provide the source through which such material has been made available to the public (www.legislation. gov.uk/ukpga/1988/48/section/30).

7. Note the image appeared in various sizes and positions on the cover page.
8. The analysis focuses on the fifty most popular reworkings which have attracted a minimum of 8 score (given that the most popular of these has received a score of 220).
9. Note that these examples have been drawn from outside the Bored Panda corpus.
10. Twitter handles used in the examples are pseudonyms.
11. These hints and reports turned out not to be true and were quickly lost from view.

References

Beck, U. (2006) *The Cosmopolitan Vision*. Cambridge: Polity Press.

Berry, M., I. Garcia-Blanco, and K. Moore (2016) UK press is the most aggressive in reporting on Europe's "migrant" crisis. *The Conversation*, Mar. 14. Available at: https://theconversation.com/uk-press-is-the-most-aggressive-in-reporting-on-europes-migrant-crisis-56083. Accessed: 12 Aug. 2019.

Blommaert, J. (2015) One crisis, three photos: How Europe started caring for refugees. *Alternative Democracy, Ctrl+Alt+Dem: Research on Alternative Democratic Life in Europe* [online]. Available at: https://alternative-democracy-research.org/. Accessed: 29 Sept. 2018.

Boltanski, L. (1999) *Distant Suffering: Morality, Media and Politics*. Cambridge: Cambridge University Press.

Bored Panda (Neje, J.) (n.d.) *Artists around the world respond to tragic death of 3-year-old Syrian Refugee*. Available at: www.boredpanda.com/syrian-boy-drowned-mediterranean-tragedy-artists-respond-aylan-kurdi/?utm_source=google&utm_medium=organic&utm_campaign=organic. Accessed: 10 Oct. 2018.

Burgess, J. (2006) Hearing ordinary voices: Cultural studies, vernacular creativity and digital storytelling. *Journal of Media & Cultural Studies* 20 (2): 201–214.

Chouliaraki, L. (2004) Watching 11 September: The politics of pity. *Discourse and Society* (Special Issue: Interpreting Tragedy: The Language of 11 September 2001) 15 (2–3): 185–199.

Chouliaraki, L. (2006) *The Spectatorship of Suffering*. London, Thousand Oaks, and New Delhi: Sage Publications.

Chouliaraki, L. (2010) Post-humanitarianism: Humanitarian communication beyond a politics of pity. *International Journal of Cultural Studies* 13 (2): 107–126.

Chouliaraki, L. and T. Stolic (2017) Rethinking media responsibility in the refugee "crisis": A visual typology of European news. *Media, Culture and Society* 39 (8): 1162–1177.

De Fina, A. (2016) Storytelling and audience reactions in social media. *Language in Society* 45: 473–498.

Georgakopoulou, A. (2015) Sharing as rescripting: Place manipulations on You-Tube between narrative and social media affordances. *Discourse, Context, and Media* 9: 64–72.

Georgakopoulou, A. (2016) From narrating the self to posting self(ies): A small stories approach to selfies. *Open Linguistics* 2: 300–317.

Georgakopoulou, A. and K. Giaxoglou (2018) Emplotment in the social mediatization of the economy: The poly-storying of economist Yanis Varoufakis. *Language@Internet* 16: 1–15.

Giaxoglou, K. and T. Spilioti (2018) Mediatizing death and suffering: Rescripting visual stories of the refugee crisis as distant witnessing and mourning. In Burger, M., J. Thornborrow, and R. Fitzgerald (Eds.), *Discours des réseaux sociaux: enjeux publics, politiques et médiatiques*. Bruxelles: De Boeck, pp. 65–92.

Giaxoglou, K. and T. Spilioti (2020) The shared story of #JeSuisAylan on Twitter: Story participation and stancetaking in visual small stories. *Pragmatics: Quarterly Publication of the International Pragmatics Association (IPrA)* 30 (2): 277–302.

The Guardian Media Group (2007) *Guidelines: The Guardian's Editorial Code*. Available at: http://image.guardian.co.uk/sys-files/Guardian/documents/2007/06/14/EditorialCode2007.pdf. Accessed: 20 Oct. 2018.

Hoijer, B. (2004) The discourse of global compassion: The audience and media reporting of human suffering. *Media, Culture and Society* 26 (4): 513–531.

IOM (2015) *Global migration trends factsheet: International Organisation for Migration (IOM)*. Available at: http://gmdac.iom.int/global-migration-trends-factsheet. Accessed: 29 Sept. 2018.

Jaworski, A., R. Fitzgerald, and O. Constantinou (2005) Busy saying nothing new: Live silence in TV reporting of 9/11. *Multilingua* 24: 121–144.

John, N. (2017) *The Age of Sharing*. Malden, MA: Polity Press.

Jones, R. (2012) *Discourse Analysis: A Resource Book for Students*. Oxon: Routledge.

Jungblut, M. and I. Zakareviciute (2019) Do pictures tell a different story? A multimodal frame analysis of the 2014 Israel-Gaza conflict. *Journalism Practice* 13 (2): 206–228.

Kurdi, T. (2018) *The Boy on the Beach: My Family's Escape from Syria and Our Hope for a New Home*. New York: Simon & Schuster.

Milstein, C. (Ed.) (2017) *Rebellious Mourning: The Collective Work of Grief*. Chico, Edinburgh, and Baltimore: AK Press.

Mortensen, M. (2017) Constructing, confirming and contesting icons: The Alan Kurdi imagery appropriated by #humanitywashedashore, Ai Weiwei, and Charlie Hebdo. *Media, Culture and Society* 39 (8): 1142–1161.

Nussbaum, M. (2007) Cosmopolitan emotions. *New Humanist*, May 31. Available at: https://newhumanist.org.uk/articles/470/cosmopolitan-emotions. Accessed: 30 Nov. 2018.

Olesen, T. (2017) Memetic protest and the dramatic diffusion of Alan Kurdi. *Media, Culture and Society* 40 (5): 656–672.

Pantti, M. and M. Tikka (2014) Cosmopolitan empathy and user-generated disaster appeal videos on YouTube. In Benski, T. and E. Fisher (Eds.), *Internet and Emotions*. New York and London: Routledge, pp. 178–193.

Rae, M., R. Holman, and A. Nethery (2017) Self-represented witnessing: The use of social media by asylum seekers in Australia's offshore immigration detention. *Media, Culture and Society* 40 (4): 479–495.

Renard, C. (2018) Du "Massacre des Innocents" au "Petit Aylan". Analyse d'images percutantes. *France Culture, Savoirs.* Available at: www.franceculture.fr/peinture/du-massacre-des-innocents-au-petit-ilan-histoire-dimages-percutantes. Accessed: 30 Nov. 2018.

Schultz, D. (2012) *Politainment: The Ten Rules of Contemporary Politics: A Citizen's Guide to Understanding Campaigns and Elections.* USA: Amazon.com.

Smith Dahmen, N., J. Abdenour, K. McIntyre, and K.E. Noga-Styron (2017) Covering mass shootings: Journalists' perceptions of coverage and factors influencing attitudes. *Journalism* 12 (4): 456–476.

Sontag, S. (2004) *Regarding the Pain of Others.* London: Penguin.

Svensson, J. (2014) Power, identity, and feelings in digital late modernity: The rationality of reflexive emotion displays online. In T. Benski and E. Fisher (Eds.), *Internet and the Emotions.* London and New York: Routledge, pp. 17–33.

Topinka, R.J. (2016) Terrorism, governmentality and the simulated city: The Boston Marathon bombing and the search for suspect two. *Visual Communication* 15 (2): 351–370.

Vis, F. (2015) Examining the hundred most shared images of Aylan Kurdi on Twitter. In Vis, F. and O. Goriunova (Eds.), *The Iconic Image on Social Media: A Rapid Research Response to the Death of Aylan Kurdi.* Sheffield: University of Sheffield, pp. 27–31. Available at: http://visualsocialmedialab.org. Accessed: 18 Sept. 2018.

Vis, F. and O. Goriunova (2015) The Iconic image on social media: A rapid research response to the death of Aylan Kurdi. In Vis, F. and O. Goriunova (Eds.), *The Iconic Image on Social Media: A Rapid Research Response to the Death of Aylan Kurdi.* Sheffield: University of Sheffield. Available at: http://visualsocialmedialab.org. Accessed: 18 Sept. 2018.

Young, G.K. (1987) *Taleworlds and Storyrealms: The Phenomenology of Narrative.* Dordrecht: Martinus Nijhoff.

Zelizer, B. (2010) *About to Die: How News Images Move the Public.* Oxford: Oxford University Press.

Media Sources

Bouckaert, P. (2015) Dispatches: Why I shared a horrific photo of a drowned Syrian child. *Human Rights Watch Blog*, Sept. 2. Available at: www.hrw.org/news/2015/09/02/dispatches-why-i-shared-horrific-photo-drowned-syrian-child. Accessed: 10 Oct. 2018.

CNN (2015) Photographer describes "scream" of migrant boy's "silent body". *CNN* [World], Sept. 3. Available at: https://edition.cnn.com/2015/09/03/world/dead-migrant-boy-beach-photographer-nilufer-demir/index.html. Accessed: 25 Jan. 2019.

Daily Mirror (Rossington, B.) (2015) Photographer who took picture of drowned toddler Aylan Kurdi says she had to "make this tragedy heard". *Daily Mirror* [World News, Refugee Crisis], Sept. 4. Available at: www.mirror.co.uk/news/world-news/photographer-who-took-picture-drowned-6380991. Accessed: 29 Sept. 2018.

The Guardian (2015) *The Guardian*'s decision to publish shocking photos of Aylan Kurdi. *The Guardian*, Sept. 7. Available at: www.theguardian.com/commentisfree/2015/sep/07/guardian-decision-to-publish-shocking-photos-of-aylan-kurdi. Accessed: 29 Sept. 2018.

The Guardian (Meade, A.) (2016) Charlie Hebdo cartoon depicting drowned child Alan Krudi sparks racism debate. *The Guardian* [World, Europe], Jan. 14. Available at: www.theguardian.com/media/2016/jan/14/charlie-hebdo-cartoon-depicting-drowned-child-alan-kurdi sparks-racism-debate. Accessed: 15 Oct. 2018.

Hürriyet Daily News (2016) Dogan News Agency nets two photo awards. *Hürriyet Daily News* [Turkey, Local]. Available at: www.hurriyetdailynews.com/dogan-news-agency-nets-two-photo-awards-97014. Accessed: 29 Sept. 2018.

The Independent (Harrold, A.) (2015) Charlie Hebdo publishes a cartoon of drowned Syrian toddler Aylan Kurdi. *The Independent* [World, Europe], Sept. 14. Available at: www.independent.co.uk/news/world/europe/charlie-hebdo-cover-cartoon-jokes-about-death-of-drowned-syrian-toddler-aylan-kurdi-10499645.html. Accessed: 10 Oct. 2018.

The Independent (Withnall, A.) (2015) Refugee crisis: Turkish police officer who found Aylan Kurdi's body describes "terrible loss". *The Independent* [World, Europe], Sept. 6. Available at: www.independent.co.uk/news/world/europe/refugee-crisis-turkish-police-officer-who-found-aylan-kurdis-body-describes-terrible-loss-10488681.html. Accessed: 29 Sept. 2018.

TIME (2015) Alan Kurdi's story: Behind the most heartbreaking photo of 2015. *TIME*. Available at: http://time.com/4162306/alan-kurdi-syria-drowned-boy-refugee-crisis/. Accessed: 29 Sept. 2018.

TIME (Laurent, O.) (2015) What the image of Aylan Kurdi says about the power of photography. *TIME* [Lightbox], Sept. 4. Available at: http://time.com/4022765/aylan-kurdi-photo/. Accessed: 12 Oct. 2018.

Appendix 1

Table 7.2 UK newspaper headlines – Thursday, September 3, 2015

Newspaper	Front page	Image
Daily Express	EU blamed for migrant chaos. Europe's border crisis is totally out of control.	Image of a group of migrants walking en masse (right-hand side)
Daily Mirror	EUROPE'S REFUGEE CRISIS (in red) A three year-old boy washed up on a holiday beach in Turkey . . . the heartbreaking human face of a tragedy the world can no longer ignore UNBEARABLE	Image of a gendarme carrying the boy in his arms covering the entire front page
London Evening Standard	MIGRANT CRISIS: 13-HOUR EUROSTAR ORDEAL	
The Daily Telegraph	Plight of migrant children stirs Europe's conscience	Image of a soldier carrying a toddler (not Alan Kurdi) and people in a queue in the background
The Guardian	The shocking, cruel reality of Europe's refugee crisis – Boy among 12 Syrians who died in boat tragedy – Picture raises questions over EU's response.	Image of a gendarme carrying the boy in his arms on the left-hand side of front page.
Daily Mail	Tiny victim of a human catastrophe (in large letters on the right hand side of the image)	Image of a gendarme carrying the boy in his arms covering the entire front page.
The Independent	SOMEBODY'S CHILD The tide of desperate humanity seeking safety in Europe is rising. Yesterday's victims include this Syrian boy, drowned in his family's attempt to reach Greece from Turkey. The EU is deadlocked: our Prime Minister is in denial. A vast human catastrophe is unfolding. Do we really believe that this is not our problem?	Image of a gendarme carrying the boy in his arms covering the entire front page

8   Small Stories of Mourning and Affective Positioning

Summary

The starting point for this book has been that mourning is a response to loss as much as the taking up of responsibility; it is situated in between the unsayable and the sayable, the singular and the iterable, the private and the public, the personal and the collective. The liminality of mourning makes it a unique site for the study of the narrative, affective, and identity form(at)s and positioning negotiations that are part of the *techne* of reckoning with death, the dead, and our very own emotional selves (see Chapter 1).

One of the main arguments in this book has been that mourning is deeply ingrained in social life and needs to be approached as narrative practice embedded in other practices in line with discourse and sociolinguistic perspectives in narrative analysis (De Fina and Georgakopoulou, 2012). A narrative approach to dying, death, and mourning allows insights beyond the popular thesis that these topics are taboo in contemporary society and turns attention to the conditions of their tellability or storyability, shareability, and visibility in different contexts as well as to the dynamics of their circulation. Such an approach also makes it possible to examine continuities and shifts in mourning practices in relation to broader processes, such as secularization, globalization, or mediatization, and to avoid judgments and sweeping generalizations about the nature of mourning performances (see Chapter 2).

This book has focused on mourning in social media, with an overarching interest in how people use social media to share dying, death, and grief and what kinds of storying and participation practices online become associated with these types of sharing across different platforms. Ultimately, the aim of this study has been to shed light on the continuities and shifts but also on the promises and limits of engaging with death, dying, and grief in contemporary networked societies beyond utopian or dystopian views of the web (see Chapter 3).

Although a large body of accumulating research on digital mourning has celebrated the positive potential of mourning online, noting for instance the contribution of such practices to the re-emergence of a sense of community (Walter et al., 2012) and their benefits for the bereaved in the process of coping with their loss (Sofka et al., 2012), media representations of sharing mourning online have tended to portray them uniformly as inauthentic and trivializing displays of grief. These contrasting views attest to the two sides of ideologies of social media, utopian and dystopian (Fisher and Wright, 2006), which tend to reflect individual preferences and values instead of offering a balanced assessment of the technology's impact on digital death and mourning. This book has sought to stir clear of both cyber-utopianism and dystopianism, advocating the need for the empirical and situated study of such heterogeneous and dynamic social practices.

The case studies selected for discussion ranged from small-scale to large-scale social media events of dying, death, and mourning: from practices of auto/biographical storying of (terminal) illness in a vlog (Chapter 4) and the poly-storying of grief for the loss of a popular young adult on a Facebook memorial group (Chapter 5) to practices of shared mourning via hashtags and images illustrated in reactions to the terrorist attack on *Charlie Hebdo* (Chapter 6) and to migrant death in the case of the iconic death of three-year old Alan Kurdi (Chapter 7).

The common threads bringing together the four case studies have been the interrelated questions of (i) how dying, death, and grief are mobilized across different types of loss and contexts as *small stories* and (ii) how these stories are drawn upon as resources for negotiating specific kinds of *identity* and *affective positioning* that help modulate distance from or proximity to a death event and the dead, audiences (known and unknown; online and offline), and the emotional self. As I have shown, in "an age of sharing" (John, 2017), social media extend the domain of dying, death, and grief into events and spectacles open to participation, where digital media affordances can be capitalized for amplifying personal-affective as well as collective-symbolic meanings and for increasing connectedness, visibility, and value (narrative, social, and economic).

A Narrative Approach to Mourning

This book has put forward an empirical framework for the study of mourning as narrative inspired by a number of current research approaches in narrative, discourse, and sociolinguistic studies, including (i) the *small stories* research paradigm pioneered by Georgakopoulou (2007, 2015) for the study of non-canonical stories as crucial sites of subjectivity in everyday interaction; (ii) interactional approaches to the study of *positioning* at three analytically separable levels for analyzing the construction of the self in narrative tellings (Bamberg, 1997; Wortham, 2000; De Fina et al., 2006; Depperman, 2013); (iii) the analysis of *sharing* as a metaphor we live by (John, 2017) that can be empirically studied at distinct levels (Androutsopoulos, 2014); and (iv) the framework of *mediated narrative analysis* introduced by Page for the analysis of online, large-scale, multimodal *shared stories* (Page, 2018).

The framework proposed in this book analyzes mourning in social media along three interrelated practices of sharing, namely *selecting*, *storying*, and *positioning*, and introduces the concept of *affective positioning* as a necessary extension to identity positioning. Affective positioning is defined here as the linguistic and discourse modulation of the level of *proximity* to or *distance* from the death event and the dead, the audience (known and unknown), and the sharer's own emotional self and offers an empirical window into affect as an integral part of narrative performance and identities. In what follows, I summarize the key insights that have emerged from the analysis of the different case studies using this framework.

Selecting Practices

The study of *selecting practices*, that is the choices about which aspects of a particular personal experience or an event to share, clarified which types of dying, death, grief – and hence lives – gain visibility in online contexts. It was observed, more specifically, that it is predominantly sensational and already newsworthy personal experiences, such as the suffering and loss of promising young adults, or spectacular death events, such as terrorist attacks or the death of a child, that also gain popularity and public visibility online. Disenfranchised grief seems to remain restricted to closed groups, as previous studies have shown (Hård af Segerstad and Kasperowski, 2015; Refslund Christensen et al., 2017). This suggests that any claims about a generalized positive impact of social media on making death more generally visible in society and contributing to changing long-established attitudes to it must be considered as exaggerations – at least for now. In addition, a preference for selecting specific facets of death as shareable content, namely post-mortem types of content, relating to memorialization was noted. This does not mean, of course, that other aspects are not shareable, but it does seem to be the case that other kinds of content attract lower levels of attention.

At the micro-level of crafting small stories of mourning, selections of shareables were found to vary depending on the situated affordances indexed as much as indexing the type of loss, the sharer's relation to the dead and the networked mourners, and platform-specific norms of sharing.

Storying Practices

In terms of *storying practices*, the different modes of small storying identified were found to be associated with the different narrative positions, namely the positions of *teller*, *co-teller* of, or *witness* to disruptive episodes and events of life and death. Assuming responsibility for the sharing of a personal experience from the position of a *teller* allows sharers to select moments as part of a story they curate themselves, claiming some control over their post-mortem legacies, as shown in the case of the cancer vlogger (Chapter 4). Positions of *co-tellership* foster collective small storying through which mourning is construed as a collective experience, as illustrated in the case of the Facebook memorial group (Chapter 5). Finally, positions of *witnesses* were found to be associated with more mimetic types of small storying, as part of displaying alignment or dis-alignment to shared values, as in the case of the shared reference stories circulated via the hashtags #JeSuisCharlie and #JeSuisAylan (Chapters 6 and 7).

The four case studies have pointed to the *poly-storying*[1] of mourning, i.e. the creation of a shared story about an event through the accumulation of sequentially contiguous, though independent, contributions of multiple tellers in platform-specific spaces, such as the comment space underneath a YouTube video (Chapter 4), the wall of a Facebook memorial group (Chapter 5), or interconnected hashtags and reply threads on Twitter (Chapters 6 and 7).

The temporality of small storying was found to vary depending on the type and purposes of mourning performances. For example, in cases of personal sharing discussed in Chapters 4 and 5, the temporal focus of stories was found to shift from the here and now or recent past (*breaking news stories*) to the past (*recounts*) and even the future (*projections*) as sharers negotiated emerging identity and affective dilemmas and modulated their distance from or proximity to the experience or event and the addressees of their sharing.

In the case of the cancer vlog (Chapter 4), more specifically, the mode of small storying was found to shift as the vlogger's illness deteriorated. While at the start of the vlog, recounts of the general impact of the illness on the vlogger's life arguably signalled a more reflective and distant stance to the cancer, the shift to breaking news stories about the very recent past (for example, a few hours before the broadcast) or her here and now in a later phase marked a change in the vlogger's affective positioning to a more proximal and intense emotional engagement with her illness, her audience, and her own self as things became increasingly more serious and life threatening.

The association between storying in the here and now and affective positions of proximity was also noted in the case of small stories of global mourning in reaction to highly mediatized death events. These stories shared in the ecstatic mode of instantaneity afforded sharers the possibility of witnessing global events in a sense of proximity to those involved and to other witnesses.

And yet such connections between storying and affective positions are not straightforwardly generalizable but rather always need to be empirically substantiated. This became evident in the examination of the

Facebook R.I.P. group (Chapter 5), where stories focused on the here and now were, in fact, found in posts shared as immediate reactions to the sudden news of the death, marking some level of distance to the event and even disbelief. As sharers started to reconstruct their relationship and bonds with their dead friend, their storying began to be oriented to the future, seeking their 'angel' friend's support in forthcoming sports activities, contests, or other important life transitions and indexing positions of renewed affective intimacy to the dead. In this group, stories reproducing the temporal rhythms of the sharers' everyday life, termed *habitual small stories*, emerged as the typical mode of small storying, underscoring the sharers' commitment to keep their deceased friend in their everyday life as an absent present.

Positioning Practices

Different types of small stories were found to be in association with different types of *positioning*, fostering specific modes of story participation through *viewing* a story as it unfolds (in the case of the vlog), *co-creating* a tribute mosaic (in the case of the Facebook group), or *aligning* to shared values (in the case of hashtag stories). Across the different cases discussed in this book, sharing dying, death, and mourning as small stories invited participants to take up specific positions indexing identities of the 'good mourner': the *appreciative* mourner inspired by the impact of a lived life, the *dutiful* friend committed to everyday commemoration of a beloved peer, or the *solidary* and *cosmopolitan* mourner taking part in iconic death events.

In addition, small storying was associated with different types of practices of negotiating affective dilemmas and tensions inherent in emotional performances. These included dilemmas around (i) the uniqueness versus the representativeness of a personal experience or the local versus the supra-local and symbolic value of a big-scale death event; (ii) the possibility for (dis)identification and (dis)alignment with shared experiences and values; and finally, (iii) the projection of emotional control versus loss of control over personal affective sharing or the projection of local emotional values and frames for evaluating vicarious experience. These practices were analyzed through a focus on *affective positioning*, which extends the investigation of identities into their affective constituents located in three interrelated levels, including the event and the characters involved, the audiences, and the emotional self.

The cues used to construct and negotiate different types of affective positioning were empirically identified in each of the cases examined and included both verbal and non-verbal cues. Verbal cues included the use of evaluative expressions, spatial, temporal, and personal deixis, and metacommunicative devices, such as openings and closings, while non-verbal cues included the use of body postures, gestures, head movements, and breathing in the case of video-stories or images often in reworked versions.

The degree of distance or proximity taken with respect to dying, death, or grief varied not only across the different cases examined but also within these, pointing to the dynamic affective trajectories of sharers and groups of sharers. Overall, a relative distance to these different types of crises was arguably expressed through assuming and maintaining positive stances to transgressive experiences as sources of inspiration and motivation for those left behind. At the level of audiences, sharing dying, death, and grief in social media was characterized by a pervasive tendency to construct relationships of proximity to networked publics, either by inviting them to take a peek into the intimate details of life with illness or by seeking some form of connection with a small community of mourners or a larger group of witnesses to spectacular death. Finally, affective positioning in relation to the emotional self was found to revolve around the negotiation of relatively empowering positions as a teller, co-teller, or witness, reflecting sharing norms that privilege the display of affective control over transgressive and difficult experiences in public (or semi-public) contexts.

Based on the cases discussed in this book, mourning in social media emerges as a narrative practice which involves sharers' strategic performances of affect for authenticating their online sharing and presence. These performances are an integral component of complex private–public identity constructions aimed at engaging and connecting with networked audiences in the context of platform-specific norms of sharing.

From Life-Writing of the Moment to Death-Writing of the Moment

The eclectic focus on diverse cases of digital mourning foregrounded the mobilization of modes of sharing and updating the self in social media as *life-writing of the moment* (Georgakopoulou, 2015). The analyses, which have touched upon both biographical and news engagements with the world, have pointed to the extension of these modes into sharing as *death-writing of the moment*. Death-writing of the moment reconfigures forms of experiencing and witnessing death and dying and redraws – at least to some extent – the conditions of the visibility of dying, death, and mourning. As mentioned, this visibility is limited by existing norms of shareability as much as by dominant thanatopolitics that assign differential value to lives and their grievability (Butler, 2004).

Visibility emerges as a central concern for sharers who mobilize illness, death, and grief for accruing the value – personal, social, or economic – of their digital presence as well as of their assets. This concern with visibility has developed in tandem with the development of communication media, which, as Thompson (2005) notes, brought forward a new form of visibility – *mediated visibility*. Mediated visibility differs from the situated visibility of co-presence, in that the field of vision is shaped by the particular properties and technical affordances of communication media, such as the camera angle and editing practices, but also by the language, spoken or written, that accompanies the produced images and accounts (ibid, p. 35). This new kind of "de-spatialized visibility" fostered intimate forms of self-presentation and facilitated the rise of what Thompson calls "the society of self-disclosure" (ibid, p. 38).

The advent of digital technologies has further amplified this form of visibility, making it *more intensive*, more *extensive*, and less *controllable* – despite the strategic and reflective constructions and displays it involves – given how difficult it can be to predict the consequences of public appearances and disclosures. Despite these risks, *struggles for visibility* have become central in contemporary networked societies, given the equation of visibility with presence or recognition in the public sphere, which can be instrumental in calling attention to a particular situation or for advancing a particular cause (ibid, p. 49). Recognition and value are, thus, closely connected to visibility. Thompson's discussion of visibility focused on its importance for politicians and, more particularly, for the construction of their credibility in the eyes of their voters.

In this book, mediated visibility has focused on (i) individuals bringing attention to personal experiences of illness and grief and raising awareness of what it is like for a young adult to live with cancer (Chapter 4), (ii) communities of bereaved claiming visibility for a loved one as a way of paying tribute to his life (Chapter 5), or (iii) more or less ephemerally connected groups seeking to publicly affirm shared values and identities and make visible social issues or concerns (Chapters 6 and 7).

As the visibility of death, the dead, and the bereaved increases online, sharers are faced with 'new' challenges that have to do with the navigation of a "spectrum of visibility" (Giaxoglou et al., 2017), as one crosses one's own and others' understandings of private–public boundaries. In addition, increased visibility of mourning opens it up to attacks, also known as trolling or "LOL-ing at tragedy" (Phillips, 2011), which in some cases can represent broader criticisms of grieving in public as 'inauthentic' (Phillips and Milne, 2017). At the same time, heightened visibility of death affords big-sized audiences and the scaling up of affect at an unprecedented scale and makes it possible to mobilize crowd empathy. Such mobilization is instrumental for awareness-raising campaigns and fundraising and helps create value out of mourning and memorialization or even move people into activist action.

The above claims to visibility are part of a wider turn to mediated affect in media, social media, and politics as a mode of engaging with the world and its crises – personal or collective – and as vectors of instrumentalization (political, economic, commercial; see Alloing and Pierre, forthcoming). In this context, visibility becomes associated with claims to authenticity and attempts to build intimate relationships with networked audiences.

My main argument has been to posit that despite their heterogeneity, practices of mourning in social media are shaped by and shape social media and narrative affordances for rendering dying, death, and grief tellable, shareable, and viewable in recognizable, recyclable, and portable formats. Such forms of participation should not be seen as straightforwardly attesting to a return to communal mourning, the social 'opening up' of death, or an index of public participation. They should, instead, be seen as forms of *connective mourning* (see van Dijck, 2013), whereby experiencing and witnessing death and mourning is subjected to media and social media logics of sharing and visibility.

Connective mourning takes shape in the context of an increased psychologization of social life, whereby dying, death, and grieving are often approached as events that pertain to the personal affective realm and that call up therapeutic discourses to cope with their affective implications. At the same time, in social media, a tendency for over-celebrating life events has been promoted, especially among young adults in the Western world, inviting the publicization of what was previously considered to be private (Gieseler, 2017) and pushing for the sharing of life and death moments with known and unknown audiences. In addition, the rise of cosmopolitan forms of ethics and humanitarianism prompt the mobilization of mourning in individualized acts of activism as symbolic acts of moral behaviour.

In summary, the application of a narrative approach to mourning to the four case studies examined in this book clarified the 'new' visibilities for dying, death, and mourning afforded by social media technologies of communication as much as by specific modes of small storying.

Directions in the Study of Death Online

The interdisciplinary field of death online is well placed to address questions about these 'new' visibilities and the impact of social media on the experience and public understanding of dying, death, and mourning. Further empirical studies on situated practices of death-writing of the moment needed that will continue to document and critically assess continuities and shifts in death-related practices. It is important to pay closer attention to users' individual affective trajectories across time so that the dynamic character of these activities can be further clarified. In addition, it is important to examine the different modulations of distance and proximity for performing emotion and the self through acts of affective positioning to the death event and the dead, known and unknown audiences, and the affective self in alignment or disalignment to master discourses of emotion.

In addition, given the extensive use of emoji over hashtags as an emotional coping strategy (Stark and Crawford, 2015, p. 1), empirical studies of the mobilization of emoji for sharing grief in different types of digital mourning are called for. Such studies can also provide important insights into identity and affective negotiations of negative emotions in digital environments, where positive emotions tend to be privileged. More broadly, there is still scope for clarifying the evolving conditions under which social media allow individuals and groups to connect meaningfully around dying, death, and mourning while also continuing to research the implications of the data traces sharers leave behind and the level of control they have over the shaping of their post-mortem identities (see Kasket, 2019).

In order to address these areas and questions and additional ones that emerge from the close observation of related practices, some consensus among scholars working in the field of death online is needed on the scope and analytical vocabulary so as to facilitate interdisciplinary dialogue. The narrative approach and the analytical concept of affective positioning proposed in this book could hopefully prove useful in this direction.

Future work is very likely to move beyond practices and questions of digital mourning and memorialization to techno-visions of using digital technologies for immortalization. This is currently a promise waiting to come true among futurists, who predict that one day the scientific understanding of the brain will make it possible to upload the human mind to computers and allow humans to live eternally – even if in a post-human future. Peter Thiel, an American entrepreneur and venture capitalist, has been funding research on life extension, and predicts that "death will eventually be reduced from a mystery to a solvable problem" (O'Connell, 2017, p. 180).

Irrespective of whether the post-humanist extension of memorialization to eternalization is possible or even desirable, it certainly illustrates the extension of the domain of control over not just life but also death. In Don DeLillo's book *Zero K* (2016), which offers a reflection on the transcendent promise of biomedical advances for the cryogenic control of death – as much as a meditation on the afterlife of art – death is represented as a cultural artefact and the end of the world something that everybody wants to own (274).

While the dystopian and utopian implications of digital technologies continue to be a source of fascination and critical attention, there is still plenty of scope for reflecting on how best to face the raw realities of death and grief collectively and how to mobilize social and political attention to broader social issues and precarious lives.

Directions in the Study of Affect Online

Death-writing of the moment forms a rich site for the study of affect online. So far, the study of emotion online has predominantly revolved around the main strategies for addressing the inadequacy of computer-mediated environments for communicating and interpreting emotion, given the lack of the rich non-verbal cues available in face-to-face communication. Scholars have drawn attention to the usefulness of emoji[2] as an instrumental digital communicative resource that helps add tone, emotional voice, and nuance to our messages (Evans, 2017). The use of emoji has rapidly extended into all domains of life, including domains of death and mourning. Given the playful and creative connotations of emoji use, the embedding of emoji in mourning messages is often criticized as trivializing mourning, as in the case of the use of an emoji of a crying face in the report of a Cincinnati news station about a child's suicide or the use of a bomb emoji by Cher in a tweet she posted as an immediate reaction to the news of the Brussels attack in 2016 (Seargeant and Giaxoglou, 2017). Putting aside the various kinds of reactions and criticisms of light-heartedness raised by uses of emoji, their mobilization as a resource for "emotion work", i.e. the efforts expended as part of managing the expression of emotions in order to fulfil a social role (Hochschild, 1979), has become an integral part of digital communication. At the same time, however, their increased commodification as part of large tech companies' commercial strategies, noted by Seargeant (2019), needs to be taken more seriously into account in empirical work on emoji. As Stark and Crawford (2015) point out: "emoji create new avenues for digital feeling, while also remaining ultimately in the service of the market" (p. 1). The commodification of emotion is not, however, restricted to these pervasive visual-digital objects, even if this is one of the most visible signs of this trend. It also extends to the digital communication of affect, as attested in the regimentation of modes of affective positioning afforded by the specific types of storying and participation fostered by social media.

If "affect is what sticks" (Ahmed, 2010, p. 29), online affect is what 'screams' for attention and what makes people engage in some form or other with shared content. Across the different types of death-writing of the moment proposed earlier, highly affective experiences and events (e.g. illness, dying, mourning) are predicated upon claims to authenticity, a notion which has become a currency in online sharing. This domain of online activity, therefore, points to the close connection between the injunction to share and the injunction to be 'authentic' online. Emotional sharing does not happen in a vacuum: it draws on existing cultural frames about what counts as an appropriate, acceptable, and recognizable emotional expression in response to death, dying, and grief. In Western networked societies, emotional sharing is largely shaped by and shapes styles of psychologized individualism which privilege the display of autonomy, uniqueness, individuality, and growth and the rights of the psychological self, developed through early socialization in soft forms of individualism, especially among the middle classes (see Kusserow, 2004).

A concern with developing methodologies for the empirical study of affect has been growing in media and cultural studies (Knudsen and Stage, 2015; Stage, 2017). The concept of affective positioning proposed in this book can complement these efforts by drawing attention to the linguistic, discourse, and visual cues used to construct particular kinds of relationalities and mobilize affective flows across different contexts. The empirical framework proposed here calls for moving beyond the study of emotion as psychological states, such as joy, sadness, anger, or as linguistically realized at utterance or sentence level to an analytical approach that connects affect to narrative performance and views it as indexical of socio-cultural ideologies of emotional norms and sociability. More specifically, a focus on affective positioning can address emerging questions about the way emotion is being instrumentalized for driving content creation online and user engagement, ending up in reconfiguring the construal of personal and social realities and experience as *affect*.

As Stark (2015, p. 17) notes, the interactionist study of emotion is expected to occupy a major place in technical, policy, and design debates on information privacy, given the central role that emotion plays in the way users construct private spaces online as a complex, subjective experience.

Directions in the Study of Narrative

Death online is a rich site for the study of the emergence and circulation of stories. The examination of death-related practices online in this book brought to the fore the use of small stories as a resource for different kinds of affective positioning that help authenticate emotional types of sharing. In addition, it foregrounded the increasing trend for video- or image-based stories as part of the wider turn to the visual, calling for increased attention to story curation practices and creating new types of participation positions for story recipients as story viewers.

In addition to paying close attention to the specifics of storying practices and their associated strategies for performing the networked self and constituting publics, it is also worth investigating practices surrounding the sedimentation of stories and their use as frames for interpreting personal experience and events. As noted in Chapter 4, stories of personal experience are often celebrated as the hallmark of authenticity, but in a world where 'stories' are increasingly commoditized as part of the commercial interests of advertisers and tech companies (Georgakopoulou, 2019), more critical perspectives to their constitution are needed that can pinpoint further the specifics of the technological, socio-cultural, and political embeddedness of narrative practices.

This book foregrounds the importance of narrative analysis as a critical perspective to the study of specific domains of social life. The focus has been on mourning, given that mourning has never been purely a matter of emotion, but has, rather, constituted a site of social reproduction as well as an arena of social contestation in which ideologies of gender, class, and social status are played out (Seremetakis, 1991; Wilce, 2009).

Approaching mourning as narrative practice underscores the situatedness of identities and affect and paves the way for the study of the ideological dimensions and drivers of (inter)subjectivation in contemporary socio-political formations.

Notes

1. The term *poly-storying* is discussed in Georgakopoulou and Giaxoglou's (2018) study on the emplotment of economist Yanis Varoufakis, where it was understood as "the availability and/or remixing of different plots involving Varoufakis, as well as of the different possibilities for networked audiences to contribute to them" (p. 38). The term as used here chimes with the notion of *inter-reactions*, described in Chapter 7 of this book as a form of public communication which involves the sharing of individual contributions as part of accumulating comments on and across threads and sites and in which the act of sharing is an act of story participation and where usernames can be inserted to publicly involve others in the digital interaction. These aspects of sequencing and addressivity are also captured in Page's (2018) description of Facebook and YouTube comment threads and Twitter reply threads as *polylogal*, where a comment can respond to either a post or to another comment in a thread, using markers of addressivity rather than turn sequentiality to signal thematic adjacency, although in this case, aspects of story-participation are left aside.
2. As Riordan (2017) has shown, both face (emoji representing facial expressions) and non-face emoji (emoji representing objects) are used as tools for emotional work, communicating emotions that are primarily positive in nature (p. 560).

References

Ahmed, S. (2010) *The Cultural Politics of Emotion*. Edinburgh: Edinburgh University Press.

Alloing, C. and J. Pierre (forthcoming) Affects et émotions numériques: matérialité(s) et instrumentalisation(s). *Communiquer: Revue de communication sociale et publique* 10 (10): xx.

Androutsopoulos, J. (2014) Moments of sharing: Entextualization and linguistic repertoires in social networking. *Journal of Pragmatics* (Special Issue: The Pragmatics of Textual Participation in the Social Media) 73: 4–18.

Bamberg, M. (1997) Positioning between structure and performance. *Journal of Narrative and Life History* (Special Issue: Three Decades of Narrative Analysis) 7 (1–4): 335–342.

Butler, J. (2004) *Precarious Life: The Power of Mourning and Violence*. London: Verso Books.

De Fina, A. and A. Georgakopoulou (2012) *Analyzing Narrative: Discourse and Sociolinguistic Perspectives*. Cambridge: Cambridge University Press.

De Fina, A., D. Schiffrin, and M. Bamberg (Eds.) (2006) *Discourse and Identity*. Cambridge: Cambridge University Press.

DeLillo, D. (2016) *Zero K*. London: Charles Scribner's Sons.

Depperman, A. (2013) Editorial: Positioning in narrative interaction. *Narrative Inquiry* 23 (1): 1–15.

Evans, V. (2017) *The Emoji Code: The Linguistics Behind Smiley Faces and Scaredy Cats*. New York: Picador.

Fisher, D.R. and L.M. Wright (2006) On utopias and dystopias: Toward an understanding of the discourse surrounding the internet. *Journal of Computer-Mediated Communication* 6 (2): n.p.

Georgakopoulou, A. (2007) *Small Stories, Interaction and Identities*. Amsterdam: John Benjamins Publishing Company.

Georgakopoulou, A. (2015) Small stories research: Methods-analysisoutreach. In De Fina, A. and A. Georgakopoulou (Eds.), *Handbook of Narrative Analysis*. Malden, MA: Wiley-Blackwell, pp. 255–272.

Georgakopoulou, A. and K. Giaxoglou (2018) 'Emplotment in the social mediatization of the economy: The poly-storying of economist Yanis Varoufakis'. *Language@Internet* 16, Article 6: 1–15.

Georgakopoulou, A. (2019) Designing stories on social media: A corpus-assisted critical perspective on the mismatches of story-curation. *Linguistics and Education*. https://doi.org/10.1016/j.linged.2019.05.003.

Giaxoglou, K., K. Döveling, and S. Pitsillides (2017) Networked emotions: Interdisciplinary perspectives on sharing loss online. *Journal of Broadcasting & Electronic Media* 61 (1): 1–10.

Gieseler, C. (2017) Gender-reveal parties: Performing community identity in pink and blue. *Journal of Gender Studies* 27 (6): 661–671.

Hård Af Segerstad, Y. and D. Kasperowski (2015) A community for grieving: Affordances of social media for support of bereaved parents. *New Review of Hypermedia and Multimedia* 21: 1–2, 25–41.

Hochschild, A. (1979). Emotion work, feeling rules, and social structure. *American Journal of Sociology* 85: 551–575.

John, N.A. (2017) *The Age of Sharing*. Cambridge: Polity Press.

Kasket, E. (2019) *All the Ghosts in the Machine: Illusions of Immortality in the Digital Age*. London: Robinson.

Knudsen, B.T. and C. Stage (Eds.) (2015) *Affective Methodologies*. London: Palgrave Macmillan.

Kusserow, A. (2004) *American Individualisms: Child Rearing and Social Class in Three Neighborhoods*. Houndmills and Basingstoke: Palgrave Macmillan.

O'Connell, M. (2017) *To Be a Machine: Adventures among Cyborgs, Utopians, Hackers, and the Futurists Solving the Modest Problem of Death*. London: Granta Publications.

Page, R. (2018) *Narratives Online: Shared Stories in Social Media*. Cambridge: Cambridge University Press.

Phillips, W. (2011) LOLing at tragedy: Facebook trolls, memorial pages and resistance of grief online. *First Monday* 16 (12): n.p.

Phillips, W. and R.M. Milner (2017) *The Ambivalent Internet: Mischief, Oddity, and Antagonism Online*. Malden, MA: Polity Press.

Refslund Christensen, D., Y. Hård af Segerstad, D. Kasperowski, and K. Sandvik (2017) Bereaved parents' online grief communities: De-Tabooing practices or relation-building grief-ghettos? *Journal of Broadcasting & Electronic Media* 61 (1): 58–72.

Riordan, M.A. (2017) Emojis as tools for emotion work: Communicating affect in text messages. *Journal of Language and Social Psychology* 36 (5): 549–467.

Seargeant, P. (2019) *The Emoji Revolution: How Technology Is Shaping the Future of Communication*. Cambridge: Cambridge University Press.

Seargeant, P. and K. Giaxoglou (2017) What effect is social media having on the way we mourn global tragedies? *Open Learn*. Available at: www.open.edu/openlearn/languages/what-effect-social-media-having-on-the-way-we-mourn-global-tragedies. Accessed: 9 Aug. 2019.

Seremetakis, N. (1991) *The Last Word: Women, Death and Divination in Inner Mani*. Chicago: University of Chicago Press.

Sofka, C., I.N. Cupit, and K.R. Gilbert (Eds.) (2012) *Dying, Death, and Grief in an Online Universe: For Counselors and Educators*. New York: Springer Publishing Company.

Stage, C. (2017) *Networked Cancer: Affect, Narrative and Measurement*. Houndmills, Basingstoke: Palgrave Macmillan.

Stark, L. (2015) The emotional context of informational privacy. *The Information Society: An International Journal* 32 (1): 14–27.

Stark, L. and K. Crawford (2015) The conservatism of emoji: Work, affect, and communication. *Social Media + Society* 1 (2): 1–11.

Thompson, J.B. (2005) The new visibility. *Theory, Culture & Society* 22 (6): 31–51.

van Dijck, J. (2013) *The Culture of Connectivity: A Critical History of Social Media*. Oxford: Oxford University Press.

Walter, T., R. Hourizi, W. Moncur, and S. Pitsillides (2012) Does the internet change how we die and mourn? Overview and analysis. *OMEGA: Journal of Death and Dying* 64 (4): 275–302.

Wilce, J. (2009) *Language and Emotion*. Cambridge: Cambridge University Press.

Wortham, S. (2000) Interactional positioning and narrative self-construction. *Narrative Inquiry* 10:1: 157–184.

Index

Printed in the United States
by Baker & Taylor Publisher Services

Printed in the United States
by Baker & Taylor Publisher Services